Frontiers in the Gilded Age

The Lamar Series in Western History

The Lamar Series in Western History includes scholarly books of general public interest that enhance the understanding of human affairs in the American West and contribute to a wider understanding of the West's significance in the political, social, and cultural life of America. Comprising works of the highest quality, the series aims to increase the range and vitality of Western American history, focusing on frontier places and people, Indian and ethnic communities, the urban West and the environment, and the art and illustrated history of the American West.

Editorial Board

Recent Titles

White Fox and Icy Seas in the Western Arctic: The Fur Trade, Transportation, and Change in the Early Twentieth Century, by John R. Bockstoce
Growing Up with the Country: Family, Race, and Nation after the Civil War, by Kendra Taira Field
Grounds for Dreaming: Mexican Americans, Mexican Immigrants, and the California Farmworker Movement, by Lori A. Flores
The American West: A New Interpretive History, Second Edition, by Robert V. Hine, John Mack Faragher, and Jon T. Coleman
Legal Codes and Talking Trees: Indigenous Women's Sovereignty in the Sonoran and Puget Sound Borderlands, 1854–1946, by Katrina Jagodinsky
An American Genocide: The United States and the California Indian Catastrophe, 1846–1873, by Benjamin Madley
First Impressions: A Reader's Journey to Iconic Places of the American Southwest, by David J. Weber and William deBuys

Forthcoming Titles

Welcome to Wonderland: Promoting Tourism in the Rocky Mountain West, 1920–1960, by Peter Blodgett
Lakota America: A New History of Indigenous Power, by Pekka Hämäläinen
The U.S.-Mexico Borderlands, by Eric Meeks

Frontiers in the Gilded Age

Adventure, Capitalism, and Dispossession from Southern Africa to the U.S.–Mexican Borderlands, 1880–1917

Andrew Offenburger

Published in cooperation with the William P. Clements Center
for Southwest Studies, Southern Methodist University

Yale
UNIVERSITY PRESS

New Haven & London

Published with assistance from the income of the
Frederick John Kingsbury Memorial Fund.

Yale University Press books may be purchased in quantity for educational, business,
or promotional use. For information, please e-mail sales.press@yale.edu (U.S. office)
or sales@yaleup.co.uk (U.K. office).

Set in Bulmer type by Westchester Publishing Services.
Printed in the United States of America.

Library of Congress Control Number: 2018961531
ISBN 978-0-300-22587-7 (hardcover : alk. paper)

A catalogue record for this book is available from the British Library.

This paper meets the requirements of ANSI/NISO Z39.48-1992 (Permanence of Paper).

10 9 8 7 6 5 4 3 2 1

For Lindsay, Casey, and Audrey

Contents

Acknowledgments

THE MOST REWARDING ASPECT OF researching and writing a book that connects multiple regions has been working with a tremendous group of colleagues, descendants, and friends. As I think through the range of professional and personal interactions required by this study, my only regret is that these pages will be the lone place where all of these people gather together, at least in spirit. I have benefited from many collaborations, from graduate school to Miami University, and I hope this book meets the expectations of those who have been so generous with their time.

From my dissertation committee I acquired the tools of the trade and learned how to think historically. My advisor, John Mack Faragher, never hesitated to support a project that challenged conventional ways of viewing the American West and its borderlands. Without his expansive vision of the West, this project would have never developed beyond its early stages. The other members of my committee—Glenda Gilmore, Robert Harms, and Gilbert Joseph—completed an academic dream team for this project while also serving as models of collegiality and generosity.

Organizations and institutions at Yale supported this research and created the space necessary for intellectual exploration. The Howard R. Lamar Center for the Study of Frontiers and Borders provided a scholarly home in New Haven. Its meetings of "westerners," led by my advisor and with accompaniment by Jay Gitlin, pushed the tempo of my research at brown bag lunches every Wednesday. The Program in Agrarian Studies and its *agraristas* influenced my thinking in profound ways. James Scott and K. "Shivi" Sivaramakrishnan cultivated this broad and dynamic community of scholars with far-ranging conversations and terrific food. The Yale Group for the Study of Native America, coordinated by Alyssa Mt. Pleasant and Ned Blackhawk, helped me place the Yaqui Indians of

Sonora within the larger field of Native American and indigenous studies. The single largest influence on this book came from the Beinecke Rare Book and Manuscript Library, which funded a total of six months of research in its holdings and enabled me to read far and wide in its U.S.-Mexican borderlands holdings. George Miles, Curator of the Western Americana Collection, was a fellow westerner and perpetual resource who always found time to help me navigate a vast sea of bibliographic holdings. The Lamar Center, the Agrarian Studies Program, and the Gilder Lehrman Center for the Study of Slavery and Abolition funded various components of my research.

Other faculty, colleagues, and friends affiliated with Yale made graduate school a transformative experience. This includes Alice Baumgartner, Ann Biersteker, Ally Brantley, Christine DeLucia, Jacob Dlamini, Arielle Gorin, Allison Gorsuch, Mary Greenfield, Holly Guise, Tiffany Hale, Ryan Hall, Todd Holmes, Andy Horowitz, Khalil Johnson, Jenny Kline, Sarah Koenig, Matthew Kustenbauder, Daniel Lanpher, Michael Mahoney, Christine Mathias, Catherine McNeur, Sandra Sanneh, Ashley Riley Sousa, Taylor Spence, and especially Henry Trotter, whose collegiality and inquisitiveness greatly influenced my academic trajectory.

Beyond New Haven, the Western History Dissertation Workshop held at the Autry National Center in 2012 helped me make sense of inchoate ideas. Discussant Richard White's critique of a chapter draft was helpful, firm, and fair, the kind of feedback that scholars crave. The Newberry Borderlands and Latino/a Seminar, led by Benjamin Johnson and Geraldo Cadava, enabled me to sharpen parts of chapter 1. A Richard E. Greenleaf Visiting Scholar Library Award at the University of New Mexico offered an opportunity to consult key sources in chapters 4 and 5. A one-month research fellowship at the Huntington Library informed the overall framework of this book, as did a month spent at New Mexico State University's Manuscripts and Archives. Finally, a Newberry Consortium in American Indian Studies Graduate Student Fellowship funded oral history interviews with the Yaqui Indians.

A number of additional scholars and friends have been generous with their time. I would like to thank in particular Kirstin Erickson as well as

Adam Arenson, Rita Barnard, Katherine Benton-Cohen, Cathleen Cahill, Bill Deverell, Norman Etherington, Sterling Evans, Raphael Folsom, Jane Holden Kelley, Clement Masakure, Katherine Morrissey, Raquel Padilla Ramos, Ian Phimister, Brenden Rensink, Christopher Saunders, Jennie Sutton, Shukri Toefy, Samuel Truett, Andrew van der Vlies, and John Wunder. The fortuitous convergence of my research topics with those of Charles van Onselen and Carel van der Merwe was immensely helpful in the latter stages of this project.

A postdoctoral fellowship at the Clements Center for Southwest Studies at Southern Methodist University in Dallas helped turn a nebulous, multisite manuscript into a cohesive book. Andrew Graybill, Sherry Smith, and Ruth Ann Elmore made the center a wonderland for extended conversations and revisions. Fellows Gavin Benke, Doug Miller, and Sami Lakomäki and Senior Fellow Rachel St. John made me want to extend a one-year stay to infinity. Two senior scholars, Virginia Scharff and Mauricio Tenorio-Trillo, critiqued a former version of the manuscript, and I received their comments at a daylong workshop, with additional feedback from participants Luis Garcia, Jill Kelly, Carla Mendiola, Monica Rankin, and Joel Zapata. Outside of SMU, others in Dallas made that city feel like home, including Jennifer and Michael Carp and the Leung-Tsai family.

At Miami University I received institutional funding from the Office for the Advancement of Research and Scholarship for supplementary work in South African archives in addition to faculty leave to finalize the manuscript. Furthermore, I benefited from the intellectual environment and camaraderie of the Department of History and from the critical feedback and support of numerous colleagues, in particular Elena Jackson Albarrán, Steven Conn, Wietse de Boer, Lindsay Schakenbach Regele, and Susan Spellman. The department also funded last-minute editorial needs, including transcriptions by Benjamín Alonso Rascón (whose expert guidance in Sonora was vital to archival explorations) and research assistance by Adriana Obiols at Tulane University's Amistad Research Center and by Madihah Akhter in the Burnham Papers at Stanford University.

Editors and professionals at Yale University Press have enhanced this manuscript with critical feedback. Thank you to Christopher Rogers and

Erica Hanson, who oversaw the early stages of submission, and especially to Adina Berk, Eva Skewes, and Lawrence Kenney, my copy editor, for shepherding these pages through the latter processes of publication. I am thrilled that this book appears in the Lamar Series in Western History.

From beginning to end I valued interacting with descendants of this book's subjects, from requests for private archives to conversations and oral history interviews. I am indebted to them for willingly sharing papers and stories from the past. In Sonora, I especially relied on Teodoro Buitimea Flores, Juan Silverio Jaime León, Cornelio Molina Valencia, and Jesús Matuz González. One family in the Yoeme pueblos—María Cristina Gómez Valenzuela, José Gregorio Álvarez Cocmea, and Fátima Guadalupe Álvarez Gómez—made the interviews possible; I am moved by their kindness and generosity. Boer descendants included Michele Bottaro, Bill Brookreson, Barbara Fonseca, Coleman Ganoe, the late Joann Ganoe, George "Dogie" Jones, John Stinnett, JoAnn Tessandori, Benjamin Viljoen III, Christo Viljoen, and the late Jeannine Viljoen. In Chihuahua, Noé Casas Rodríguez and the Methodist community of La Trinidad welcomed an outsider interested in their church's Congregational heritage, and Pablo Hoffmann openly discussed his ancestral roots. Descendants of the Eatons, Sue Martine and Mary Edgar, provided privately held materials. Rod Atkinson, a descendant of Frederick Russell Burnham, generously critiqued a rough draft of chapter 2.

Family ties linked my subjects to their descendants, and they similarly sustained this project by providing a retreat from the world of Gilded Age frontiers. Thanks to my sister and her family, Janae Jaynes-Learned, Chris Learned, and Connor Jaynes, and to my parents, Chuck and Carla Offenburger and Jeffrie Story. Dad, a semiretired columnist, instilled in me a journalist's gumption to ask questions and an appreciation of personal stories; this book's reliance on them is not coincidental. While trying to balance writing and lecturing responsibilities, I often recalled Carla's teaching wisdom. And Mom fielded frequent questions on Spanish grammar and translations, especially when I deliberated issues relating to the oral history interviews in chapter 5. My parents' collective influence, their words of encouragement, and their occasional financial assistance maintained this project's momentum.

If one force carried this study from beginning to end, it was my wife, María. She inspires me daily. She and our daughters, Lindsay, Casey, and Audrey, withstood the secondhand effects of my labor on this book, including four relocations, prolonged absences for archival work, and closed doors while producing these pages. The word "love" fails to capture what I feel for them, though it does help explain why extended kin networks in the late nineteenth century—like an academic's family in the twenty-first century—crossed oceans, or sought refuge in mountains, in spite of the unknown.

A Note on Orthography

THIS STORY PRESENTS MANY CHALLENGES, but word selection and spelling proved especially difficult given the geographical breadth of these characters. As a general rule I have chosen to err on the side of clarity for readers unfamiliar with a given region. At times this has compelled me to use antiquated terms. For example, for the sake of narrative simplicity I have sacrificed the contemporary word "Afrikaner" and have relied on its outdated synonym, "Boer."

There are some exceptions to this guiding principle, where I encumber the reader with additional names, words, or spellings, as with the Shona and Ndebele of today's Zimbabwe and the Yaqui Indians of Sonora. In the African context I have used current phraseology and discarded wide variations of previous spellings. Concerning the Yaquis, given my desire to represent their interpretations of the past, which challenge outsiders' views, I felt it necessary to include occasional words and phrases to reinforce their indigenous perspectives.

For the remainder of the terms and phrases chosen, I have opted for simplicity and ask for leniency when an occasional historical term might clang in readers' ears. This unfortunately includes the adjective "American" when referring to the United States, a word I have tried to use sparingly for my Latin American colleagues who rightly recognize its broader connotation.

Term Used	Meaning
Boer Republics	the two independent republics, before British annexation, of the Transvaal (with the cities of Johannesburg and Pretoria), and the Orange Free State (with Bloemfontein)
Cape Colony	the southwestern portion of South Africa, with Cape Town as its administrative center

Term Used	*Meaning*
caujome(m)	rebel Yaqui(s) resistant to collaboration with the Mexican state
Colony of Natal	kwaZulu-Natal, and its capital, Pieter-maritzburg
Mashonaland	region where the Shona lived in Southern Rhodesia, northeast of Matabeleland
Matabeleland	region where the Ndebele lived in Southern Rhodesia, southwest of Mashonaland
South African War	the war (1899–1902) fought between the British Empire and the Boer Republics; alternatively called the Anglo–Boer War or the Second Boer War
southern Africa	the region of Namibia, Botswana, Zimbabwe, Mozambique, South Africa, Lesotho, and Swaziland; here, I use the phrase to signify the British Cape and Natal Colonies, the Boer Republics, and Southern Rhodesia
Southern Rhodesia	today's Zimbabwe, comprised of then-Matabeleland and then-Mashonaland
torocoyori(m)	Yaqui sellout(s) or traitor(s); those who collaborated with the government, and especially fellow Yaquis who served in the Mexican army
U.S.–Mexican borderlands	the states immediately bordering the international boundary
Yaqui Valley	the fertile region in southern Sonora around the Yaqui River, which flows into the Gulf of California
Yoeme(m)	Yaqui(s)
yori(m)	non-Yaqui(s)

Frontiers in the Gilded Age

Introduction

TWO AMERICANS THOUGHT THEY COULD resolve a conflict that had vexed northern Mexico for decades, if not centuries. Ever since the 1890s a land company financed by U.S. citizens had been appropriating territory, belonging to the Yaqui Indians (Yoemem) in Sonora, just south of Arizona. With support from Mexico's state and federal governments, the company had dispossessed the Yoemem of sovereign lands by developing hundreds of thousands of acres in the fertile Yaqui Valley. The onset of Mexico's Revolution in 1910, though, gave the oppressed an opportunity to rebel. They seized it, raiding company properties and private landholdings as part of a campaign to demand the restitution of their sacred territory. In an effort to bring stability to the region early in the Revolution, two U.S. citizens offered separately to negotiate an agreement to reconcile the Yaquis' land claims, Sonora's need for economic stability, and the Americans' financial investments. The proposals were impolitic, if not brash. With U.S. interests aggravating matters in Sonora, many Mexicans wondered, why should American citizens, of all people, handle a matter of such delicate national interest?

This particular historical moment, thus narrated, conforms to a trilateral framework of Mexican, U.S., and indigenous sovereignties familiar to borderlands scholars. Yet the paragraph above suppresses complicating extraregional dynamics that do not fit a traditional borderlands model. As odd as the separate proposals from American interlopers may have appeared to Mexicans, the two individuals' deeper connections—to southern Africa—prove even stranger. One offer to broker an agreement came from Benjamin Viljoen, an American only by recent naturalization. A Boer

1

general, Viljoen had attained fame during the South African War (1899–1902), after which a British victory forced many of his compatriots to seek refuge in foreign lands. Viljoen himself helped establish a colony in Chihuahua after 1903. With his unique military experience and perspective as a dispossessed person, Viljoen thought he could appeal to the Yaquis "so that they did not fight in vain, and [to show] them how much better off they were than the Boer people."[1] The other offer originated with the American-born Frederick Russell Burnham, who had fought for the British Empire in Southern Rhodesia in the 1890s, where he combatted similar indigenous revolts on behalf of Cecil Rhodes. Burnham later managed the American company expropriating Yaqui lands in Sonora. He lobbied his colonists and investors to weather Yaqui attacks, not to abandon the region, and to begin an anti-Yoeme military campaign, all under the guise of negotiating peace. In so doing he drew upon his previous experience in southern Africa and the American West. "If our little handful of settlers in Rhodesia had abandoned Mashonaland . . . just before the 1st Matabele War," he wrote, "Rhodes could never have raised $40 million in his lifetime. . . . We built [the] U.S. by sticking. My forbears helped in sticking to Minnesota, Kentucky, Texas, . . . many are *willing* to take *some* risks."[2]

If curious, the connections between these regions were not historical anomalies. They formed part of a larger pattern. This book focuses on these global connections to show how the American West, southern Africa, and northern Mexico shared a unique kind of frontier history. From 1880 to 1917 the Mexican North was one site among many where U.S. expansion transformed from a model of territorial acquisition to one of economic aggression and resource extraction, a historical process that shared people and themes with southern Africa in heretofore underrepresented ways. Capitalists, adventurers, missionaries, and indigenous peoples—and their ideas—crisscrossed far-flung territories to create a global frontier network that emerged in the Gilded Age. Not unique to the United States, this network often overlapped with British imperial possessions and found cohesion among American and British subjects through a shared frontier ideology based in social Darwinism. These frontiers typically showcased power grabs for minerals or other riches, glittering with potential and inspiring grandiose dreams, yet they also exposed the flawed and immoral strategies people sometimes used to attain what seemed rightfully theirs. At the same time, these regions exhibited the human capacity for accommodation, resistance, and resilience that indigenous peoples summoned when threatened or when they identified strategic opportunities.

I began to uncover this larger history when researching the Boer colony of Chihuahua. Like the Mexicans who had asked why Americans, of all people, should negotiate peace between Mexico and the Yoemem, I wondered why Boer colonists would land in Chihuahua, of all places. Boers? In *Chihuahua?* The past was not complying with established historical categories. Investigating the colony's history required initially engaging with three historiographies: South African, Mexican, and American. As I circled out to understand the global forces that led to the South African War and how many Americans' expansionist plans overlapped with the British Empire's, I realized the special place Mexico, like southern Africa, occupied in capitalists', adventurers', and missionaries' minds. The resulting portrait of the U.S.–Mexican borderlands from 1880 to 1917 no longer fit within a tradition established by borderlands historians. This was not solely about America's role in the Mexican Revolution after 1910, or cross-border capitalist expansion, or adventurism and filibusterism, or foreign relations, or American missionaries abroad, or migration between global locales, or indigenous sovereignty, or the absurdity of cartographic lines determining nationality. It was all of these. As a result, I sensed a blind spot in previous borderlands histories. What happened to international and transnational connections *beyond* Mexico and the United States in this era? Ironically, historians had reduced outside complicating factors to identities shaped by the border itself: either as "Mexican," "American," or "indigenous" or as other peoples affected by migration. If not dismissed altogether as a historical quirk, southern African connections ended up on the cutting-room floor.

In this book I reassemble these clippings to reveal a transnational frontier history in the U.S.–Mexican borderlands. Chapter 1 provides the ideological framework that gives shape to the entire narrative. It examines how Americans, fearful of the frontier's closing in California, regarded

Mexico as a logical next step in U.S. expansion. This frontier worldview and the booster literature it inspired coincided with themes found in British imperial adventure fiction, suggesting how both frontier and empire comingled after 1880. Chapter 2 shows how one individual (Burnham) embodied these themes and connected the American West, southern Africa, and northern Mexico. Burnham typified a generation of like-minded individuals, and Richard Harding Davis placed him alongside William Walker and Winston Churchill. Burnham devoured adventure literature as a boy in Minnesota, he idealized his British roots, and he acted on these dreams, serving Cecil Rhodes and fighting Ndebele warriors in one context before working for the mining engineer John Hays Hammond and challenging Yaqui sovereignty in another. Chapter 3 analyzes the Mexican North from the perspective of James and Gertrude Eaton, American missionaries to Chihuahua, who imagined themselves as part of an extranational community. The Eatons had to find ways to spread their Protestant message in a Catholic world, and they relied on gendered networks and their position as immigrants to befriend Mexicans and other foreigners alike. Chapter 4 follows some of the Eatons' dearest friends in the region, the Boer colonists in Chihuahua, and highlights how the colony symbolized the transnational connections of this place and time. Landing in Chihuahua was no historical anomaly. The Boers, as emigrants without a home, wanted to settle along a frontier, far enough from urbanizing areas to allow a new beginning with humble means, yet close enough to markets to prosper financially. Rail networks between northern Mexico and the U.S. Southwest made this possible. Finally, chapter 5 narrates the conclusion of this global frontier, as a Boer emigrant (Viljoen), an American adventurer (Burnham), and others discussed in earlier chapters aligned with American investors in Sonora, clashing with Yoemem in the Yaqui Valley.

My choice of narrative focus inevitably obscures the roles of other worthy historical actors. To draw the links on opposing sides of the Atlantic I needed to rely on the writings and perspectives of transnational explorers, capitalists, and farmers—all migrants—and to set these in contrast with the indigenous voices of the Yaqui Indians they ultimately encountered. The focus on these settler/indigenous dynamics in the Mexican North consequently meant I could not digress into other worthy aspects of this history, such as contemporaneous African American intellectual migrations, or Chinese immigration to these regions, or the larger context of Ndebele resistance in southern Africa, or the rise of Mexican working classes. The latter issue, especially important given the setting in the borderlands, unfortunately fell beyond this book's covers, but whenever possible I relied on secondary literature to contextualize the world peones inhabited and the forces that shaped their experiences. Significant contributors do appear: mining employees (chapter 1), the first converts of the Eatons (chapter 3), and farmers on irrigated lands in Chihuahua and New Mexico (chapter 4), among others. The longer trajectory of Mexican laborers, though, including the rise of Chicano identity in the borderlands after the Revolution, does not figure here. This book, after all, paints an unusual picture of a familiar region and then explains why the story is not strange at all but matches a global pattern of American frontier history.

Terminology: "Frontier," "Borderland," and "Empire" in Mexico

Considering the triangulated connections I explore and the divergent historical traditions between regions, some discussion of terminology, historiography, and methodology is necessary. The power dynamics of this history persuaded me to strategically use the word "frontier," a troubled term. I do so reluctantly to capture the mindsets of the book's characters. For decades western historians have noted the bias of "frontier," evident in Frederick Jackson Turner's now-infamous thesis.[3] Such a perspective champions the advance of Euro-American cultures, undergirds U.S. exceptionalism, and marginalizes indigenous actors, at best. As I wrote this history it became abundantly clear to me how many of the characters accepted such a worldview without question. It felt disingenuous to downplay the power of this ideology during the Gilded Age for the sake of a contemporary historiographical preference. In order to constrain the power of "frontier" to skew the historical narrative I employed a number of methodological strategies (discussed below).

Historians tend to refer to these regions as "borderlands," particularly when dealing with the lands surrounding the U.S.-Mexican boundary. Drawing on a perspective established by Herbert Eugene Bolton, Turner's protégé, borderlands studies critique cartographic imaginaries by emphasizing the permeability of borders and by understanding these regions as part of an ongoing historical process, or as a contestation of space, rather than as a geography "settled" by a unidirectional force of conquest.[4] This interpretation inspired and initially cultivated this book, as I tracked the migrations of Americans, Mexicans, Yaquis, Boers, and Britons between Mexico and the United States.[5] As the research deepened, though, the overlapping frontier and imperial ideologies—and the power the international border exerted over the book's actors—so saturated the sources that I felt characterizing this Gilded Age story as a frontier history to be more accurate. Nevertheless, I do use "borderlands" in geographical terms, when referring to the states adjoining either side of the international boundary. Boers and Yaquis alike fully recognized its power.

Equally influential, American capitalist expansion shaped countless lives in this region and others, and an important question arises as a result: did this constitute an American empire? During this era western expansion transformed from a system of territorial acquisition, common in the earlier nineteenth century, to one based on capitalism and the domination of foreign markets at the dawn of the twentieth century. Historians have approached this from a number of perspectives, typically under the rubric of empire and almost exclusively by focusing on the annexation of Hawaii or in the Spanish–American and Philippine–American Wars. Mention "American empire" to most historians today and these wars come immediately to mind, thanks to the seminal works of a number of scholars in the field of American studies.[6]

Though these books and others often acknowledge that U.S. expansion after 1898 had its roots in manifest destiny in the nineteenth-century, few works show how the latter mutated into the former.[7] For example, Walter Nugent effectively gives a cogent multicentury analysis of American expansion from Thomas Jefferson to Theodore Roosevelt, but his approach, as a series of juxtaposed case studies, does not detail the transformation of these "imperial habits."[8] The work of the geographer Neil Smith addresses the intellectuals that morphed western geographic expansion into economic power in the American Century as "a solution and successor to the economic geographic limits of European expansionism."[9]

The most thorough historical explanation of the transition between expansion into the western half of the American continent and later events in the Philippines can be found in Walter LaFeber's *The New Empire*, but LaFeber's scholarship, like Smith's, favors a top-down approach and generally misses the unique role Mexico played in this era.

Mexico after 1848 has been all but forgotten in the historiography on American expansion, but it loomed large in capitalists' minds after the Civil War.[10] This book uses cultural history to narrate how local actors experienced this shifting dynamic on the ground and to analyze the cultural evidence these people generated, what Ricardo Salvatore has called the "enterprise of knowledge" in the context of U.S.–Latin American relations. Elite politicians like Theodore Roosevelt and Francisco Madero may appear in the story, but so do everyday "cultural mediators whose texts and visions have left an important and enduring imprint in the metanarratives of U.S. expansionism."[11] While many of the works cited refer to this process as an imperial one, I hesitate to call it empire for reasons discussed in chapter 1. For this study I prefer "economic expansion," given the presence of southern Africa, where "empire" in that context was exponentially more violent and ubiquitous.

Historiography: The International West

At the heart of this book beats the American expansionist impulse that defined the long nineteenth century. The Northwest Ordinance of 1787 set the model for land acquisition and the admission of territories and states, thereby creating a system of nationalist expansion. By the 1840s, as sectional divisions strained the nation, an ideology of manifest destiny promoted and justified western migration and colonization. The West therefore aggravated sectionalism at the same time that it contributed to national growth. Once the Civil War erupted, the Republican-dominated Congress pushed through three key pieces of legislation—the Homestead Act, the Pacific Railway Act, and the Morrill Act, all in 1862—that lured Americans, armed with ideology and technological developments, from the Old Northwest to California. This process was itself international (a fact all too commonly

overlooked), with the United States expanding west through broken or nul-
lified treaties with Native American nations, through conquest in the
Mexican–American War (1846–48), and through a process of settler colonialism. That the United States assumed the continental shape it has today
was not, despite the cries of boosters in the 1840s, foreordained.

Between this march west and the foreign brand of investments and
intervention that characterized the middle twentieth century, Americans
fretted over the so-called closing of the frontier. Having reached the Pacific,
they wondered, what would next power the nation's progress? A number
of people looked to fulfill their golden dreams in other regions. In this case,
those who aimed to develop lands in northern Mexico had—it is no
coincidence—substantial ties to other regions under similar development
processes, among them southern Africa. This book consequently returns
Mexico to the center of a historical movement that connected the American
West to other global locations: Hawaii, Alaska, the Philippines, Nicaragua,
Chile, and Australia.[12] A few select studies within this growing interna-
tionalist tradition have examined in particular the overlapping connections between the U.S. West and the British imperial world.[13] Yet these
works view their particular international connections in a binary framework, whereas the subjects I treat here conceived of their travels in global
terms but with local familiarity.[14] Burnham, the would-be peace commissioner, once wrote from southern California to a friend, "Yeaton is now off
to Venezuela with an old time prospector whom I knew in Tombstone forty
years ago. They are going down to the district where Bob Adams of Alaska
has made the big gold."[15] To reflect this global dynamic, I triangulate a
western frontier tradition with southern Africa and northern Mexico.

These frontier zones gave adventurers a place to enact their dreams,
however problematic, and to brandish a romanticized frontier ideology. An
awareness of performing the frontier infused everyday actions into it. Burnham and Viljoen embodied this in overt ways regardless of their different
countries of birth, the former writing what can best be described as a
romance autobiography as well as a dreamy frontier history of the Yaqui
Valley, and the latter composing cowboy-esque fiction set in the South
African War while simultaneously performing in the Boer War Show at the
St. Louis World's Fair in 1904.

Such self-awareness, of playing the frontier while living it, may not be unique to the time period I cover here, but it certainly was most evident in the Gilded Age, and this partially grew from the era's overt emphasis on masculinity. Few personified this cultural phenomenon more than Theodore Roosevelt, who interacted with most of the characters I discuss, from a shootout with one of many Boer emigrants to sustained conversations with Burnham and others. Roosevelt, too, connected global frontiers and was lionized by a coterie of transnational adventurers, settlers, and military men. On the prospect of living in a world without frontiers, Roosevelt wrote to Burnham, "Africa and particularly Asia will see us through in this generation. Frankly, I am glad I shall have crossed the Great Divide before the last frontier has vanished."[16]

Methodology

Given that the characters in this book, like Roosevelt, were prone to embodying a hypermasculinity, to denigrating indigenous peoples, and to romanticizing the American frontier, I offset their bias by employing three methodological strategies. First, when possible I emphasize the experiences of the women and children that often accompanied these settlers and indigenous resisters. From the outset it was clear that families and their shifting roles formed an important part of capturing change over time. For example, Burnham's insistence that his family accompany him to Southern Rhodesia in the 1890s stood in stark contrast to his later adventures in Mexico. Faster and cheaper transportation mainly accounted for this, though a number of other factors contributed. Southern Rhodesia, so far away—reached by steamer, train, and then stagecoach—did not allow for the cross-border jaunts that kept the Mexican North so close to southern California.

The dynamics of gender and families make their most forceful appearance with the Eatons. Struggling to convert Catholics and socially isolated from most laborers in Chihuahua, the couple explicitly targeted women and children as a way to build their church. The significance of kin networks with the Eatons and with their Boer colonist neighbors resonates with Yaqui stories foregrounding gendered narratives. I have previously used a "home lands" framework, first advanced by Virginia Scharff and

Carolyn Brucken, to understand the importance of family in the colonial and capitalist encounter.[17] This model proposes understanding history as a way of making, maintaining, and breaking home spaces or places where peoples inevitably compete for resources. The definition of "home" as both domestic residence and region of belonging therefore puts families into the same conversation as states. Readers will see the home lands theme emerge in subtle ways in every chapter.[18]

Second, I sought indigenous perspectives of this past by conducting oral history interviews with Yaquis in Sonora. To many of the non-Yoeme actors in these chapters, native peoples were either obstacles to the future or they were relics of the past. Yet indigenous peoples like the Yaquis determined the outcome of this history. They understood and defined their regions on their own terms, often indifferent to settlers' attitudes about civilization. Government officials may have presumed that native peoples stood in opposition to progress, but, as the case of the Yoemem demonstrates, they frequently used the very technologies and beliefs introduced by Euro-American settlers to demarcate and develop their own cultural practices, showing resilience in the face of overwhelming forces.

Indigenous interaction, accommodation, resistance, and adaptation most forcefully come to the fore in chapter 5, where the Yaquis struggle to maintain sovereignty against the many characters of the preceding chapters. If anything, this book should contribute to a deeper understanding of the outside interests against which they fought: a millionaire mining engineer and his network of investors, a ruthless military man prepared to defend U.S. and Mexican claims on indigenous lands, a glory-seeking Boer veteran having the ear of Mexico's new president, and the ideological argument that all of these men held, namely, that indigenous societies were doomed, quite simply, to extinction. To think that this moment of Yaqui and Mexican history registers today as a mere blip on the historical radar underscores how long and fraught the Yaqui experience has been in dealing with outsiders over the past five hundred years. The ways in which Yoemem worked with and against aggressors in 1910–13 repeated previous patterns of accommodation and resistance, more accurately described as indigenous resilience, but chapter 5 offers new views into how families were both targets of ethnic cleansing and simultaneously the source of effective survival strategies.[19]

Digging into the history of the Yaquis gave me a profound appreciation for the Yoeme past and present, and it required additional care and sensitivity around the question of bias in the historical record. Scholars of Native America and Africa, like the subjects of their studies, contend with this daily. To compensate for the prejudices of colonial officials, adventurers, and capitalists, who were more likely to leave behind written records and memoirs, I relied on my Yaqui participants' oral histories. Anecdotes, tales, traditions, and myths can be slippery sources, for sure, and so I listened for general themes to emerge from the collected stories. This contributed an invigorating perspective on the Yaqui wars of the nineteenth and early twentieth centuries, one unrecorded in most history books. Owing to the relative inaccessibility of Yoeme perspectives and because I analyze them in the final chapter, I have deposited the audio recordings and transcripts with the Museo de los Yaquis in Cócorit, Sonora.

I also actively sought descendants of all my other historical subjects—capitalists, adventurers, Boers, Mexicans, and missionaries—and conducted interviews and informal discussions about their ancestors while also requesting privately held documents. The details of these can be found in the corresponding chapters and footnotes. Interacting with the descendants proved exciting yet produced some insomnia at times, as I wrestled to balance critical interpretation with respect for my interviewees' vested interests. Most of the events I discuss here transpired more than a century ago, but the family ties remain strong. In cases of uncertainty I stuck to the sources, and I hope that where family members may disagree with my interpretation they will nevertheless respect the care I took to uncover the past.

My third methodological strategy safeguarded against nationalist bias. As borderlands historians are trained to do, I consulted archives (mainly in Spanish and English) in multiple locations relevant to this history: New Haven, Boston, Johannesburg, Stellenbosch, Chihuahua, Hermosillo, Las Cruces, Albuquerque, Los Angeles, Dallas, Reno, and Tucson. When sufficient evidence enabled viewing history from more than one perspective, I attempted to represent competing interests from multiple vantage points.

These methodological adjustments come to the fore and recede as the narrative progresses, but the historical characters and the themes resonant across continents tie the five chapters together. I suspect that other scholars may recognize similar frontier connections to other parts of the world, to areas beyond my own specialization, and I can only hope that these may broaden the research begun here. Indeed, rather than cast these transnational connections aside as oddities or quirks of history, we historians should take seriously the forces that placed them there. Do historical anomalies exist? I'm not sure. But by refusing to dismiss them without thought, the history of the U.S. experience in the Mexican North suddenly resonates with the themes of capitalist development that shaped southern Africa, as U.S. investors shied away from territorial acquisition and sought less ostentatious models of economic expansion. This migrating practice beyond the nation's borders was carried by common actors, powered by currents that linked the frontier West to British imperial worlds.

To uncover this past, we board a catamaran to cross Lake Pátzcuaro in central Mexico in 1888. An American artist and engineer, Francis Hopkinson Smith, rides with six natives and a guide he calls Moon, who holds the tiller to steer the vessel toward a small village. Smith has heard rumors that a European masterpiece—a Titian painting—hangs, unrecognized and unappreciated, in a remote village chapel. Overcome by curiosity, and like many Americans of his day, Smith seeks to find this treasure in the Mexican countryside, unaware of the historical and narrative currents beneath him, propelling his adventure.

ONE

The Titian in Tzintzuntzan

Frontier Adventures and the Development of Latent Wealth

AN AGED BELL TOWER MARKED FRANCIS Hopkinson Smith's destination. It bobbed on the horizon as he, his guide, and six native rowers traversed Lake Pátzcuaro in a catamaran, 160 miles west of Mexico City, in 1888. Born in Maryland, Smith was an artist, writer, and engineer of note. Two years earlier, he had constructed the foundation of the Statue of Liberty. Having an interest in relaxation and an artist's eye trained for beauty, Smith had embarked on a vacation south of the border, intent on painting and writing a memoir, presenting to his readers "what would appeal to the painter and idler" without going "very far below the surface."[1] Nevertheless, superficial leisure alone had not inspired his adventure to the nearby village of Tzintzuntzan. A story had.

Smith had read an article in *Harper's New Monthly* by another painter and author, Charles Dudley Warner, who told of a masterpiece hanging on the crumbling walls of the town's church. In the article, published the previous year, Warner recalled feeling as if he had "stepped back into the sixteenth century" in the churchyard, shaded by centuries-old olive trees.[2] After entering an inner sanctum Warner found himself standing in front of the unidentified painting. He described in detail "the treasure of Mexico," a fifteen-foot "Entombment" of Christ, possibly painted by Titian, he conjectured, "lost to the world and unappreciated."[3] Warner analyzed the image, finding true beauty, though he "[could not] say how much was due to the contrast of the surroundings," noting the "ignorant natives and the priest who guards it . . . attributing to its presence here . . . a supernatural influence."[4] Warner sketched the painting, reprinted in *Harper's*, and asked readers if the work was "really a Titian," hoping "some investigation abroad" might "settle the question."[5]

With Warner's questions firing his imagination, Smith stepped out of his catamaran and took in the new world before him. The residents of Tzintzuntzan witnessing his arrival looked on "with wonder-stricken faces," he wrote, "as curious a crowd of natives as ever greeted the great Christopher [Columbus] himself."[6] Smith translated the stares as ignorance, unaware perhaps that a fair-skinned English speaker carrying a white parasol and lugging an easel might constitute a spectacle in its own right. Between the visual of Tzintzuntzan itself and its inverted projection on Smith's retinae, the everyday life around him transformed into fantasy. Smith fancied himself an adventurer akin to Allan Quatermain, the fictitious hero of Rider Haggard's classic novel *King Solomon's Mines* (1885), the precursor to today's Indiana Jones. He walked through the village, noting the imposing walls, some "broken by great fissures." He peeked through the cracks to find "abandoned tenements overgrown with weeds and tangled vines."[7] Around him everywhere wilderness attempted to reclaim civilization. Smith, wielding his paintbrush in lieu of a machete, would slice through the overgrown myths to rescue the long-lost masterpiece and uncover the hidden wealth in darkest Mexico.

The similarities between the American myth of a Titian in Tzintzuntzan, on the one hand, and British imperial adventure novels like *King Solomon's Mines*, on the other, testify to the ways in which American expansion into Mexico in the late 1800s overlapped with British imperial culture during the age of Queen Victoria. This dual ideology, with frontier roots and imperial overtones, similarly guided U.S. economic expansion in the late nineteenth century. In this chapter I analyze the Titian-in-Tzintzuntzan myth and its history to interrogate the gilded tales that drove U.S. capitalist development to the "treasure house" south of the border in the late nineteenth century.[8] The possibility of uncovering hidden riches in Mexico appealed to artists, engineers, and miners alike, and the narratives that drove these people south—and overseas—became all the more seductive with the construction of railroad lines between the United States and Mexico after 1880. From the perspective of the Mexican government, American dreamers of the capitalist persuasion brought with them much-needed knowledge, technology, and financing. The boom times that followed the laying of railroad tracks enabled the nation to grow economically, but they also set the stage for political instability and the nation's uneven development.[9]

With his guide, Moon, by his side, Smith passed empty rooms "infested with lizards and bats." He commented that underground passages near the church had been recently discovered by foreigners, yet hidden once again by natives. Secrecy surrounded him. Inside the church Smith and Moon encountered the padre seated "in the darkest corner of a low-ceiled room . . . surrounded by half a dozen Indian women."[10] When his desire to view the painting was rebuffed, Moon convinced the padre by producing gifts, including some type of alcohol—perhaps pulque—and five pesos. The priest relented. As Moon, the padre, and Smith made their way to an inner sanctum, Smith became "aware of an especial espionage over us, which was never relaxed for a single instant." The natives were "suspicious of strangers who come from a distance to see [the painting], they worshipping it with a blind idolatry easily understood in their race."[11] Once in the interior room, Smith encountered the massive painting, lighted by a single open window that allowed daylight to disperse the darkness. Overwhelmed by the artistic beauty, Smith allowed passion to overtake reason; he concluded that the painting was a Titian. The artist-adventurer opened his easel "and began a hurried memorandum of the interior. . . . The picture absorbed me. I wanted to be shut up alone with it."[12] He surveyed the room, now left alone for the moment by the padre and Moon, and in order to "make a closer study of the texture of the canvas and the handling of the pigments, I mounted the bureau itself and walked the length of the painting, applying my pocket magnifying glass to the varnished surface. Looking closer I found the over-glaze to be rich and singularly transparent, and after a careful scrutiny fancied I could separate into distinct tones the peculiar mosaic of color in which most of all lies the secret of Titian's flesh. In the eagerness of my search I unconsciously bent forward and laid my hand upon the Christ."[13] Unaware of his transgression, Smith was startled by "two Indians," one of whom "advanced threateningly, [as] the other rushed out shouting for the padre. In an instant the room was crowded with natives clamoring wildly, and pointing at me with angry looks and gestures."[14]

Trapped on the bureau by rapture, Smith took orders from the nimble-minded Moon, who tried to justify the touching of the surface. The artist was previously unable to paint, Moon claimed, and in a dream Smith had been instructed to make a pilgrimage, whereby his abilities would be restored. Apparently more open to spiritual reasoning, the angry padre and the natives softened, the "change in their demeanor was instantaneous."[15] Moon thus tricked the purportedly gullible natives into letting Smith leave unharmed.

Smith's tale—of ignorant and threatening Indians, of reclaiming European heritage in the form of an artwork, of bribing a priest to enter the inner sanctum, of beholding the Titian masterpiece, of painting a reproduction of it, and of barely escaping an angry mob of natives with the help of his guide—reeks of late Victorian colonial ideology. Smith tried to live as a romantic adventurer, finding wealth and value in lands lost to time.

His story is noteworthy not for its unique thrill but for its ubiquity. It was neither the first nor the last expedition to find the "lost" Titian in the Mexican countryside. In addition to his and Warner's previous expeditions, the Titian-in-Tzintzuntzan myth was continued by an English businessman and adventure seeker, John Gladwyn Jebb, who claimed that the painting was protected, like all of the treasures of the Aztecs, in one of the "out-of-the-way corners of the sierras where sometimes stray fragments of strange, wild stories can be heard about temples yet devoted to Aztec gods, which are hidden away in mountain fastnesses, and whose whereabouts are known only to the few tribes who, through all persecution and change, have kept the faith of their fathers."[16] Whereas Smith fancied himself a modern-day Christopher Columbus, Jebb claimed to be the first European to penetrate a "mountain abode of unmixed Indians."[17] And, like Smith, Jebb remarked on the silence of the distrusting natives, who "can keep their secrets well" and who "jealously guarded" their treasure.[18] Jebb also bribed the priest to view the painting, its beauty radiating amid the darkness. Like all of his predecessors, Jebb escaped an "angry throng of excited Indians."[19]

Warner's, Smith's, and Jebb's accounts did not end this tradition of exotic adventure and treasure recovery. A photographer picked it up for his journalistic exposé in *World Wide Magazine* (1900); an anonymous author published a full-page piece covering page two of the *New York Sun* (1906); and a poet proclaimed in 1923, "But suddenly a window opens wide, / And afternoon pours in its golden tide / Showing us there upon the old stone wall / Of Titian's genius masterpiece of all."[20] Despite the proclaimed authenticity of each tale, rumors that a Titian hung in the church persisted for eighty years and followed identical storylines, regardless of the fact that, in 1891, a Mexican art historian had attributed the artwork not to Titian but to the Spanish artist Baltasar de Echave.[21]

These various versions of the myth do more than replicate a particular story. They function as quests and use similar narrative constructs made famous by *King Solomon's Mines*. (It is no coincidence, therefore, that Jebb, one raconteur of the myth, was in fact close friends with the novel's author, who wrote the introduction to Jebb's posthumous memoirs. The pair had even planned on searching for Montezuma's rumored treasure together in Mexico.) Set in British South Africa, Haggard's novel follows Allan Quatermain and his accomplices as they attempt to recover diamonds and riches from the terrible grasp of the fictitious King Twala.[22] To do so, the treasure seekers outwit the natives by pretending to be "white men from the stars" with the power of gods. Vastly outnumbered, Quatermain convinces a rival faction leader under King Twala to ally with the Europeans and to lead them to the legendary treasure chamber. Their guide accedes and takes them all the way to an inner sanctum adorned with the skeletons of past leaders. Thus presenting the British journeymen with specters of the ancient past, the guide moves a lever and a hidden stone door rises to reveal the great treasures within the mountain. After marveling at the riches, Quatermain and his associates soon become trapped and must escape through a hidden tunnel to a river and thence to safety.

This sketch of the plot illustrates a schematic of Victorian adventures: rumors of lost treasure, unwitting natives who do not understand or deserve its wealth, an adventurer who braves the wilds to recover the riches, and a sacred chamber complete with a trick lever that bestows the hidden riches upon the worthy warrior. The parallels between *King Solomon's Mines* and Titian-in-Tzintzuntzan are clear. Not only do Warner, Smith, Jebb, and others venture into purportedly unknown territory; they, too, must convince natives and bribe a priest to allow them into the inner sanctum, to open the window, to cast light onto darkness, and to appreciate a treasure once lost to civilization. One self-proclaimed adventurer in Mexico attested even to having been assaulted by the natives, awakening in a cave, and crawling through a hidden tunnel, à la Quatermain, to a water-bound escape.[23]

At the core of these various legends and expeditions resides a Victorian imperial culture, but digging beneath the surface of adventure fiction uncovers the origin of this myth, connected to painters affiliated with the Hudson River School, a group of nineteenth-century American artists with a romanticized vision of the U.S. West. To get at this western foundation one must consult the archives of the nineteenth-century artist Howard Russell Butler, whose unpublished papers take credit for inspiring the myth that would captivate American audiences for decades.

Born in New York in 1856, Butler grew up as the child of two artists. He attended Princeton University and, upon graduating, combined his interests in the arts and sciences by joining the Princeton Geological Expedition of 1877 to the Rocky Mountains as an assistant photographer. Thereafter, Butler could not settle on a profession, working first in the telegraph business and later becoming a patent lawyer. Artistic inclinations tugged at him, and in 1884 he pulled out a sheet of paper, drew a line down the middle, labeled one half "Law" and the other half "Art," and made a balance sheet that would determine his future career. His choice of art came quickly. "I have found joy and health and much inspiring subject-matter for oils, water colors and pastels in various parts of the West and Mexico," he later wrote.

Attracted by landscapes in frontier regions, Butler traveled to central Mexico in 1884 at the invitation of Frederic Church, famous for his association with the Hudson River School and with other prominent artists like Albert Bierstadt. Church had been drawn to Latin American landscapes for some time, and the opportunity to paint alongside the famous artist gave

Butler a boost in finding his unique vision. This generation of painters—
Church, Bierstadt, Frederick Catherwood, James Whistler, and others—
traveled throughout the American West and Latin America, producing
vast landscapes on enormous canvases. The anthropologist Deborah
Poole has noted that this artistic tradition coincided with increasing commercial interests beyond the nation's shores, culminating in what she
called the "visual property of empire."[24] As their works were most prominently displayed in the East, the artists of the Hudson River School and
their apprentices exposed New Englanders to lands unknown to them beyond the Mississippi and far south of the Rio Grande. Church's invitation
to Butler must have thrilled the young apprentice, who had decided only
recently to pursue a career as a full-time painter.

Butler and Church traveled in Mexico together and to Tzintzuntzan,
where they encountered the "Entombment." Butler used the large work as
a study for several sketches and paintings. This was the first of two trips
for him, and his reminiscences of the visit do not contain many of the adventure tropes found in later iterations of the myth. In contrast to the ex-
plorer fleeing the village full of dangerous natives, Butler and his traveling
companion spent three days there, renting a small house from one of the
residents. His encounters with the priest align with the myth in the popular press (the padre apparently accepted bribes and was appreciative of flattery), yet Butler's account of his final day examining the painting adds
depth to the caricature of superstitious Indians. As he finished a replica,
the priest asked for his recommendations on preserving the original.
Butler, through his interpreter and companion, mentioned that "there are
certain spots which look like old varnish which should be removed. The
priest asked where and rising, I went to the end of the room where the
picture was and mounting on a cupboard, pointed to the spots in question. An uproar in the back of the room made me turn and Perry shouted
'For God's sake, don't touch the picture.' The priest and the many peons
in the back of the room were greatly excited. I asked Perry what I had
done and he explained that the priest said that those spots were the blood
of the savior, which had miraculously appeared on the picture. This was
the miracle of Tzintzuntzan!"[25] Butler recorded this story toward the end

of his life in an unpublished autobiography. Though memory can often-times deceive, his experiences in 1884, especially of the angered natives, appear to have formed the myth's foundations. (Interestingly, the indigenous actors in Butler's papers are agitated less by any "native superstition," as later storytellers would portray them, than by their belief in *Christian* superstition about the apparition of Christ's blood.) Butler acknowledges himself as the inspiration for later tales, and it is furthermore likely that he invited Warner to view the famous painting in 1887, leading to the *Harper's* article and to the arrival of Smith in 1888. The painting stayed intact for decades until, in 1944, the parish church burned to the ground.[26] To this day the most detailed color replica of the "Entombment" remains the facsimile that Butler painted on his trip with Church (fig. 1).

The origin of the myth denotes the dual nature of how Americans, and in this case American painters, viewed Mexico in the late nineteenth century. First, it shows how they found artistic inspiration and romanticized frontier lands on both sides of the border. Artists easily transferred their skills from representing the West on landscapes to incorporating Mexican works in their oeuvres. This transformation from understanding the West to seeing potential in Mexico would motivate similarly capitalist and entrepreneurial agendas.

Second, the myth's origin and circulation in the borderlands make evident the significance of these stories regardless of their originality, whether started by Butler, used by Smith, or reprinted as original adventures by others after the turn of the twentieth century. The persistence of this legend proves its salience to both British and American audiences, which consumed the adventure mystery long after it arguably was solved in 1891. Magazine and newspaper editors, book publishers, and the reading public devoured the recurring Titian-in-Tzintzuntzan myth because it appealed to and reflected Victorian British and American frontier sensibilities. Such tales of Mexico introduced the country as an exotic wonderland to American readers, drawing on a tradition of established tropes in British imperial adventure novels.[27] Furthermore, the appeal of the story—its central irony—revolves around unrecognized, unappreciated riches awaiting recovery. In this way the mystery of a lost Titian constituted but one

Figure 1.   A study sketch of a supposed Titian painting, 1888. Howard Russell Butler Papers, 1874–1936. Archives of American Art, Smithsonian Institution.

variation of a theme—latent wealth—used most effectively by boosters in the United States with an interest in capitalist development.[28]

Artistic Discovery, Gender, and the Claiming of Mines

Few themes wielded as much influence on U.S. expansion into Mexico as the reclamation of lost wealth, and one couple embodied the connection between the artistic theme and the economic realities of development: the novelist Frances Christine Fisher and her husband, James Tierney. Fisher's and Tierney's experiences in Mexico expose the inconsistencies between the literary symbols and ideologies used to narrate the quest for wealth, on the one hand, and the realities of the journey, on the other.

Born in Salisbury, North Carolina, in 1846, Frances Christine Fisher grew up a member of the aristocratic old South. Her father, a miner, railroad president, and Confederate colonel, died in the Civil War when she was fifteen. Thereafter, Fisher lived with her aunt, in whose presence she acquired her Catholic faith and honed her abilities as a writer.[29] Fisher's first few novels unfolded among an aristocratic milieu in southern landscapes. Regional fame soon followed. She had written eighteen novels by 1887, when, at the age of forty-one, she wed James Tierney, a mineralogist for the Northern Pacific Railroad. The newlyweds honeymooned in Mexico, looked for investment opportunities there, and returned to the State of Durango intermittently over the next ten years in search of wealth: he for minerals, she for narrative. The years in Mexico influenced Fisher's writing, evident in themes like the country's landscapes, the author's deepening Catholicism, and her explorations of plantocracies, capitalist development, and patriarchy. Each characterized her works from this era, but it was her *Picture of Las Cruces* (1894) that garnered early critical acclaim, a work that exemplifies the cultural undercurrents guiding U.S. expansion.[30]

The Picture of Las Cruces recounts the adventure of an American painter, Ralph Ingraham, who hears of a lost painting by Diego Velázquez in the dark recesses of an hacienda not far from Lake Pátzcuaro.[31] Ingraham, suspicious of the tale, decides to seek the truth if for nothing more than the thrill of it all. "Adventures, perhaps," he justifies to himself, "would be even more desirable than possible Murillos and Titians."[32] At the ranch near Lake Pátzcuaro the hacendado invites Ingraham into an inner room and provides the artist with his moment of discovery: "As they paused before a painting that in the obscurity could only be dimly perceived, he unbarred one of the heavily-shuttered windows opposite. Throwing it open, a flood of light poured over the canvas, and Ingraham, stepping back, uttered an uncontrollable exclamation. 'How beautiful!' he cried; and then, 'It *is* a Velasquez, by heaven!' . . . A Velasquez, buried here on this remote Mexican hacienda!"[33]

Daylight exposes the masterpiece, not a painting of Titian's Entombment but one of "the Marquesa," an ancestor from Spain; it also unveils the true beauty of the hacendado's daughter, Carmen, standing nearby. While Ingraham admires the painting, he is overcome by the striking resemblance between Carmen and the Marquesa. Each captivates him. Art, like beauty, requires recognition. A European masterpiece hanging on the walls of an hacienda—like a Titian among Indians—demands recovery. For, as Ingraham himself realized before setting out to find the painting, he "could not but own that there was a singular fascination in these stories of mines of fabulous richness waiting only the magic touch of capital to develop them . . . and even of the buried treasure of which so many tales are rife in Mexico."[34] Likewise, Carmen's beauty had passed heretofore unknown. Her strong resemblance to Spanish aristocrats, if not royalty, gives her new value in the countryside. Ingraham, who discovered the likeness, insists on painting her portrait, dressed as the Marquesa, for it is only through the American's paintbrush that the hidden Spanish beauty can be reclaimed from rural obscurity (fig. 2). Through the artistic rendering Ingraham claims ownership of her heart. "She was his by every possible claim," Ingraham thinks as he later competes for her love, "his, as he had declared, not only by right of discovery, but by right of awakening to knowledge of herself. And when was it ever heard that the bold adventurer who rescues and awakens the sleeping princess yielded her to another?"[35] By Ingraham's right of discovery, the artist owns the painting. The man claims the woman. The American miner justifies ownership of Mexican minerals.

Fisher not only fixed capitalist values onto Mexican landscapes; she imbued them with feminine properties. Consistent with American frontier expansion centuries past, authors and American capitalists gendered the Mexican landscape as female, a virgin and romantic land awaiting recognition, penetration, and exploitation.[36] The country appears in both nonfiction and fiction as radiant, a "sweet dream of my heart," my "dark-eyed Mexico."[37] The conquest of land and riches so evident in the Titian-in-Tzintzuntzan myth and in the Mexican novels of Fisher resounded with Arthurian tales of conquering a woman's affections. One commercial guide to Sonora, for example, proclaimed in 1897,

> The wealth of a nation a thousand-fold lies
> Beneath the gay blossoms that gleam on your breast;
> . . .
> Ah, there is a ransom for all the world's kings,

Figure 2.   Ludovico Marchetti, untitled illustration accompanying Christian
Reid [Frances Christine Fisher], "Le Tableau de las Cruces." *L'Illustration*,
August 18, 1894, n.p.

Which needs but the sinew, the muscle and bone
Of the rough, hardy miner, with knowledge imbued,
To seize the rare treasure and make it his own.
To give to the world this great store from your heart,
Till men everywhere shall your richness proclaim,
And speak of your opulent beauty sublime,
With a tremor of joy at the sound of your name![38]

The tradition of exploration, expansion, serenading a virgin land, and penetrating her lands to extract her riches continued from the earliest of frontiers, to the West, and then south.[39] These tales exuded a colonialist ethos that rationalized the exploitation of resources and people in the development of native lands. The trope of lost treasure guarded by indigenous populations thus resonated in turn-of-the-century American literature on Mexico as it did in tales from other frontier zones. Mexico became one more stop on an imperial adventure circuit.

Youth literature especially reinforced these imperial values and regenerated ways of seeing foreign lands. By the 1890s children's adventure tales highlighted the nation among other global imperial locales. In the "Knockabout Club" series, for example, two globe-trotting boys in Mexico find "nothing less" than "the treasure of the Aztec King!"[40] English and American literature thus entwined the nation within an imperial formation. The continuities between British informal empire in Mexico and U.S. expansion southward expressed themselves most vividly in such adventure tales. These outgrowths of imperial logic proliferated in the last half of the nineteenth century, when more than thirty British and American novels were set in this dreamscape, past and present.[41]

While latent wealth or treasure may appear to be the central element of these stories, the presence of native peoples operates as their fulcrum. Legends of the lost Titian portray natives as gullible, superstitious, and ignorant of the wealth around them, hanging on their very walls. As one scholar wrote in 1901, ["The] Indians of the region, while they cannot appreciate the painting as a work of art, nevertheless are so strongly attached to it through superstitious veneration, enhanced by its recent fame, that nothing will induce them to part with it, although enormous sums have been offered."[42] Native communities therefore became the ubiquitous other, a stock character appearing in treasure tales from colonial and imperial encounters. Peasants in Tzintzuntzan thereby filled the same role played by fictitious Bantu chiefs on the opposite side of the ocean. The continuities between lost valuables—paintings, precious gems, and mines—guarded by indigenous peoples formed a substantial corpus of folklore and mythology in zones of cultural encounter.

In reality, the curious peasants of Tzintzuntzan were Purépecha, founders of the pre-Columbian Tarascan state that was separate from the expanding Aztec Empire by 1300.[43] Expansionist in their own right, the Tarascan people were far from silent observers and must have tired from a regular cavalcade of quixotic adventurers—all white, all male—intent on fulfilling their fantasies at the Tarascans' expense: Church, Warner, Smith, Jebb, a photographer, a reporter, and so on. Though they would not have had access to the myths published in English beyond their borders, the Tarascans were clearly onto the game. When Smith first visited in 1888 he noted that the priest, unenthused by the artist's arrival, had been forewarned of Smith's interest in the "Entombment" by a group of indigenous emissaries.

As these stories indicate, American artists and capitalists viewed it as their natural right, even duty, to develop untapped resources south of the border. Promoters of investment opportunities ostensibly derided rumors of lost treasure as a way to increase the legitimacy of their own cross-border searches for wealth; but in so doing they merely perpetuated the underlying message of imminent riches. As one investment pamphlet for the Mexican Central Railway commanded, "Stop Chasing Rainbows! Come to Mexico and Find the Veritable Pot of Gold" (fig. 3).[44]

The push and pull of American capital induced social, economic, and cultural encounters that would further unite the borderlands in profound ways. U.S. expansion into Mexican markets, however, did not result in unilateral exchanges. Fisher's husband, James Tiernan, witnessed the unvarnished reality of life on the ground, which often challenged the rhetoric of annual company reports and capital stock figures. In 1894 he traveled to conduct an inventory of a company's gold, silver, and lead mine in Topia, Durango, and to resolve a lawsuit between investors, local officials, and land agents.[45] Tiernan drew on his experience as a former mineralogist for the Northern Pacific Railroad and later as a colonization agent for the Richmond and Danville Railroad in North Carolina.[46] On his journey through the countryside he was reminded of his wife and her recent publishing success and soon-to-be-released *The Picture of Las Cruces*.

Figure 3. Cover of *Brief Sketches in Mexico: Its Large Cities and Points of Interest* (Mexico: Edgard Bouligny, 1893). Beinecke Rare Book and Manuscript Library, Yale University.

Tiernan dined with government officials in Mexico City and, following the standard capitalist playbook during the Porfiriato, met with President Porfirio Díaz, "the greatest dictator now living," he wrote.[47] Díaz promised to send him a letter of introduction to officials in Durango, and Tiernan reciprocated with a copy of one of Fisher's novels. "I am pleased that you and your associates are doing so much to assist in the development of our country," the president said, "and you shall have justice done."[48]

Tiernan soon descended from the rarefied heights of presidential politics to travel to Topia—two days by stagecoach and six by horseback. The population there, he discovered, "is the very roughest to be found."[49]

Once at the mine Tiernan discovered a reality far removed from mines awaiting the simple touch of American capital, of hidden paintings easily revealed by opening a window. The "cream of the mines" had been "skimmed off to enrich persons connected with this operation but the company has had nothing but the payment of the bills," he wrote. One female employee was "stealing every cent she can," and a mill operator unwilling to overexert himself, "being the only one who understands the leeching process, which is complicated, . . . is taking advantage of his knowledge to do nearly as he pleases."[50] Local conditions outmaneuvered absent foreign investors with elite credentials and golden dreams. The well-paid laborers created ways to maintain power and regulate conditions in the mine. With regard to the obstinate mill operator, Tiernan found himself "in the same subservient position that all the other managers were in, and that was, to submit to him in everything."[51]

The confident mine manager quickly learned that investors, boosters, and company reports presented but one side of the reality of American investments south of the border. When Tiernan died in 1898, Fisher took full possession of the couple's languishing investments, and by 1915, after the onset of the Mexican Revolution, her remaining holdings amounted to nothing. Reality proved far more difficult than the pots of gold promised by the Mexican Central Railway. Such booster literature, as well as the general tenor of perspectives of Gilded Age Mexico, attempted to entice investors with railway, mining, and colonization schemes.

Tiernan and Fisher encountered difficulties in Durango, and American investors likewise had trouble inducing waves of southern migration akin to those in the U.S. West. When the Mexican Revolution began, dreams of imminent wealth vanished for the typical investor and certainly for the common family. Writing on the failures of immigration, a British investor reported, "Hundreds of poor families were induced to leave the States of the Middle West and emigrate to occupy the 'desirable lots' of the land companies." Abandoned household objects sat silently in Mexican customshouses. "It was terribly pathetic, . . . the big deal packing-cases with their poor contents: the little household things of the settlers—crockery, babies' clothes, packets of seeds, and little home-made things like knitted comforters; the family Bible and a few books of the Sunday-school type—some of them prizes—all carried to the new home in glorious Mexico!"[52] Others also saw the effects of golden dreams deferred. "Some investors had returned wiser," wrote one contemporary, "but never was one known to return richer."[53] As early as 1894 American consuls began warning their citizens to be wary of "alluring statements . . . to emigrate [sic] to Mexico," that "disappointment is the result of emigration undertaken upon insufficient or misleading information."[54]

The statistics of U.S. investment in Mexico were equally misleading. Although between 1884 and 1910 it appeared that U.S.-backed holdings increased Mexican rail lineage from 3,682 to 15,360 miles and that by 1902 Americans owned 80 percent of railroads, historians then and since have recognized that such startling figures did not lead directly to tremendous profits. In 1917 the economic journalist Clarence Barron remarked that "for years the Atchison folders printed the Mexican lines almost as their own. Today on the Atchison folders connections north even into Canada may be traced, but Mexico is a foreign country upon which the railroads need not waste paper in maps or timetables. A thumbnail corner in the Santa Fe map shows Mexico and on it from Mexico City to the Rio Grande on the coast is a wilderness broken only by the harbor of Tampico."[55] Writing forty years later, the historian David M. Pletcher concluded that "not a single major line [in Mexico] justified its advance publicity" and that "the profits which they described so glowingly were a mirage, a fantasy of their overheated imaginations."[56]

With the nationalization of the railways in 1909 it would thus appear that, for all the writing on the dominance of U.S. empire by railroads, Mexico actually made a decent investment by allowing American capital to develop its national railways. As John Coatsworth has shown, the source of investments notwithstanding, construction of railroads was essential to the growth of the Mexican economy, more so than in the United States.[57] Given the advantage of hindsight, history has confirmed that, so far as overall U.S.

investment in railroads is concerned, Americans earned far less than their dreams had projected. Investors, so assured of vast profits based on the largesse of previous rail construction in the U.S. West, were misguided by their own ideology, a dynamic lampooned by the great British novelist Anthony Trollope.[58] The fact that Americans owned 80 percent of the railroads of Mexico by 1902 therefore does not reflect an omnipotent force on the ground. Financial control of the railroad companies simply did not flood the vast majority of stateside bank accounts, nor should it unquestionably substantiate American influence for historians. If this holds true for the railways, historians should be leery of interpreting "empire" purely from company reports and economic indicators without context.[59]

In terms of U.S. emigrants the numbers are even less convincing. The Mexican Census of 1900 reported 15,265 resident Americans, a mere 0.1 percent of the nation's 13.6 million inhabitants. The U.S. consul-general to Mexico, Andrew Barlow, estimated that of these, "It is said that the average residence [is] three years. It is certain that the American population of Mexico is floating to a certain extent . . . I do not believe there is any great amount of profit on American capital invested in Mexico at present," he reported.[60] Nevertheless, throughout this entire period promoters continued to draw on language fresh from the pages of booster materials to the Southwest and California, using frontier rhetoric as a recruiting tool. They bet that relying on a westering logic could easily cross a line in the sand. This "western turn South," begun in the middle nineteenth century and mature by 1880, thereby pitched the southern republic as the next frontier, encouraging hardy homesteaders and capitalists alike to venture across the border.

The Western Turn South, 1853–80

Before 1880, when railways facilitated cross-border capitalism, the borderlands had remained a series of isolated outposts caught between many competing peoples, among them: Spanish, Mexican, French, Comanche, and Apache.[61] After the Mexican–American War (1846–48) and with the Treaty of Guadalupe Hidalgo (1853) the United States added to its territory nearly half of its southern neighbor and began a period of economic and cultural transformation of the borderlands. Territory in the present-day Southwest became available to adventurers, scientists, administrators, and immigrants to explore, study, govern, and develop. Capitalists looked even further south; expansionists and war hawks cried for "All Mexico!"[62] After 1880 this ad hoc movement gained steam with the extension of railroad lines north and south of the border. The increased circulation of capitalists, entrepreneurs, miners, ranchers, bandits, scoundrels, and boosters—not always mutually exclusive and seldom immigrants—brought an American dream to the borderlands. This movement peaked between 1890 and 1910 as artists searched for hidden masterpieces and capitalists looked for lost mines. Scores of Americans sought their own riches along the U.S.–Mexican frontier.[63]

Economic ambitions dovetailed nicely with aggressive political agendas. Secretary of State William Seward, who had coordinated the 1867 purchase of Russian America, supported "the ever-increasing expansion of the American people westward and southward. Five years, ten years, twenty years hence," he argued, "Mexico will be opening herself as cheerfully to American immigration as Montana and Idaho are now."[64] Like the West, these lands lay contiguous to the continental United States. The diffusion of American culture into the Southwest and Mexico, and vice versa, proved facile and yet raised a troubling set of questions for politicians, capitalists, and intellectuals. Should the United States continue expanding? If so, how? And how could the U.S. body politic incorporate the foreign influences of colonized subjects? No single answer satisfied all Americans, many of whom feared with a sense of urgency the closing of the western frontier. Some wanted to follow the pattern of territorial acquisition that had served national interests so well in the West. Others promoted the domination of foreign markets without military intervention. Behind each possible solution, however, loomed an ideology of expansion and a transforming United States.

This transition was powered by the age-old quest for riches, but the language of progress and development that created the American West provided an ideological template for boosters in the borderlands region.

Railroad, mining, and irrigation experts believed that what had worked for the West could transform the Southwest and Mexican North. They promoted their cause with boisterous jubilation, dreaming of a day when the United States would annex its southern neighbor, if not Canada too. Yet rhetoric fell far short of reality. As one historian has noted in the case of Canada, "Most Americans remained indifferent to these proposals, and most Canadians were hostile to them. But proposals for annexation continued to appear, and the closing American frontier was usually an integral element in the arguments."[65] So it was with Mexico. The impact that boosters had in the press and in corporate promotions far outweighed the general will of most U.S. residents. This dichotomy misinformed the general public and especially Mexican officials, and it has misguided historians ever since. Nevertheless, the lofty rhetoric and golden dreams of American investors accompanied much of what was said and what happened in the borderlands.

Throughout the second half of the nineteenth century Americans and adventurers looked at the Mexican countryside as a great secret to future wealth beyond the western frontier. After gold was found near Sutter's Mill in California in 1848, prospectors' paths often wove through Mexico and the Southwest, exposing these dreamers to the borderlands' geography and its potential mineral wealth. Prospectors stood to gain the most by staying one step in front of the current mineral rush. Thus, after the secret of California had spread to the kitchen tables of the Middle West and the corporate boards of the East Coast, the prospecting fringe and other fortune hunters began to eye the new Southwest and adjacent lands south of the border. Miners in California "strained their eyes for prospects rendered more glittering by distance and vagueness," remarked Hubert Bancroft. "Stories of the precious mountains of Sonora, the gold nuggets of the Gila, and the silver bullets of the Apaches, so current on the Mexican border, found ready acceptance among this class of fortune-hunters, who dreamed only of sudden and easy acquisitions."[66]

Augmented by booster propaganda and early travelers' accounts, Mexico began to take shape in American minds as a logical extension of the American West, and vice versa. Emphasizing the similarities between industries and environments on both sides of the border naturalized the southern extension of western dreams. To gold rushers in California, the analogy took hold, given the regions' vast mineral wealth and environmental continuities. "It is *but natural* to go to California after visiting Sonora," wrote one visitor. "The history of the Southwest leads one out of Mexico, through Sonora, and on to Southern California. . . . The State of Sonora, Mexico, belongs to the Southwest."[67] Once established, these ideological channels guided western dreams further south. Miners with northern Californian experiences in the gold rush, for example, conceived of Baja California and Sonora as the next frontier.[68] The connections between the ports of San Francisco and Guaymas, Sonora, also elicited comparison, for Guaymas grew as a direct result of eastern and Californian investments. One traveler recalled, "Every steamer from San Francisco lands at Mazatlan and Guaymas from 100 to 200 passengers, many of whom, disappointed in more northern regions, desire to establish themselves in the rich mineral fields of the south."[69] U.S. capitalists began working old, abandoned mines in earnest after the 1870s, and by the end of the century Americans owned almost three hundred mines valued at $68 million, a figure that would increase fourfold by 1911.[70]

Along with growing U.S. interests in Mexico and the California gold rush, a nascent class of mining engineers began to traverse lands on both sides of the border and beyond. These young professionals often received training in Europe and moved within an informal, international network of engineers, adventurers, and investors who, like prospectors, crossed paths in California, Nevada, and Idaho as much as they did in southern Africa, Mexico, Australia, and the Alaskan Klondike. Their assessments of the profitability of domestic and foreign mines shaped U.S. investments and how Americans understood these lands. This was especially so with regard to Mexico. As one booster later quipped, "Old 'Forty-Niners' will remember the California market in the times before the war. Sonora is the California of Mexico, and history repeats itself."[71]

Men like John Hays Hammond exemplified the international reach of American mining engineers and the ties between western and global mineral frontiers. Born in San Francisco in 1855, Hammond grew up in gold rush California, learning of minerals and mirages by working the tailings of Chinese miners. "As I washed the gravel, sometimes finding as much as fifty cents' worth," he wrote of his boyhood, "dreams of fortune filled my head. I imagined myself a real miner, hiring hordes of Chinese to work for me. I was caught by the lure of gold."[72] Hammond studied at Yale College and then at the Mining Academy at Freiberg, Germany, before working for the U.S. Geological Survey under Clarence King to assay mines in Arizona, Nevada, and California. With this training and contacts through Freiberg alumni, Hammond was hired to manage a mine at Minas Nuevas in Sonora in the early 1880s. Between 1893 and 1900 he oversaw mining accounts for Cecil Rhodes's British South Africa Company and became entangled in regional politics of the British Empire.[73] After 1900 Hammond directed the operations of Daniel Guggenheim's smelters throughout northern Mexico. Like his professional peers, Hammond exported the past and the present of the American West into lands beyond U.S. borders.

For most of the early years after annexation, the Southwest lingered in national purgatory, what one popular writer described as a part of "the United States which is *not* United States."[74] Colonization companies such as the Lower California Company of New York, which formed in 1867, attempted to place American settlers in the borderlands. They hoped that, as one railroad company later claimed, "the American will find in Mexico infinitely more pleasant and hopeful conditions than the American of forty years ago found in Kansas and Nebraska."[75] For some, the designs of investors and colonists in Baja California, Sonora, and other north Mexican states seemed like "the story of Texas all over again!"[76] Unlike Texas, though, early attempts at American colonization in the Southwest and Mexican North never accelerated on par with expectations.[77] The failure to attract settlers before 1880 proves that the United States could not easily realize its own golden dreams in the borderlands through rhetoric alone. Sectional tensions related to the admission of western states and the resulting Civil War had discouraged many eastern investment houses from developing arid lands, and doubly so while mines near San Francisco continued to produce gold in quantity. Capitalists initially demurred when approached to fund pipe dreams beyond the Southwest; the French Intervention and the reign of Maximilian (1861–67) had undermined financial stability. Thus, with little colonization by capital-friendly families throughout the U.S.–Mexican borderlands, English-speaking easterners conceived of the Southwest as on the edges of the nation's geography, politics, economy, and culture.

To meet the challenge of populating the arid Southwest and the borderlands, promoters less frightened by risk drew upon previous successes in California and the Pacific Coast. The answer seemed obvious. "A railroad," wrote one surveyor, "will work the same magical change here that the iron-way does everywhere in the fertile lands of North America."[78] With the joining in 1869 of the Union Pacific and Central Pacific Railroads fresh in their minds, and with the great land grab that the creation of the first transcontinental line enabled, American capitalists were convinced that building railways could generate immense profits. Necessary or not, railways promised to alleviate many of the ills facing the Southwest: stiff resistance by Chiricahua Apaches and other Native Americans, sparse settlement by Anglo-Americans, little opportunity to produce for the U.S. market, and scant educational and religious influence. Railroads, developers hoped, would repeat before long their successes in the rest of the West. After the Civil War and Reconstruction, investors clamored to form companies and to purchase lands and rights of way in the Southwest and Mexico. Construction of the Atchison, Topeka and Santa Fe Railroad (ATSF) began in 1868, reaching the Colorado state line in 1873, Pueblo in 1876, Santa Fe in 1880, and El Paso in 1881.[79] The route followed the general contours of the Santa Fe Trail and El Camino Real. Rails replaced trails.

By 1880 the ATSF and the Southern Pacific connected the new Southwest to the rest of the nation, but anxieties unsettled investors, politicians, and elite Americans. Reality was catching up to unprecedented economic growth, and Americans feared waking from their frontier dreams along Pacific shores. William Henry Bishop, an affluent American and traveler in his early twenties, encapsulated this concern when he posed himself a question in 1881: "What is a world to do when it has no longer a West?"[80] Bishop had graduated from college in 1867 and spent his younger years traveling the world, a passion that would ultimately lead him to teach Spanish

and French for a decade, followed by a consular position in Italy in the early
twentieth century. These experiences nurtured Bishop's literary ambitions. He published articles and short stories in elite magazines. In 1881 the
thirty-four-year-old sailed from New York to Cuba and Mexico and then
journeyed by horse and rail into the Territory of Arizona. Along the way
he searched for a changing West, asking rhetorically, "When the race has
quite arrived at this farther shore, will it stop here? or will it possibly start
round the world again? Will it go on yet many times more, always beginning with the highest perfection yet attained, weaker types dying out in
front to make room, till it shall become in its march a dazzling army of
light?"[81]

For a century territorial expansion had provided the answer to Bishop's
overblown question. Americans enjoyed unprecedented growth through
ad hoc settlement, treaties made and broken, the removal and resettling of
Native Americans, military conquest, colonization companies, federal
funding of railroad development, and congressional support through legislation such as the Homestead Act of 1862. By the 1880s, though, fears of a
"closing frontier" forced investors to consider alternative forms of creating
foreign markets.[82] For the first time expansionists could not move into contiguous lands by ignoring the sovereignty of Native American societies
and claiming the lands to be empty. Canada and Mexico, states formed out
of European empires, bordered the United States to the north and south,
the Pacific Ocean to the west. Some, like William Seward, championed the
full annexation of North America. But to expand north or south required
additional justification from those who sought to exploit the neighboring
nations' resources. By itself, manifest destiny no longer sufficed as an
ideological explanation.[83]

The geographical argument—of the Mexican North as a natural extension of what is now the U.S. Southwest—buttressed expansionist agendas. Contiguity supported the capitalist drive in several ways. First, like
the U.S.-Canadian border, no geographical feature clearly divided the two
nations. The Rio Grande marked the Texas boundary, but west of El Paso
the two nations did not reach an agreement on the boundary until 1853.[84]
For the entire nineteenth century the border existed only on maps and along

imaginary lines between stone markers. Second, the Sonoran desert provided ecological continuity across the international line. Irrigation experts on both sides of the border collaborated to reclaim the land. Third, mineral deposits in southern Arizona and the north of Sonora created a "copper borderlands," among others, that justified industrial cross-border connections.[85] Many forty-niners who had passed through the Mexican North and rushed to California soon suffered from crushed dreams; they then looked back to Sonora, Baja California, and the interior Mexican states for the next mineral rushes. These geographic ties across the border worked to naturalize expansion to the south. Lines of logic, like rails of steel, connected the U.S.–Mexican borderlands and directed Bishop as he traveled throughout the region.

Beneath Bishop's feet lay the logic in material form. American syndicates financed the rail lines on which he rode. In 1880 two American groups received concessions from the Mexican government to build railways from Mexico City to the northern border. The first, a Boston company, completed the Mexican Central Railway in four years, connecting Mexico City with Chihuahua, Ciudad Juarez, and, via the ATSF, El Paso and the rest of the United States. The second, under the same management as the Denver and Rio Grande Railroad in New Mexico and Colorado, connected Mexico City to Laredo, Texas.[86] On the most basic level these rail lines improved transportation between and among nations, while they also functioned symbolically as part of a "civilizing mission" that elite Mexicans used to justify the nation's "economic and political ambitions." The same could be argued for U.S. railroad and economic expansion south, as well as, Michael Matthews has noted, for European powers in Africa and Asia.[87]

Once completed, these lines opened Mexico to tourists and especially to rising middle-class travelers. Between 1880 and 1884 the distance of rail lines more than quintupled, from 674 to 3,682 miles. The latter amount would quintuple again by 1910 largely owing to American investments.[88] By comparison, the United States contained more than 90,000 miles of tracks by 1880. The new links with the Mexican Central and Mexican National Railways prompted older western and California routes to start adding excursions south of the international border, "embracing not only

that territory of the States south, west, and north, but extending a tribu-
tary tour into the peculiarly attractive land of Mexico."[89] After the com-
pletion of the Mexican Central in 1884, the ATSF promoted the Mexican
lines "almost as their own."[90] Before long, elites like Bishop and tourists
began to travel—and to write about—northern and central Mexico, inscrib-
ing it into the national imagination.[91]

A third group of investors, formed as the American and Mexican
Pacific Railway, attempted to construct yet another rail line across the Mexican North, beginning at the Gulf Coast of Texas and ending at Topolob-
ampo Bay on the Gulf of California in Sonora. William G. Le Duc, a surveyor
and former U.S. commissioner of agriculture, wrote favorably of the enterprise and touted its potential. The vast majority of boosters agreed with
Le Duc that the development of the region represented the steady march
of civilization. Fully confident that "what has occurred elsewhere in the territory acquired by the United States from Mexico will occur here," Le
Duc prognosticated in Darwinian fashion that "the crooked wooden stick
shod with iron and attached to the heads of the patient cattle will be replaced
by the steel beam and mould-board, or the sulky plow; the brush scratcher
by the steel-tooth harrow; the machete by the axe and brush scythe; the
threshing-floor, where the grain is trampled out by cattle and horses, by
the steam thresher; and the hooked sickle by the header and self-binder;
school-houses will be seen, and modern civilization, with all its wants and
demands, will take the place of ignorance and barbarism."[92] Le Duc's report thrilled the railway's board of directors, which boasted that the completed railway, when connected with the Gulf States line, would follow the
"first transcontinental route ever explored in America."[93] While the board
eagerly embraced historical tradition by invoking the sixteenth-century
path trod by the Spanish conquistador Álvar Núñez Cabeza de Vaca, it
certainly wanted to avoid his experiences as a castaway, starving and naked,
and as a slave to indigenous peoples.

Le Duc's and Bishop's accounts offer an important turning point in
the drive by the United States to Mexico, for both their similarities and their
differences. Each subscribed to the triumphant theory of social Darwinism, so prevalent in the West and other frontiers worldwide. This imperial

logic exculpated conquest by emphasizing historical and cultural progress. In the case of Mexico this argument caricatured the nation as one
in perpetual revolution and political tumult, a country weakened by racial mixing, or *mestizaje*, a land of open opportunity for a superior civilization. The ideology substantiated arguments for benevolent conquest in
the earlier nineteenth century. "It will only be when we shall have thus
taken possession of Mexico," wrote a Texas Ranger, "that an end will be
put to civil warfare within her borders, and her degraded population become elevated into prosperous, intelligent, and peace-loving citizens."[94]

By their differences, however, Le Duc's and Bishop's texts evince a
rupture of consensus on the nature of American expansion. Whereas Le
Duc believed that developers need only replicate strategies from the American West, Bishop began to note the impracticality of such an approach.
As he traveled, Bishop met with local officials and expatriates, who often
compared development in Mexico to that in the American West, but he did
not share their optimism, casting the Mexican nation as "the very antipo-
des of our own, though adjoining it." Development, he wrote, "must not
be sought in a parallel situation of things in the United States, but rather in
such countries, perhaps, as Russia and India, with a large peasant population to be developed, instead of a new population to be created." Bishop
caught a glimpse of how to export the westering process, to avoid the less
savory aspects of its history while still acquiring the maximum amount of
resources. "We have built railroads in advance of settlement, and depended
upon immigration to fill up in their wake," he recalled of the American
West. "Mexico has but an infinitesimal immigration, and presents no great
inducements to it at present. It must depend upon the local carrying trade
and natural development of the industries and commerce of the country."[95]
Bishop did not question his intentions or their potential consequences. He
trusted the purity of economic reach—to him, a benign relationship between nations.

His Mexican counterparts expressed resignation. Colonel Nicolás
España of the army, one of Bishop's informants, was fatalistic about the reach
of capital. "You will not annex us with bayonets," he said to Bishop in 1881,
"you will annex us with dollars. . . . I feel that it is the manifest destiny of

Mexico to be taken by the United States."[96] The colonel's view reflected a national concern that accompanied line construction, and some officials worried about a causal link between railroads and annexation.[97] Ever since the inauguration of President Díaz in 1876 American companies had gained unfettered access to Mexican markets. Generous concessions to American syndicates characterized the Porfiriato, an era steeped in social Darwinism and a firm belief in *progreso*, or national betterment. Under the president and his allies the Mexican Congress modified laws in December 1883 to open lands for foreign ownership and settlement. To stateside investors the opening of the region rang with prophetic tones. One capitalist recalled Díaz's appeal in biblical rhetoric: "Take . . . take this country we have just won; build your irrigation works; reclaim these lands; bring civilization into this new country; and make of Sonora, as you can, the garden spot of the world."[98] Dollars and pesos flowed like milk and honey.

Another strategy that Mexican diplomats and representatives used to craft their nation's image involved participating in a series of world and regional fairs. Between 1893 and 1900 Mexico attended several U.S. expositions, at times of its own accord and at others at the invitation of the host cities. Díaz and his supporters, such as Matías Romero, the Mexican ambassador to the United States, made constant appeals to northern investors for national development. This was not merely a benevolent gesture but one calculated to secure the north Mexican states from falling prey to territorial conquest or, worse yet, secession. Like their American colleagues, wealthy Mexicans appealed to investment through western logic and language. At a banquet held in his honor in New York in 1891, Romero predicted, "When the settlement of the last territory of the United States shall make it difficult to find a new field for profitable enterprise, . . . the capital which this country is now so rapidly accumulating, and its enterprising activity, will have to look for new ventures. It will be an act of foresight to enter at once into the large and rich field offered by Mexico, at the very doors of the United States."[99]

Romero, speaking in 1891, painted a picture of imminent wealth so clearly for investors that it could have been bested only by a true Titian in Tzintzuntzan. Industry giants with gilded dreams differed little from artists searching for true beauty. All coveted Mexico, the beautiful. Only three years removed from Romero's sales pitch, Smith's quest for a lost Titian embodied the aspirations of businessmen and the new strategy of Bishop: locate wealth, extract it, and return with minimal complications. This was especially true of the Mexican North, specifically in the states of Chihuahua and Sonora, where investors concentrated their ventures for the proximity to the international border.

Alongside Romero that night in 1891, Walter S. Logan attempted to harness the logic of the western turn south to his advantage. Logan promoted his company, the Sonora and Sinaloa Irrigation Company (SSIC), to the captive audience of potential investors. While railroad executives expected the locomotive to "work the same magical change" that it had in the American West, Logan proposed channeling this logic into irrigation works.[100] Reclaiming arid lands in the Southwest and Mexican North had become a family business of sorts. His brother developed irrigation works along the Gila River in Arizona Territory, while he, "the apostle of irrigation," aimed to replicate his success along the Yaqui River of Sonora. The logic of western strategies working south of the border so gripped Logan's mind that he wrote, "When I began to formulate my ideas in reference to the lands under the Yaqui I found that I was unconsciously and unavoidably using the same language and the same forms of expression as I had formerly used in reference to the Gila." Logan characterized the Gila and Yaqui Rivers as twin siblings, "and all that concerns them is so much alike that whatever can be said of one is almost always equally applicable to the other."[101]

The realities of American economic and cultural expansion into the new Southwest and Mexico, however, challenged these hopes. From this obstacle came Bishop's realization—a generation ahead of his time—that settlement in Mexico could not replicate simply the past of the American West. Most promoters believed that land tracts south of the border required colonists, and the harsh environment offered few incentives to women and families. In an effort to foster women's interest in the region, railroad tours promoted special accommodations for single female passengers. One tour's brochure from 1891 highlighted its chaperone, "a lady of culture and refinement" who offered "protectorship" and who "not only ministers to [women's] comfort in countless ways . . . but has a watchful eye for those delicate attentions which might escape the observation of the sterner sex." The tour company reassured its female readers that "no lady or party of ladies need hesitate for a moment to join one of these tours on account of the inability of husband or brother to act as escort. The presence of the Chaperon removes every impediment that would deter a timid woman from undertaking a journey alone, and places them on a footing as independent as that enjoyed by the men."[102]

Promoters and investors aimed to package Mexico to both women and men as a land of immense opportunity, one with latent wealth, and a dark region awaiting American light and progress. They portrayed it as the next frontier. Mexico lay far enough from the higher costs of more developed areas yet close enough to access these same areas by rail, a kind of transnational frontier sprawl. For decades this scenario had appealed to many emigrant groups from the United States and beyond: vanquished Confederate soldiers, Kickapoo Indians, Mormon colonists, German farmers, freed African Americans, and even, by 1903, Boer settlers from South Africa. Authors, boosters, and politicians in both borderland nations based their arguments on the assumption that the United States needed continual expansion, be it by land or by markets.

This migratory westering experience fed directly into the frontier's southern—and overseas—extension.[103] One contemporary at the dinner held for Romero pointed out, "'Westward! Ho!' is still a talking cry, but not the only one. All the borders of the earth are being explored. Australia is filling up. Somebody writes a new book on Africa every month. But Mexico is on the very eve of her great change; she is almost there."[104] These international intonations point to the ties between U.S. capitalist development and Victorian imperial cultures. As France, Germany, Holland, Portugal, and England became global imperial powers in Africa, Latin America, and Asia, the United States began to transition from expansion by conquest to one driven primarily by economic interests. In pursuit of its southern neighbor, the United States followed the example set by England's "informal empire" there in the early nineteenth century.[105] Each power's presence grew from similar impulses—more economic, less territorial—and each characterized Mexico, past and present, as a slumbering giant awaiting the golden touches of capitalist development. One can therefore see a continuity between British and American portrayals of the nation: myths of its exotic appeal, its Oriental otherness, its dark-eyed *señoritas* and chivalrous *caballeros*, myths of immense wealth waiting to be uncovered, of vast treasures lying in sleepy pueblos, of foreign antiquities and mines from Spanish colonial days awaiting the return of a rightful heir or adventurer. These were not mere fables of fantasy fiction; they inspired mining engineers like Hammond, irrigation promoters like Logan, railway corporations like the Sud-Pacífico de México, and artistic adventurers like Smith.

These and other flawed dreamers shared many traits and troubling beliefs as they sought riches throughout the world. Indeed, their ideological paths overlapped as much as their real-world travels, and a great number found their way to Chicago for the World's Fair of 1893 to marvel the latest inventions and surround themselves in a spirit of can-do. Historians may generally recognize the fair as a turning point in U.S. history, following the model that Turner proposed in his presentation there, claiming the frontier had closed three years previously.[106] To many contemporaries hoping to uncover latent wealth, though, it marked the beginning rather than the end of their adventures. Two such individuals personified this hopeful beginning and crossed paths that year, each susceptible to the seduction of frontier tales.

The first, an eastern physician and investor, Nathan Boyd, left Chicago and traveled by rail to southern New Mexico. He sought to purchase properties to exploit rising land prices as a result of anticipated irrigation developments. Once in Mesilla, New Mexico, Boyd visited the home of Demetrio Chávez, a successful merchant who had already achieved the American dream by his early forties.[107] Regardless, when Boyd arrived at the merchant's doorstep, he did not see the elegant estate of a successful merchant. He described Chávez's house as "an old-time adobe house" located in "an oasis in the heart of a vast desert."[108] While his initial interest was in land speculation, Boyd could not help noticing something else at Chávez's house. "On first entering Don Demetrio's house," he later wrote, "I noticed two pictures on the wall of the ante-room." The room "was badly lighted, and at first I did not recognize what they were, but on having the heavy wooden shutters to the window to the room opened I saw that the pictures were very old and remarkably perfect and beautiful paintings." One, he guessed, was Giuseppe Mazzolini's copy of Titian's portrait of his daughter Lavinia. The other, he wrote, looked like a painting remarkably similar to a known masterpiece: Guido Reni's portrait of La Cenci.[109] Years later Boyd sent the portraits to the National Gallery of Art along with detailed speculation on the Mazzolini painting he had purchased. It turned out he hadn't uncovered a priceless treasure. Yet in 1893 Boyd sought to unearth latent wealth in a newly accessible land. Fresh from the World's Fair and riding the rails of progress to Mesilla, he also sought to convert dry lands to fertile valleys through the magical touch of capital.[110]

A second sojourner in Chicago, Frederick Russell Burnham, embodied more than anyone the frontier and imperial ethos of his era. His childhood dreams led him away from Minnesota to the Southwest, to Southern Rhodesia, and then to the Mexican North. The romanticized frontier literature he devoured as a boy in the Midwest provided him with a framework for understanding his African and Mexican adventures, as western and imperial worlds overlapped. Burnham and other Americans were not inspired by frontier ideals alone; they would circulate among imperial actors themselves, people like Cecil Rhodes and Haggard, on their quest to convert cultural beliefs into mineral wealth and reclaim lost caches of treasure.

Working Frontier Dreams

Frederick Russell Burnham and the Global West

HUNDREDS OF MILES FROM THE NEAREST RAILROAD, in April 1893, Frederick and Blanche Burnham and their son, Roderick, jostled back and forth on a buckboard led by four mules. The horizon stretched out before them, their destination not yet visible, the territory unfamiliar. Shrubs and occasional vegetation dotted an otherwise rocky, dusty landscape, inhabited by native peoples unknown to the Burnhams. The family traveled with a few other parties encountered along the way. Accustomed to the clanks and creaks of their mules' harnesses, Frederick Burnham found comfort in the austere setting, but one day odd sounds announced the approach of a stranger. Burnham turned to dart a glance. He slowed his cart as the person drew near.[1]

The man rode alone and wore "a stiff-brimmed Stetson hat made from beaver fur," Burnham wrote years later. When the stranger noticed that Burnham sported the same hat, he stopped his mules, skipped introductions, and asked, "When did you leave the West?"

Burnham responded with levity: "Just ahead of you."

The stranger played along: "It was daybreak, as near as I can remember."

"Almost you are a Texan," jested Burnham, "and almost a short grass puncher."[2] Burnham and the unknown man "exchanged jokes," he wrote, "but, with Western reticence, [we] refrained from asking names."[3] Weeks later he learned the stranger was Maurice Gifford, a famed soldier who had fought with British forces in the Red River Rebellion in Canada, just north of present-day Minnesota and South Dakota.

45

The interaction between Burnham and Gifford occurred not in
Canada or in the American West or in the Mexican North, regions where such
an encounter might have been more common, given the dialogue, but thousands of miles away, in a stretch of land between the Transvaal and Matabeleland in Southern Rhodesia. The two figures connected through a
casual familiarity with cowboy culture in a location far removed from traditional western frontiers. The similar hats, the shared sense of humor, and
the stiff, staccato dialogue forged a bond between Burnham, a self-described
cowboy and scout, and Gifford, an imperial soldier. Of different origins,
both men were heading to Fort Victoria, in today's Zimbabwe, then an outpost of the British Empire, to defend settlers and investors of Cecil
Rhodes's British South Africa Company (BSA Company).

As a private venture granted a royal charter by the British government, the BSA Company could act on the government's behalf to make
agreements with indigenous populations, explore their lands, settle new
populations, and develop natural resources. In practice this arrangement often led to dispossession and the attempted conquest of native societies, and company papers recognized as much. The company charter
proclaimed, "The condition of the natives inhabiting the said territories
will be materially improved and their civilization advanced, and an organization established which will tend to the suppression of the slave trade in
the said territories, and to the opening up of the said territories to the immigration of Europeans, and to the lawful trade and commerce of Our subjects and of other nations."[4] To attain these goals, the company relied on
men like Burnham and Gifford to protect its settlers from Ndebele warriors
resisting empire and fighting for their lands.[5]

No one had recruited the American. He and his family had arrived
on the scene unexpected, hoping, as Blanche wrote to her family, to settle
in a "new Utopia in the heart of Africa."[6] Frederick's abilities to scout—to
follow the trail of enemies and to read signs in the landscape for military
purposes—soon earned him a place in the BSA Company's frontier corps.
For the young American, fighting for Cecil Rhodes would fulfill a boyhood
dream; for the company, Burnham seemed uniquely qualified for the post.
It needed willing soldiers to spearhead an attack on Matabeleland in order

to unearth potential gold fields and reassure investors that the company's reality matched its grand claims back in London. Raised in Minnesota during the Dakota War of 1862, employed as a messenger for Western Union in California in the 1870s, and weathered among old-time scouts fighting Apache Indians in Arizona during the 1880s, Burnham had prepared to fight in imperial zones in southern Africa. He represented the rise of Gilded Age frontiers as he and his family moved on a global circuit, of sorts, after 1893: to southern Africa for two wars (the 1893 Anglo-Ndebele War and the 1896 Ndebele Uprising), to the Alaskan Yukon (1898–99), back to southern Africa for the South African War (1899–1900), followed by an expedition to West Africa (1901) and other adventures before returning to southern California and the U.S.–Mexican borderlands after 1904.

The history of Burnham and his family shows how a frontier ideology based on capitalist development and a masculine sense of the American West made these far-flung regions interchangeable to those who sought them. At the same time, the papers and archives that Burnham left behind disclose more troubling aspects of such an ideology, one steeped in social Darwinism and ethnic purity that enabled the Burnhams to chase wealth by dispossessing indigenous populations, whether the Ndebele of Southern Rhodesia or the Yoemem in Mexico. The archives also raise valid questions concerning Burnham's reliability as a historical figure. While the full truth of some of his stories may never be known, his desire to emphasize certain anecdotes over others makes clear his wish to self-identify as a frontier scout. These tales—tall or not—demonstrate the connection between Burnham's dreams and the reality that awaited him in southern Africa and the U.S.–Mexican borderlands. Through his life and work, Burnham wanted to find out, as he wrote to his mother en route to Durban in 1893, "if any of my dreams can be worked out even in part. If they cannot, then I will return and put them behind me forever. If they can, then I will work them till I die."[7] His two memoirs, *Scouting on Two Continents* (1926) and *Taking Chances* (1944), argue for the relevance of his frontier ideology to a globalizing world, but his private papers contain darker aspects of a romanticized frontier and the intertwined roles of imperial expansion and dispossession. To examine the life of Frederick Burnham is to explore the world of global frontiers in the Gilded Age.

From Minnesota to Matabeleland

Born in May 1861 to missionary parents in Tivoli, Minnesota, Burnham grew up distant, but not removed, from the nation's unfolding Civil War.[8] Cornstalks and sermons marked his childhood on the northern plains. His father, Edwin, an ordained minister, worked as a part-time mill operator and preacher, serving the American Home Mission Society (AHMS), a Presbyterian organization with extended networks in southern Minnesota, the Middle and Far West, and around the world. Burnham's mother, Rebecca, was born in England and moved with her family to New York in 1845 before settling in Minnesota Territory a few years later. However full of energy, Edwin's early proselytizing fell short of spectacular. One merchant described him as a man "who does not seem to have much talent in managing a meeting, & his talent in preaching is quite small, but I think he will improve."[9] Nevertheless, Edwin honed his craft, and he impressed others at AHMS enough to receive an appointment to Wilton, St. Mary's, and Tivoli. As he traveled his circuit, Edwin's adopted hometown of Wilton grew along with the young minister. Bridges, sawmills, and Sunday schools appeared in the vicinity during his first two years alone. Rebecca likely met Edwin when her father, a deacon in Mapleton and Sterling Center, requested additional service for his growing congregation.

Two aspects of Burnham's early life especially influenced the boy's future. First, as the son of a missionary family young Frederick was exposed to religious dogma. Second, owing to his family's location the boy would become familiar with, and fascinated by, Native Americans. He spent the first nine years of his life in Minnesota and Iowa, formative years that glowed in his mind later in life and shaped the narrative arc that he would use to write about his adventures in distant lands. The books and stories he was exposed to as a child in the Middle West unlocked in his mind enchanted worlds in the American West and in Africa. "The charm of that first old tale of Africa read to me as a boy on the frontiers of Minnesota never failed," he wrote just before his death. "Years later, when as a hardened scout I crossed into the lines of the enemy in the very region described in that book, the picture in my mind's eye of Katy Boardman reading by candlelight to a ring of pioneer children sprang before me as vivid as the rosy tints of dawn on the African veldt."[10] Burnham, like others alongside him in later years, imbibed the romanticism of those boyhood adventure tales and memories.[11]

His frontier dreams began to take hold in the 1870s, after his family moved to California. When his father died suddenly in 1873, his mother and young brother returned to the Midwest, but twelve-year-old Frederick stayed behind for a time to work off a family debt. For the remainder of his childhood Burnham drifted between southern California, the Southwest, Mexico, and the Midwest, holding a number of jobs, from a horseback messenger to a prospector to a deputy sheriff in Arizona. When he encountered a boyhood friend, John Blick, in the Far West, Burnham reconnected with Blick's sister, Blanche, and in 1884 the two wed in the Blick family's home land of eastern Iowa.

Burnham would later think of this period of gestation west of the Mississippi as critical to his budding frontier philosophy, and the few sources from this early period indicate that his western incubation was equally driven by material needs. Ricardo Salvatore, writing on adventurers in South America, identifies this impulse as "the complex relationship between business and knowledge in the era of informal empire. In both cases, the entrepreneur-explorers were personally engaged in the production, diffusion, or application of knowledge and left a vast collection of representations (mostly photographs) of the territories and populations transected by the new railroads."[12] Burnham acted as one such cog in Salvatore's "representational machine" through his articles and memoirs. After their wedding, Blanche stayed with her family in Iowa while Frederick worked in the Southwest, trying to generate enough money to support a family, aware of the financial necessities beneath a romanticized frontier sheen. As he explored mining interests and prospected, Burnham wrote to his wife about potential developments, keenly attentive to financial affairs. One potential investor, he wrote, "has got money & I hope will find a good mine here if I had time could stay here to catch on to something with

them & make money." Two weeks later he wrote of meeting two men in
Denver, one "who clears $200k per month" at a mine, and describing the
other as a "$25000 a year man."[13] While frontier visions may have driven
Burnham to go West, he did so—like his father and his mother's immigrant family before him—accompanied by financial pragmatism.

Burnham eventually found a mine that provided him a significant
profit, enough to meet immediate needs and afford him a chance at big
dreams, and in 1892 he saw news that fired his imagination.[14] He read of
the BSA Company under Rhodes, the great empire builder for England in
southern Africa, and of the company's workings in Matabeleland and
Mashonaland, expanding British dominion. Burnham followed Rhodes's
progress through the newspapers and was, in his words, thrilled "to the
core of my being" at the thought of joining his hero, who "so completely
fulfilled and satisfied all my ideals of what a real man should be that I gave
him my enthusiastic devotion and service."[15] On the day after Christmas,
1892, the young American, along with Blanche and their six-year-old son,
Roderick, set off to live on the frontiers of his youth's imagination. Funded
by profits from the sale of Burnham's mine interests in Arizona, they traveled to Chicago and sailed from New York to London and then to the British Colony of Natal on the eastern coast of southern Africa.[16]

As Burnham was beginning his adventure by passing through Chicago the year of the World's Fair, others were already in Southern Rhodesia hoping to amass riches and return triumphant to the Columbian
Exposition as mining magnates. "Everybody was going to make money
quickly," wrote one settler about his time in Rhodesia, "and everybody
meant to meet everbody [sic] else at Chicago. It was the Mashona adieu."[17]
Participants hoped to replicate the discovery of minerals that had led the
South African Republic to become the world's center of gold production.
Similar to the many New York and Boston capitalists who had hoped to
take the western frontier south into Mexico, investors in London and Cape
Town sought to extend the British mineral frontier, but to the north.

The Burnhams arrived and acclimated in Durban for three weeks.
They purchased supplies, and then, as they traveled beyond British rule to
Johannesburg, they witnessed a region transformed by industrialization

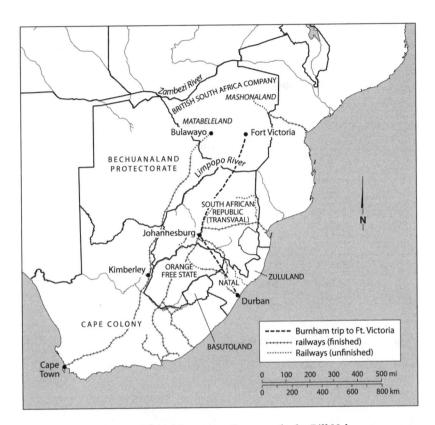

Figure 4.   Southern Africa in the 1890s. Cartography by Bill Nelson.

(fig. 4). Mine development, railroad construction, conflicts with indigenous populations, and capital investments changed what had been a remote region—in the South African Republic, one of two Boer states—into a central hub of wealth thrust into the global spotlight. Adding precious minerals to the mix only intensified political tensions among indigenous Africans, rural Boer farmer-citizens, British administrators in London and the Cape Colony, and foreign settlers like the Burnhams.

The discovery of diamonds in what would become Kimberley and gold south of Johannesburg enticed many in the United States to attempt to strike it rich, especially for those who had missed the great California rush of 1849. Though separated by continents and decades, the mineral

booms in southern Africa and the American West were different only by
degree, not by kind. Within six years of the discovery of diamonds in 1867,
for example, thousands of Boers, Britons, and foreigners worked the dig-
gings, along with thirty thousand indigenous Africans there.[18] The disparity
between a tiny minority of foreigners among an overwhelming majority of
native peoples created exceptional tensions between social groups in the
African setting, though xenophobia and racism certainly proliferated in
both contexts. A second similarity concerns historical timing. Diamonds
in Kimberley facilitated the gold rush near the Witwatersrand River ("the
Rand") similarly to how gold in California had facilitated the silver rush of
Nevada's Comstock Lode.[19] Economic and logistical structures of a first
bonanza therefore aided a second rush, intensifying regional development
in both southern Africa and the American West.

However far from home, the Burnhams were not isolated as foreigners. Southern Africa at this time constituted one stop along a network of
global frontiers. In *American West, Global Frontier*, David Wrobel argues for an expansive view of the trans-Mississippi West as "one developing frontier, one colonial enterprise, among many around the globe,"
and the connections with southern Africa support this interpretation.[20]
The inverse of Wrobel's claim also holds true. "One of the joys of life on
this frontier," wrote Burnham, "was the mingling of the adventurous and
hardy from every corner of the world. If there was a single colony of the
British Empire that was not represented I have yet to hear of it."[21] This
resulted in scenes—like the one of the Burnhams on their buckboard
meeting Gifford—where a singular nationalist narrative falls apart. For
example, when Burnham later scouted for the BSA Company with three
other Americans and an Australian, he and others communicated by using
"the Australian 'Coo-ee'" and the western "cowboy yell."[22] Men would perform Wild West tricks in "William Tell fashion," and when the time came to
track the Ndebele king Lobengula in the Anglo–Ndebele War (1893), the
company relied on trackers that included Khoikhoi, San, Boers, Australians,
Americans, Canadians, and frontiersmen "from all parts of the world."[23]

These concurrent frontiers—in the West, the Southwest, southern
Africa, the Klondike, Australia, and so forth—were not merely developing

simultaneously. A loose network of adventurers, settlers, miners, and families often bound them together. An "ideal mining man," wrote Gray Brechin, could move "as easily amid the smelters of South Africa's Rand and Butte, Montana, as in the palaces and bourses of the European capitals or the New York Stock Exchange. One month would see him prospecting on a Russian droshky and the next on a Mexican burro."[24] The South African historian Charles Van Onselen has taken up the example detailed in Brechin's work to show how the mining engineer John Hays Hammond connected these regions and engaged in a militant form of "cowboy capitalism."[25] The Burnham and Hammond families would become close before long. Both worked, lived, invested, and moved alongside many of the same people and families in southern Africa, London, southern California, and the Mexican North. Their circle of friends and colleagues included Haggard, the renowned American writer Richard Harding Davis, Gifford, the British war hero and founder of the scouting movement Robert Baden-Powell, and Theodore Roosevelt along with lesser-known individuals who tied these regions together: Andy Hammond (in Arizona and Rhodesia, no immediate relation to John Hays Hammond),[26] Roy Leslie Magoon, a dentist (Rhodesia, Arizona, and the Klondike),[27] Mr. Bowan, "a Michigan man" (Rhodesia, London),[28] and Captain W. M. James (Arizona and Rhodesia).[29] At times these networks could lead to fascinating observations, as when Burnham casually referred to a friend in Venezuela linking up with two others from Tombstone and Alaska.[30] International connections also created comical situations. In the Klondike, Burnham stumbled across Major Terry Laing, "my old Rhodesian friend and respected opponent in many a hard stampede," and the two challenged each other to a friendly race to Dawson, Alaska, only later to leave the Klondike and race each other to South Africa. "You beat me to the Yukon," Burnham told Laing, "but I will beat you to the Boer War. It will come and all our friends will be in it."[31]

To support these personal connections, a cottage industry of clubs and organizations appeared, including Roosevelt's Rocky Mountain Club in New York and the Adventurers' Club in Los Angeles, and several publications like *Adventure* magazine, while cultures also trailed adventurers and settlers to these distant lands in the 1890s. Burnham's sister-in-law, for example, attended a talk by Mark Twain in Bloemfontein in 1896 and later saw an American roper perform.[32] By far the most influential organizational structure to emerge from these Gilded Age frontiers was the Boy Scout Movement (partially inspired by Burnham), which combined the American frontier, British imperial experiences, and strident masculinity. It spread rapidly worldwide.

Along the Rand and beyond it, as he and his family traveled by buckboard into Rhodesia, Burnham processed the strange new land through his experiences and romanticized frontier ideals. He conceived of Boer farms as American cattle ranches, wrote of the atmosphere around Natal as being "balmy as that of California," and described a Boer entrepreneur as the "Ben Halliday of South Africa."[33] He expected southern Africa to be much like Arizona. In Matabeleland and Mashonaland Burnham described the Ndebele as being "on the war path in red Indian style," and he painted Bulawayo as "like all Cal. towns during boom days." Africa, he claimed, had its settler tragedies and was "dotted with Cherry Creeks, New Ulms, and Custer's defeats."[34]

As the Burnham family traveled north, driving their four burros five hundred miles beyond the railroad's end, they camped and slept on "coconut feather" mattresses. They supped on boiled potatoes, fried bacon, and gravy.[35] And they encountered Gifford and his Stetson hat before arriving at Fort Victoria. There, the scout introduced himself to the BSA Company and took the first step toward realizing the self-image he first crafted in the American West.

The world he encountered was infinitely more complex than he cared to understand. The region between the Limpopo and Zambezi Rivers, ruled by a dispersed confederacy of Shona-speaking peoples, had experienced a prolonged peace in the early nineteenth century. The confederacy had built a series of large stone fortresses, or *zimbabwes*, collectively known as Great Zimbabwe, from which the contemporary state takes its name. By the 1830s, military instabilities in the Zulu kingdom to the southeast pushed splinter groups north and west. One such group, the Ndebele, settled around the Matobo Hills and exacted tribute among the Shona. Never fully conquered, the Shona were pushed to the north and east, yet they maintained some control in isolated pockets. Rhodes, Burnham, and the Anglo settlers of the company therefore were only the latest to arrive and attempt to consolidate control of a once-flourishing society. When these new arrivals encountered the impressive *zimbabwe* architecture, they assumed they had been made by a long-extinct white race.[36] The BSA Company, its military, and its settlers therefore simplified this complex history into a binary problem with, to them, a simple solution: the Shona made peace and the Ndebele made war, but white settlers were destined to rule.[37]

To make sense of the region, Burnham classified its inhabitants according to a hierarchy, and here the folksy frontier charm gave way to a racist *mentalité*. Like many of his era, Burnham accepted the tenets of social Darwinism, a philosophy that took Charles Darwin's biological thesis on evolution, survival of the fittest, and applied it to diverse societies. Proponents believed that the world's peoples could be ordered by race, with Anglos, Aryans, or Americans (or "whites") as leaders of civilization. Social Darwinists often characterized indigenous peoples of the Americas and Africa interchangeably as societies doomed to extinction on the basis of their "primitive" characteristics. To Burnham's mind, such logic equated the western migration of Euro-American settlers with the march of the British Empire from the Cape to Cairo, in which the scout was helping to lay "a stepping stone in the stride of the northern march of the race."[38]

Burnham saw himself on the cutting edge of empire, and he did not shy away from justifying violence while dispossessing indigenous populations. "There is a prevalent notion that the sword must never be used because it destroys & all ways are alike," he wrote later. "It would be just as logical to say to the surgeons you may use lotions & balm & sponges & plastics etc. to cut off a crushed leg—but the knife never. Is a slow rotting limb less painful even if the patient survives than a quick strike of the surgeon's knife?"[39] To him, the actual hierarchy of various populations mattered less than the inevitable triumph of the "white race." To be clear, as scholars have noted, whiteness itself was in flux and ill-defined, and so late nineteenth-century attitudes about the superiority of the "white race" became slippery with the introduction of, say, Boers, the Irish, or other fairer-skinned peoples of (then) less repute.[40] Whether Burnham wrote about the Khoikhoi of the Western and Northern Capes ("yellow, beady-eyed, diminutive natives . . . are only a shade above the now extinct Bushmen in the human scale"), the Negro ("differs from Apache Indian"), Indian emigrants in southern Africa ([who were] "like our John Chinaman"), or others, Burnham primarily contended, as he did in one particular moment, "a trained white man can out stand all other races. In this instance I had won out nigger after nigger Zulu, Basutos & others."[41] In his letters home and in his later memoirs, Burnham ordered societies according to the cultural norms of his own people, especially as they pertained to masculinity, virility, and the arts of war.

At the tip of an imperial spear, Burnham fought for a "white" settler society that misunderstood and feared indigenous peoples while living among them. His in-laws, in particular his brother-in-law, John Blick, embodied this disturbing settler worldview. The Blicks had joined the Burnhams in Southern Rhodesia after the Anglo–Ndebele War to establish a foothold in conquered lands and to make, for them, an Eden in Africa. Blick's letters home convey a power rush fueled by racial ideology. As whites settled in and around Bulawayo they often bartered with neighboring peoples for personal servants. What Blick described differed little from slavery. He lashed two servants for deserting him and, bragging of his personal comfort and power, wrote, "I even have a boy untie my shoes and I call my cook 50 yds to come pour out my tea when the pot is sitting by my side."[42] Writing home, he passed along greetings to a friend and proposed a ghastly exchange: that his friend in California "lick some little nig for me and I will kill one for him."[43] To many settlers, dark skin tones signified lesser human beings, no matter the geographical or cultural context.

The inhumanity espoused by Blick took subtler forms, especially with Blanche. Writing from the Gwelo River, she made a passing observation intended to justify her own positioning. While she did employ a "boy" (she clarified, "no one except blacks are called boys here"), Blanche still could not "believe I could be mean to them." She followed this with a thought, startling for its candor: "I wish there were no blacks in Africa. It would be a beautiful country." She then remarked on her tent's proximity to native workers, a mere one-eighth of a mile away, and when alone, she confided, "I keep the loaded six shooter where I can touch it with my hand."[44]

This hierarchy was often organized by skin color, but it alone could not account for all fair-skinned peoples. The Boer Republics, in fact, often vacillated between "civilized" and "savage," depending on local circumstances. Burnham, like many Anglophiles, felt for the antagonistic Boer president Paul Kruger "as [he] had felt for some of the great Sioux chiefs who were [his] boyhood enemies. They belonged to another age; they could not adjust themselves."[45] In this, Burnham drew a distinction between the more recent colonizers (the British) and the previous ones (the Dutch), who then became "Africanized" and thus would be doomed to extinction, a notion that replicated widespread misperceptions that the general public in the United States held of Native Americans.

These strains of virulent racism—in the correspondence of Frederick and Blanche Burnham and of John Blick—exemplify how race both shaped and was shaped by the frontier experience. Frederick's views distinguished themselves in rare instances, though, by placing gender and masculinity above culture and the pigment of one's skin. Later in life he wrote of meeting Tippu Tib, a famous indigenous Zanzibari slaver and trader, and commented he was "without a doubt a very shrewd man, with many excellent qualities. It has been a good thing for white supremacy in that part of the world that others of his race were not like him."[46] Burnham thus allowed some wiggle room to escape an absolute hierarchy of race, and this occurred most often when adversaries demonstrated masculine prowess. It should be little surprise that Burnham would think, therefore, that, next to Rhodes, Theodore Roosevelt "best filled my ideal of what a man should strive to be." Real men did not attend art museums, peopled by a "funny prudish conglomeration jumbled together by sissy men & feeble minded women."[47] Rather, they embraced the rugged outdoors and the "barbarian virtues" promulgated by Roosevelt himself.[48] The deeply held belief in a man proving himself on the frontier accounted for the Burnhams' presence in Southern Rhodesia, and it was through this bravado that the scout easily joined the BSA Company's expeditions.

Within four years of his arrival, Burnham would earn fame among British and American readers for two wartime exploits. In the first, the Anglo–Ndebele War of 1893, he was one of only three survivors of an ill-fated mission to capture King Lobengula. This episode, known as the Shangani Patrol, riveted British and global settler societies. The fear of in-digenous revolt and victory—like Custer's "last stand" in 1876 and a re-curring theme in colonial cultures—preoccupied readers, who nicknamed the massacre Wilson's Last Stand. The second escapade that brought Burn-ham fame transpired in the Ndebele Uprising of 1896 when he killed a re-ligious leader purportedly stoking rebellion against colonial authority. The violence inherent in these expeditions and, indeed, the constant threat against his life gave the scout an unquestioned resolve to use mortal force. The more success he achieved in his conquests, the more it reaffirmed his beliefs in his people's supremacy.

For his efforts on behalf of the British Empire Burnham earned the British South Africa Company Medal and, for his service in the South Af-rican War, the Distinguished Service Order. Major General Frederick Carrington, among others, heaped praise on Burnham. Lauded by his su-periors and highly respected by most of his peers, Burnham became an es-teemed constituent of the British Empire. In fact, when the South African War erupted, Lord Frederick Roberts telegraphed the scout, then prospect-ing in Alaska, and requested his service as chief of scouts.

Burnham's successes in southern Africa came at a personal cost, how-ever. Blanche and Roderick accompanied Frederick to the first Anglo set-tlement in Southern Rhodesia in 1893, and later the next year other family joined them in Bulawayo. The extended Burnham–Blick family man-aged to travel the world together, but the loneliness of distant kin often crept into still hearts on quiet nights, especially with the scout in the field. Rebecca, his mother, may have exuded pride, often reading his letters to her Friday Morning Club in southern California, but she also felt the strains of absence. "Wonder how Fred and his expedition in the heart of Africa spent the day," she wrote on Independence Day, 1895. "Blanche and Nada in Buluwayo. Howard and Roderick in France. A scattered family. When shall we meet again."[49] The grandmother in California was referring to her one-year-old granddaughter Nada, "the first white child in Buluwayo."[50] Named after the fictitious heroine of Haggard's *Nada the Lily* (1892), Nada embodied, literally, the influence of western and imperial adventure novels on her father. Haggard had described his protagonist as "the most beautiful of Zulu women," and so the first white child of Bulawayo took on an imperial romancing of indigenous beauty.[51] Naming the child Nada not only represented the mishmash of Burnham's frontier dreams and his current reality but also revealed the insular network of settler imaginaries on a distant outpost of the British Empire.

Frederick's dreams did not lead to much family time. When the extended family arrived, for example, the scout joined them for only two weeks out of the first two months. Knowing this was the most amount of time they had spent together in recent memory, Blanche's sister, Grace, wrote to her mother, "I wonder that she hasn't quite died of lonesomeness."[52] Blanche especially suffered from Frederick's dreams. In 1900 she wrote that "life seems unbearable" and, later, "You don't know how I want you." In 1901, after much time apart, Frederick learned of an opportunity to explore West Africa, and he scurried off a day after receiving first news. By 1907, as her husband traveled throughout the Southwest and Mexico, Blanche came to a conclusion: "I am more convinced than ever that we ought never to be apart more than a couple of weeks at a time." She also wrote of getting better, with "consequentially less nerves, fewer moods, and more interest in life outside of my own self."[53] Blanche unquestionably supported her husband's exploits, but these infrequent comments call attention to the consequences of prolonged absence.

In his years in southern Africa, only once does Burnham relate racially motivated violence of his own, and this in a private letter to his mother. In 1895 the scout wrote about what was, for him, a humorous affair. In a region purportedly never visited before by a white man, Burnham wrote, he encountered an indigenous African suffering from a stiff neck. "I told him I was somewhat of a doctor myself and would try a cure," he claimed. He then used a magnifying glass, or "big eye," and while the victim's "face went through many contortions I burned C.C. on the back of his neck," for "Chartered Company," "so if the government ever lose him they will

know him when found." He followed this act by setting "the chief's blan-
ket" on fire to show "that a white man's eyes were strong."[54]

Among all of Burnham's correspondence, this anecdote—shared with
his mother—is inconsonant for its cruelty. Though the scout could use
ruthless force and held skewed views of race, no other letters or writings
evoke the sadism in this story. Either Burnham secretly reveled in causing
pain or he is intending to shock his mother by bragging of his power over
foolish indigenous Africans. Both of these possibilities may be true, but
the latter explanation resonates more with Burnham's identity and total immersion in the frontiers of his childhood imagination. The idea of trick-
ing a foolish native, especially by using technologies or knowledge
common to European culture, proliferated in the adventure tales of his
youth and particularly in Haggard's *King Solomon's Mines*. There, the
narrator, Allan Quatermain, fools fictional Africans (based on the Ndebele)
by promising to cause a lunar eclipse to "interfere with the course of nature" and "put out [the] sun, so that night comes down on the land at mid-
day." This may not be Burnham's only borrowing from the novel. Haggard
wrote that indigenous Africans referred to the hero Quatermain as
"Macumazahn," or "he who keeps his eyes open."[55] In Burnham's later
memoir the scout claims that, during his days in Southern Rhodesia, an
Ndebele chief made reference to him: "He always rides at night and is the
white *induna*'s eye. We call him He-Who-Sees-in-the-Dark."[56] Burnham
desired—yearned—to embody men like Rhodes and Hammond and fictional characters like Quatermain. To these ends Burnham appears to
have emphasized certain stories, based in truth, fiction, or a combination
of both, to cultivate his self-image.[57]

Considering his immersion in romanticized frontier literature, Burnham must have been beside himself in February 1895, while in London
briefly, when Haggard invited the scout and his family to his estate (fig. 5).
Haggard's wildly popular adventure novels had drawn upon his own real-
world experiences in Natal, where he worked for the minister for native affairs. His fiction expanded upon previous adventure literature to spawn a
genre situated in romanticized imperial zones.[58] Haggard himself did not
vocally ascribe to social Darwinist beliefs like Burnham, but his novels nev-

Figure 5.   Frederick Russell Burnham,
London, 1894. Wikimedia Commons contributors, "File:Burnham london 1894.jpg," *Wikimedia Commons, the free media repository*,
https://commons.wikimedia.org (accessed
April 23, 2018).

ertheless induced generations of armchair explorers to seek adventure beyond the monotonous work available in an increasingly industrialized world.[59]

Haggard, who had read of Burnham's participation in Wilson's
Last Stand, had been corresponding with the scout about it, and the novelist used their meeting in London to interview and later write the story for
publication.[60] Burnham was certainly star-struck, and Haggard was
surely flattered to know that Burnham's daughter, Nada, carried the name
of his previous protagonist. Over those few days in London, kindred spirits of western and imperial cultures formed a deep friendship that
would last decades and would lead them to shared adventures in Mexico and to investments in the Yaqui Valley (fig. 6).[61]

Figure 6.   A. Kingsley Macomber, Frederick Russell Burnham, and H. Rider
Haggard "measuring the largest bear skin in the world at Pasadena California,
March 1905." Accession 2012-M-057, box 1, FRB Papers. All three men chased
adventure and investments in the American West, southern Africa, and the Mex-
ican North. Frederick Russell Burnham Papers. Manuscripts and Archives, Yale
University Library.

After this brief celebrity encounter, Burnham returned to Southern
Rhodesia and would face the greatest challenge of his life. He rejoined his
frontier scouts to fight the Ndebele far from Bulawayo. Away from the settlers huddled in laager formation to repeal any indigenous attack, Burnham
was unaware that his daughter, Nada, had grown very ill. On May 19, 1896,
she died unexpectedly as she lay by her mother's side. Her father received
word and rushed back from the field. The incident devastated the family
and partly explains why, lonely Blanche might have been, she stopped

accompanying her spouse beyond established settlements thereafter. Understandably, Nada's death left a heavy imprint on their lives for years. "Baby would have been six years old yesterday," Blanche wrote from London in 1900. "I could not get the little darling out of my mind all day, and wished that Fred was in Bulawayo to cover her resting place with the flowers that she loved as well."[62] Haggard, feeling the loss of his new friend, sent his regards to the scout and dedicated his subsequent novel and other writings to her memory.[63]

Not long after Haggard and others first reported on Burnham's adventures, contemporaries began to question (and historians still do) the truth of some of the scout's previous claims. A few settlers and veterans interpreted Burnham's unbridled enthusiasm as grandstanding and caused British officials to open an inquiry into his participation in the Ndebele Uprising. Never reprimanded, and in fact lauded, the raising of these questions has cast a long shadow on the scout's legacy. In the 1970s, the former head of the National Archives in Zimbabwe concluded that Burnham's tales were best understood as "campfire stories." A recent biography on Burnham argues that these critiques were seriously flawed and that historians of Rhodesia have been led astray because of them.[64] Rightly or wrongly, doubts remain about Burnham's actions on the Rhodesian frontier, a place the young scout was determined to work his dreams to death, but there is no question he led a life of adventure and danger.[65] He reveled in it.

He may have claimed otherwise, but Burnham sought the spotlight. Not long after the catastrophe of Wilson's Last Stand, for example, Burnham sent an exclusive through his mother to his hometown paper, the *San Francisco Examiner*.[66] He granted extended interviews for papers in England and the United States, and he began planning to write a "technical book for officers" after he finished fighting in the South African War.[67] Burnham also sought approval from his seniors, especially Baden-Powell, to whom he offered his service in training British scouts. As he wrote in his second memoir, published just before his death, "Vanity is my secret sin."[68]

Beginning in 1899 he began crafting his own image for public consumption. In numerous newspaper interviews then and later Burnham recounted his wartime exploits. By 1906 the scout's fame skyrocketed with the publication of Davis's *Real Soldiers of Fortune*. The book featured Burnham alongside other notables like William Walker and Winston Churchill, and excerpts from it ran in a wide range of publications, from local newspapers to national magazines like *Collier's Weekly*.[69] With this boost to his public persona, Burnham molded his life experiences into a narrative structure, as any memoirist does, finding a common theme (the realization of frontier dreams) and therefore meaning among the myriad of past experiences. At this point, during his correspondence with Davis, the scout began to include an amazing family story from his childhood, a parable worthy of its frontier protagonist and an early indicator of his future prowess. By digging into this origin story one can reconstruct how Burnham used the past to shape his self-image. Objective truth, it seems, mattered less than did the meaning and symbolism that one could wring from history.

An Origin Story: The Dakota War of 1862

In 1862 Burnham, then a growing baby, lived in a region shaken by violence. The Dakota Indians, having ceded many of their lands in the Treaty of Traverse des Sioux (1851), had relocated to a narrow reservation in western Minnesota in exchange for annuities from the U.S. government. For years federal agents had funneled funds intended for the Dakota to local merchants and traders or into private hands. Infuriated by this and by the constant pressure white settlers placed on their lands, the Dakota attacked homesteads and towns in south-central Minnesota beginning in August 1862 and especially concentrated their efforts on the nearby community of New Ulm.

As Burnham recalled, when the war began his parents had moved into a log cabin twenty miles from Mankato, a location purportedly "in the path of the raiders" under "Chief Red Cloud." Short on powder and bullets, Edwin, his father, had gone to Mankato to resupply. Warriors descended on the cabin while Rebecca and Frederick ("an infant of two years") were alone. Panicked, his mother realized that "she could never escape if hampered with her baby," so she decided instantly to hide me in a stack of newly shocked corn. The corn was too green to burn, and if I should make no outcry, I might escape discovery. So she tucked me into the hollow depths of a shock and earnestly adjured me to keep perfectly still, not to move or make the slightest sound until she should return. . . . As she was young and strong and exceptionally fleet of foot, she managed to reach some hazel bush on the edge of the clearing just as the Indians surrounded the cabin. She saw the hostiles hunting all about, and then some of them started on her trail, but she was hidden by the cottonwoods as she moved swiftly along the stream. Through the increasing darkness and her desperate speed, she succeeded in outdistancing her pursuers and reaching a barricaded cabin six miles away, but long before she reached safety she saw the flames of her own home rising to the sky.

At daybreak the next morning, she returned with armed neighbours to look for her baby. She found me, as she often loved to tell, blinking quietly up at her from the safe depths of the green shock where I had faithfully carried out my first orders of silent obedience.[70]

However fascinating, Burnham's story as printed in his first memoir makes two glaring errors. It misidentifies the Native leader of the New Ulm attacks as Red Cloud (it was Little Crow), and he miscalculates his age at two years (he was fifteen months old). Beyond the improbability of such a child remaining quietly in one spot for hours on end, Burnham's origin tale becomes all the less plausible when checked against historical evidence. Locating the family at this time is critical to evaluating the scout's assertions.

Burnham claims that he was born at Tivoli "on an Indian reservation" and that his parents had moved to a new location when Dakota raiders burned their residence (fig. 7). Burnham makes two subtle but important shifts here. First, he occludes that the nearest reservation to his birthplace was not for the Dakota but rather for the Ho-Chunk (Winnebago).[71] This is significant because the Ho-Chunk did not participate in the Dakota War,

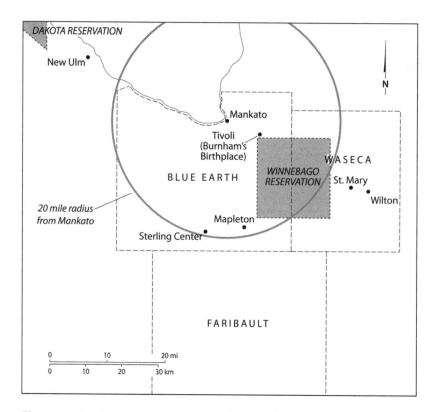

Figure 7.   Southern Minnesota in 1862. Cartography by Bill Nelson.

though they were unfairly expelled from the region after it ended. Second, his birth location, however close, was not on reservation lands.[72] Sources do confirm his birth at Tivoli, where his parents lived on a friend's property; but where was the family's log cabin that burned, some twenty miles from Mankato?[73] County land sale records place the Burnhams at the time in Wilton (Waseca County), and no other documents suggest they owned property then in neighboring Blue Earth, Brown, or Nicollet Counties, also transected by the twenty-mile radius.[74] Therefore, two viable options remain for the location of the Burnham home that was purportedly destroyed in 1862: in Wilton, where they owned property from 1859 to 1869, or in Sterling Center (Blue Earth County), where they purchased property in 1869 near Rebecca's family.[75] Neither is historically plausible.

During the August attack of 1862 few damages were reported in Blue Earth County as far east as Mankato and none in Waseca County.[76] If the family's residence did burn, the Burnhams never applied for readily available compensation from the federal government.[77] And while one missionary mentions that residents in Blue Earth counties "fled from their homes during the Indian troubles," doing so was unnecessary, he concluded, for there was never any direct threat from the Dakota.[78] The same held true for Waseca County. Rumors may have swirled about a Ho-Chunk alliance, but the "more level-headed gave little credence to these reports," wrote a Wilton resident. "After consultation, . . . it was thought best for me to return . . . to inform the people of the situation and to assure them that there was really no danger of further outrages by the Indians." In fact, locals placed a guard at the Wilton bridge to alert fleeing settlers that no danger existed and to urge them to return to their homes for the sake of their crops and livestock.[79]

Edwin Burnham's letters of the late 1850s portray the Ho-Chunk as generally nonviolent. The missionary often crossed Ho-Chunk territory on foot. "Though there is scarcely a Winebago [sic] who is sober that will do one any harm, yet in consequence of the murderous traffic in modern poison, called whisky, on the part of some reckless whites, I stand in danger of coming in contact with drunken Indians." Never threatened, Edwin considered the work "one of the easiest & most pleasant burdens I ever bore in the Christian course."[80] His understanding of the Ho-Chunk as being nonviolent before the Dakota War held true for the nearby Indians throughout the conflict.[81]

The problem with Burnham's origin story as well as subsequent tales of his is that his best anecdotes are those in which it is impossible to find conclusive evidence. If he did not invent this story, he must have heard a version of it from his father or mother, but archives and publications do not confirm this, and Burnham does not begin to share this story until after both parents' deaths.[82] Notably, a lengthy profile published in Saint Paul, Minnesota, in 1899 does not include the origin story and neither do the published memoirs of "one of the earliest settlers of Sterling township" who wrote the following year in a Mankato publication. Both pieces specifically address the scout's roots in Blue Earth County, and such a story certainly would have been of particular interest to local readers.[83] These silences are all the more notable when one considers the sensational and false claims of a separate, unpublished memoir of Burnham's, ghostwritten by a friend years later, which claims, "The home of our next door neighbor had been fired and all the occupants except a child, scalped."[84] These discrepancies raise serious doubts as to whether the story existed before Burnham saw a need for it, from his later growing fame as a frontier hero. Nevertheless, the anecdote emerged in various forms over the years, and inaccuracies in Burnham's versions were perpetuated alongside exaggerations.

Definitive evidence proving or disproving Burnham's origin story has yet to be found, but the evidence strongly points to the scout having fashioned the tale—consciously or otherwise—from bits and pieces of his childhood to match his self-image. After the Dakota War, Burnham recalls, his father was injured while constructing a new cabin, and his failing health led the family to California in 1870. This account coincides with historical records that show Edwin Burnham purchased land and a merchant store in Sterling Center in 1869, near his in-laws and about twenty miles from Mankato, and that fire soon destroyed the store.[85] Might the scout have considered his relative proximity to New Ulm and simply transformed the burning merchant store of 1869 into a burning log cabin of 1862, attacked by the Dakota? The description of his residence "on" (rather than near) an Indian reservation, the omission of that reservation as being Ho-Chunk (not Dakota), the lack of applications for restitution after the war, the historical knowledge that no attacks transpired in Tivoli, Mapleton, Sterling Center, or Wilton in 1862, and the reality that residents even turned fleeing settlers around for lack of an Indian threat all indicate that Burnham's memory constituted little more than an origin tale.[86]

Nevertheless, the veracity of Burnham's tale matters less for this book than does his use of it to fashion a single narrative from the innumerable experiences of everyday life. Nearly all of the anecdotes he relates in his memoirs concern the frontier: tales of Africa by candlelight on the Minnesota prairies, his memories of "playing tribe" as a child, his urge to go west, and even small details, like calling attention to his mother's having attended the same schoolhouse as Buffalo Bill.[87] This last claim to fame offers nothing more than the symbolic. Burnham includes the fact to supplement his frontier credentials and connect to a network of self-perceived frontiersmen. He treasured these connections. Later in life he would send his saddle gear from a 1902 West African expedition, as a token of his admiration, to the actor and humorist Will Rogers, who also had spent time in South Africa."[88] In his memoirs and in his life Burnham collected and curated frontier tales with the zeal of a new convert. A tendency emerges between his version of events in southern Africa and the origin story of his Minnesota childhood: he lived an audacious life but tended to enhance his stories to maximize danger, prowess, and strength. In short, he colored his tales to match what, for him, remained the personal ideal of the frontiersman. Like Allan Quatermain, Burnham was the son of a missionary who lived the ideals of his imagination.

However romantic, Burnham was not naive. He understood the power and consequences of realizing his dreams as early as his first sojourn to southern Africa. Behind the guns and trained scouts, he cynically noted in 1893, he and the BSA Company would push the Ndebeles north, "incidentally gobbling up their land while we spread the light of Christianity."[89] Burnham recognized the potential wealth this displacement could create, remarking to his mother, "The black [person] parts with his estates much the same as the American Indian, and I know now what the Spanish grants did for every Californian that held on to them."[90] The spoils of Burnham's participation included six thousand acres in Southern Rhodesia, the mineral rights of twenty acres, and a portion of King Lobengula's cattle in addition to other properties and exploration concessions.[91] Soon thereafter he explored north of the Zambezi River in "a quest for lost mines such as have been so colourfully imagined by Rider Haggard."[92]

Bringing the Frontier Home

The Gilded Age frontiers that attracted Burnham and his contemporaries were not unidirectional, exported from the United States. Rather, the people that traveled this circuit carried beliefs, experiences, and baggage—literal and metaphorical—with them. Burnham brought the frontier of Southern Rhodesia home to southern California. He continued a life of mine speculation and exploration working for John Hays Hammond and Guggenheim interests, primarily in Mexico. Yet he longed for the imperial culture and nature he had encountered abroad. He considered funding an ostrich farm, common in the Cape Colony, a project already under way by others in California.[93] He also reached out to Gifford Pinchot, Theodore Roosevelt, and other conservationists to attempt to pass legislation to bring wild game from Africa to the United States. He envisioned the klipspringer on the plains, the springbok in open deserts, and the gemsbok, too. The game park he hoped to establish would bring him profit on the land itself, and he always had profit in mind.[94] In July 1910 he began lobbying in earnest to pass another piece of legislation, "the Hippo Bill," sponsored by Congressman Robert Broussard of Louisiana, which would have imported African hippos into Louisiana.[95]

Racial ideologies could migrate home as easily as they could be carried overseas. Burnham felt that the United States and England could benefit from (whites') African knowledge of how to govern "the black races." In a 1906 letter to an administrator in Kenya, Burnham introduced Davis and asked for "any information concerning your methods of dealing with the natives, to what extent the laws as applied to them differ from the laws as applied to the whites, also as to what methods are used by the Government in recruiting to its service men capable of handling and managing the natives."[96] Here, Burnham appears to acknowledge the persistence of indigenous peoples, previously doomed to extinction, according to his earlier writings. Nevertheless, the scout suspected that racial governance could be transplanted from one society to the next regardless of local circumstances.

Though issues of conservation and race concerned him, Burnham still thirsted for the romance and adventure of a quest for riches. In 1922, writing from southern California to Haggard, the scout reflected upon his dreams of finding the African frontier in the Americas: "It was my intention to repeat my work in Africa and confirm again [in Mexico] the wonderful writings of Haggard and find the lost cities and buried treasure."[97]

A quotation such as this might appear metaphorical, but Burnham wrote in the literal sense. In 1905 Haggard had shared with Burnham some correspondence from an individual claiming to know the location of "lost cities and buried treasure" in Mexico. Haggard had published a novel set there (dedicated to Burnham's late daughter, Nada) and an enthusiastic reader wrote to the author offering to help locate the riches. Haggard therefore reintroduced Burnham to John Hays Hammond, who, intrigued, offered funding to create an exploration company.[98] Well aware of Hammond's concern for the bottom line, Burnham was surprised at his willingness to take a risk on the romantic quest. "Perhaps under the deliberate man of action," he wrote, "there is that other man, a dreamer and a lover of the strange, a little like Rhodes."[99]

The trip never materialized as originally planned, but Burnham and Hammond did explore much of Mexico in search of profitable mines and other enterprises. Around 1908, they learned of an opportunity not far south of the U.S.–Mexico border in Sonora that had the potential for massive profits. For decades, smaller enterprises had attempted to develop the fertile Yaqui Valley for American and Mexican homesteaders. The project had failed previously for two reasons: lack of access to tycoon-sized wealth and the persistent resistance of indigenous Yaquis. Hammond could address the first issue; Burnham, the second. The decorated scout would be in an unknown region, yet he would be in familiar territory: to defend a company's interests under the assumption that he could profiteer by taking indigenous lands and developing private enterprises on them. It was the exact same scheme he ran in Southern Rhodesia for the BSA Company.

The venture had strong financial backing, and to bring the project to reality, Burnham was forced to appease and inspire investors linked to Hammond in New York, a world totally unfamiliar to him. Ironically, this proved to be his most challenging frontier: dealing with "rich men's sons" in Manhattan and tossing about seven-figure sums.[100] By assuaging the fears of potential investors and talking of "how to handle the new settlers [and] lay off town lots without burstin a boom & having a depression as in Africa & other places," Burnham and Hammond worked with previous Yaqui Valley capitalists, the Richardson brothers, to make a million-dollar deal and thereby create a fifteen-million-dollar company.[101] With the project floated, Burnham later remarked, "My own old Mexican frontier seemed the most active region left in the world, and by night and day it was calling me back. . . . I sought out my kinsmen and some of my South African friends to join me in this enterprise."[102] Even Haggard, the novelist and a creator of Burnham's frontier dreams, invested in the company.[103]

Burnham's experience in the Yaqui Valley of Mexico gave his life purpose and focus. Whereas Southern Rhodesia became too violent for long-term investments and settlement, Burnham swore to himself that the fertile valley in Sonora would be different. It would provide a new paradise for his family and friends and fulfill the settler's dreams. As his Yaqui-related ventures commenced, a debate emerged in the press that directly addressed Burnham's contribution to American history, though no participants recognized it as such. The issue concerned the Boy Scouts of America, an organization with origins in Burnham's social circles in Southern Rhodesia.

Boy Scouts and the Socialist Critique

In 1900, after his experiences in the South African War, Burnham had sent a letter to his friend Baden-Powell of the British military. In it Burnham recommended that the British create a branch of service dedicated to the science of scouting. "It is in time of peace," he wrote, "that a small band of officers should take of this work and when a sudden war was sprung on us again every Brigade would have at least one A-1 first class scout and several second class."[104] The letter continued a friendship struck in southern Africa and solidified by the American frontier and British imperial networks. Burnham had taught Baden-Powell many of his scouting skills while involved in the Ndebele Uprising of 1896. Part of what inspired him to write his longtime friend concerned what the scout saw as an impending race war. Having just witnessed the challenge presented by the Boer Republics, and being convinced by his days in Southern Rhodesia that the white race would lead the way forward, Burnham saw an urgency to training young boys in the ways of military scouting. "It is the good strong hand of the white man above that holds this empire," he wrote to Baden-Powell, "and there is all told only a little over 40,000,000 people. It is no stretch of the immagination [*sic*] to think it might be challenged by a power some time that would call for every man."[105] Baden-Powell, who also subscribed to social Darwinism and feared that a crisis of masculinity was eroding national security, endorsed Burnham's concerns and began forming the Boy Scouts in England in 1908.[106] Within two years the movement had two hundred thousand members and had spread to the United States and other countries.

In 1911 American politicians on the left began to question the nature of this new phenomenon. In May, a writer under the pseudonym "The People" wrote an editorial lambasting the Boy Scouts, for indoctrinating subservience: "There is but one element that desires and foments wars— capitalism and it is characteristic of the hypocrisy of capitalism that . . . it should piously hold out in one hand the book which teaches of Him who proclaimed 'Peace on earth' and that spears and swords must be beaten into plow shares and pruning hooks, while with the other hand it lures the innocent youths, under the false guise of fun and adventure into a military movement."[107] Frank Weber, a member of the Wisconsin State Federation of Labor, expressed similar concerns, that the Scouts fed into the military, that an innocent boy would "become a legalized salaried, professional murderer to serve the interests of a class of privilege."[108] Organized labor distanced itself from Weber's claims, but the critique held sway with activists on the left like Margaret Sanger, and the central question of this debate emerged: what was the connection between the Boy Scouts and capitalism?[109] Were young Scouts mere agents-in-training, preparing to fight on behalf of a nation for the cause of capitalist expansion and the opening of new markets?

Burnham's name never emerged in these debates, but he embodied what socialists critiqued, and he inspired, in part, the creation of the Boy Scouts. Underneath the rhetoric of frontier romanticism and outdoors skills resided a sharpened edge of capitalist expansion. The scouting skills he wielded for the BSA Company cut through resisting Ndebele warriors in the name of empire and development. Similarly, the chance to profiteer from indigenous removals in Mexico lured him south of the U.S. border. And social Darwinism, enmeshed in every decision of Burnham's between 1893 and his death, justified his actions to himself. "In spite of their cruelty," he wrote of the Yaqui Indians to Baden-Powell in 1909, "I recognize certain fundamental virtues which they have in excess of any of our western Indians, they are a most industrious people, and we cannot deny that as the conquering race we have not always dealt justly with them. Nevertheless the inevitable march of our modern civilization could not be stopped forever by a few semi-civilized people, be they ever so brave and patriotic."[110] Burnham thus represented the "inevitable march" of capitalism, led by the virtues of masculinity. In 1927 the Boy Scouts of America elected him as an honorary scout, and in 1951 the U.S. Geological Survey christened two peaks in southern California as Mount Burnham and Mount Baden-Powell.[111] The Silver Moccasin Trail that connects these two peaks today silently memorializes the ways in which Burnham's frontier dreams mapped onto Baden-Powell's imperial adventures.

Frontier Violence Redux

Although Burnham remained fairly consistent in his beliefs from the time he first sailed to Natal in 1893 to his later life, one senses some melancholy, perhaps regret, in his second memoir, published during World War II, three years before his death. At the age of eighty-three he saw "the dawn of a better day" but wondered if the violent means to victory stained the Allied triumph, and here one may infer that Burnham was reflecting on his own violent role in the creation of modern society. "Is it mere wishful thinking," he asked, "or is it faith in the eternal integrity of Right over Might that helps us endure the iron that has entered our souls?"[112]

Burnham builds off this when he recalls a campfire conversation with Baden-Powell during which a question arose: "Because warfare pervades all nature and reaches back beyond the beginnings of man, must it therefore continue forever, and are its horrors and crimes really cancelled by its acknowledged benefits?"[113] For a brief moment the frontier warrior questions the value of force, the ramifications of his past actions, and perhaps even his notions of white supremacy. "The gift from my ancestors of superabundant physical energy and strength," he writes, "gave me a high desire to take part in what I believed to be this inevitable and glorious conquest. It took some time to moderate my exuberant optimism, but now I must admit after many years of the most strenuous experience, that all the evidence is directly contrary to my first enthusiastic convictions." While Burnham appears to be opening his mind to a new postwar order, the scout concludes that the answer must be not conquest but segregation—the separation of the races—and this in 1947, on the eve of South African apartheid.

His introspection, when it did occur, transpired mostly in his early days in southern Africa, when religion, more than race, preoccupied him. The son of a conservative Congregational minister, Burnham struggled to square his fundamentalist upbringing with the violent realities of his actions, and he rarely opened his soul beyond his innermost family. He had "torn down everything but one God," he wrote to his uncle, "finding his law and work ample and far ahead of my power to comply with."[114] One wonders how, in the course of killing dozens, if not hundreds, of Ndebele warriors, all in the name of frontier dreams and capital, Burnham could square his actions with his parents' teachings. Anti-imperialist newspapers lambasted the BSA Company for its southern African exploits, which Burnham recognized.[115] He appeared unfazed by public critique, yet his private thoughts emerged in personal musings to his mother as early as 1893:

> To part of the world we will be Apostles of civilization; to some freebooters and land pirates; to the Matabeles murderers and invaders; to the Mashonas what a lion is to a jackal, the giver of offal and stray bones[,] hence welcomed[,] not loved. To the historians in later years we will but prove the continuity of evolution in the year 93–4. To the young and adventure hunting, . . . we will be considered lucky in falling upon stirring times. Some romances can take our dreary marches strewn with the bones of our dead oxen and horses and dotted by the graves of those of us who fell, our desperate fights in dead of night, our lovely camps beside swift rivers and among blue mountains the plains dotted with noble game, the earth a paradise, the solitary scout cut off from his command and selling his life as dear as possible, the lovely girl in the garrison who is in love with the capt., the grand country conquered by a handful of men, that countless

Figure 8.   Frederick Russell Burnham and Blanche Blick Burnham at their home in Hollywoodland, California, 1930s. This photograph captures much of the Burnhams' life together. Frederick's distant gaze is counterbalanced by his heroes, friends, and family on the wall, as if in a thought cloud, behind him. Blanche, meanwhile, passes the time reading, ever by his side. Among the photographs on the wall: Cecil Rhodes, Leander Starr Jameson, Frederick Roberts, John Hays Hammond and William Howard Taft, Charles F. Lummis, Charles F. Holder, John Two Guns White Calf, Buffalo Bill, Robert Baden-Powell, and various family members. Wikimedia Commons contributors, "File:Burnhams hollywoodland home.jpg," *Wikimedia Commons, the free media repository*, https://commons .wikimedia.org (accessed April 23, 2018).

thousands may settle in peace and quiet, the buildings of an empire on our smoldering bones. All these things flash before me as I write this my last letter to you before I am off to war. But let the world class me as they choose[:] murderer, apostle, pirate, invader or what not[,] to you I am always Fred."[116]

In Burnham a direct path emerges from a romantic ideology of the frontier—he would "work his dreams," as he said—to a philosophy of racial segregation; one can also draw the connections between capitalist expansion in the U.S.-Mexican borderlands and imperial projects in southern Africa. He would bring this experience and worldview with him to northern Mexico in 1908—as would Hammond and Haggard—having found fulfillment in Southern Rhodesia. Development of the Mexican North and the Yaqui irrigation project became Burnham's new passion: to irrigate lands, to sell subdivided plots to settlers, to protect them from Yaqui raids, and to make a windfall on the twin processes of capitalist expansion and indigenous dispossession.

The son of a missionary couple in Minnesota, Burnham and his family carried a romanticized frontier with them to Southern Rhodesia and back to the U.S.-Mexican borderlands (fig. 8). They would not be the only people eyeing the borderlands as a place of dream fulfillment. Among the first to arrive, James and Gertrude Eaton landed in Chihuahua in much the same way as Edwin Burnham had in Minnesota: as trained, young Protestant missionaries ready to proselytize. Certainly proud of their American heritage, the Eatons' faith superseded national concerns and placed them in a global community that saw potential converts as believers of outdated systems, theoretically similar to Frederick Burnham's view of indigenous enemies. But unlike the scout and his parents in Minnesota, James and Gertrude Eaton worked to spread a Protestant message—among Mexicans and itinerant Americans alike—by relying on the strength of gendered networks. The Eatons would witness a Gilded Age frontier arrive and pass in the borderlands, through their work and, after 1903, through their South African neighbors.

THREE

A Borderless Faith

The Eatons' Mission to Mexico

JAMES EATON CARRIED A RAIL PASS THAT stirred his soul and stoked his imagination. In April 1882 Eaton embarked on the Mexican Central Railway from Paso del Norte (Ciudad Juárez) and rode the new line "to end of track," as the Burnhams had done in southern Africa. There, at Estación Laguna in Chihuahua, the missionary observed the frayed edges of American capital. White tents of contractors strung out along the railroad bed. The rolling *r*'s of a foreign language marked the aural landscape with difference. Workers prepared for the laying of rails. They widened and graded the road, making it flat and smooth and efficient to ease the path of development. At the end of the line Eaton transferred to a stagecoach to jostle the remaining one hundred miles of his journey to Chihuahua City.

For months the missionary had dreamed of working in foreign lands, motivated, he recognized, by the "pioneer and missionary blood flowing in my veins." After fulfilling his duties as an assistant minister in Montclair, New Jersey, and as pastor of the First Congregational Church in Portland, Oregon, in the 1870s, he and his wife, Gertrude, sought new adventures. He had dreamed of "the western frontier" and had considered leading a congregation in Santa Fe, an idea to which a family friend responded, "If you feel any inclination toward work in the southwest, why not continue along the Santa Fe railroad to El Paso, cross over the international line into Mexico where the builders of the former road have begun constructing the Mexican Central, and found a new mission of the American Board in the state of Chihuahua?"[1]

Thus began a series of thoughts and preparations that led Eaton to the "end of track" in Mexico and, in his words, to the "new South-West" and to the farthest reaches of civilization.[2] When he finally arrived in Chihuahua City, Eaton took careful measure of social, political, and economic activities of the region, which would form the base of his mission work—and the home for his family—for the indefinite future. His trip that April was thus one of reconnaissance. Gertrude, then six months pregnant, looked after their three-year-old son at her parents' house in New Jersey, eager to receive word from her husband.

What the missionary observed in Chihuahua made clear the challenges that awaited him, his family, and their work. A stark division separated most of Catholic Chihuahua from the rowdy, agnostic-at-best railroad workers from the United States. "It cuts me to the hand," Eaton wrote to his ecclesiastical superior in Boston, "to find that my countrymen are trot up in the police court & fined & imprisoned for being drunk & disorderly—far worse offenders than any of the natives." Before starting his real work in the Catholic countryside, he argued, it would be "highly desirable . . . to work for a time, and in part, in behalf of nominally [Christian] Americans."[3]

Bemused by the challenges before him, Eaton saw proselytizing to Americans as a way to establish roots in the new territory with the ultimate goal of converting Mexican Catholics. To achieve this the missionary placed special emphasis on reaching and employing women. He made this clear in an early letter from Chihuahua to the Congregational Board. "Until a few more *wives* come to give greater stability to the foreign population," he emphasized, "probably not more than a handful [of men] can be enticed for worship up a back flight of stone steps, or into a more accessible private parlor."[4] And key to this strategy of saving souls through the vectors of gender was Gertrude. Her ability to use gender as a mission strategy aligns with other recent analyses of white women on other Latin American frontiers. The historian Julie Greene has shown, for example, how housewives in the Panama Canal Zone "became willing participants in their nation's civilizing mission."[5] Gender directly contributed to expansionary impulses, whether in Latin America or elsewhere.

Together, Gertrude and James faced many challenges: converting a heavily Catholic countryside, maintaining a home in a region inhospitable to fair-skinned foreigners, and finding a way to connect with neighbors and workers. Their example demonstrates the importance of family and kin networks to the missionaries, who employed and preached to women as a means of getting beyond the thresholds of otherwise unwelcoming neighbors.[6] Yet their work, like that of the Burnhams in Southern Rhodesia, personally taxed the couple and their children. It sapped their physical and emotional strength, thus exposing the struggle for and by families along a religious borderland. At a low point in the couple's personal lives, the Eatons were rejuvenated by the arrival of "neighbors" in Chihuahua, fifty miles away: a colony of Boer settlers from South Africa drawn to the region, motivated by a need for frontier life, stability, and, like the Eatons, a location not too far removed from the United States. The Eatons' experience in founding a spiritual community lays bare the troubles of realizing American dreams in foreign lands, while also exemplifying the similarities shared by western and imperial frontiers. The distance between the rhetoric of boosters and the realities of cultural expansion proved far and wide in the borderlands.

For more than seventy years the American Board of Commissioners of Foreign Missions (ABCFM), organized by the Congregational Church, had functioned in a prototypical imperialist manner. Founded in 1810 by a group of young adherents in Massachusetts and Connecticut, the board grew from a desire, in part, to bring light to "the moral darkness of Asia," "to the Indians, or the Africans, or other disadvantaged races."[7] Cut from the same cloth as other imperial missions, the ABCFM attempted to form a joint administration with the London Mission Society.[8] Members of the early board conceived of overseas missions to Zulus and Hindus in the same way that they understood Native Americans. "From its very organization," wrote the board's editorial secretary a century later, "the American Board had the Indians in its thought. Its first address to the Christian public in November, 1811, declared the intention to establish a mission in the East in the Burman empire and in the West among the Caghnawage (Iroquois) tribe of Indians."[9] Early missions to India, to Native American lands of the

Cherokee, Sioux, and others of the U.S. South and West, to the Middle East, to China, and to Africa gave the board considerable experience by the time it turned its attention to what it called "nominally Papal lands" like Mexico in the 1880s.

Although Mexico was a field new to the Eatons and to the ABCFM, it was not ignored by Protestant missionaries of other denominations.[10] The nation's Constitution of 1857 had legalized all forms of Protestantism, and by 1883 there were more than twelve separate mission boards (e.g., those of the Southern Baptists, Presbyterians, Methodists, and other denominations) operating with 85 missionaries and 264 congregations.[11] The total number of Mexican Protestant believers hovered around a mere 2 percent of the population, and the ABCFM hoped to expand its presence in the North through the work of the Eatons and their fellow missionaries.

James Eaton set foot in Chihuahua in a time of great promise for the region, given the arrival of the railway, but sporadic indigenous resistance challenged the soundness of economic investments there. In response to persistent incursions and violence on both sides of the border, in July 1882 Mexico and the United States agreed to a binational treaty that gave each nation cross-border rights in pursuit of Apache and Comanche raiders. The treaty eventually lessened the threats to the extension of rail lines, which in turn improved the response time for troops to defend against indigenous attacks. Enhanced mobility in the form of new roads, while a flashpoint of resistance, helped to secure the region, as well.[12]

The railroad had as large an impact on the local economy as it did on security. Long a neglected region far from Mexico City, Chihuahua and other northern states began to flourish with the arrival of significant investments in the 1880s. Agriculture and mining improvements went hand in hand with the laying of rails. Between 1888 and 1907 per capita revenue in Chihuahua increased 135 percent. As a result, education also improved. Mary Kay Vaughan has shown that expenditures in Chihuahua's public primary education increased from .02 pesos per capita, the lowest in the nation in 1874, to .98 pesos per capita, third-highest in the nation in 1907. Public school enrollments increased by 838 percent for that same period, leading to the state having the sixth highest literacy rate by 1910.[13]

The Eatons therefore arrived at an ideal time to recruit new students, though the targets of their efforts deeply distrusted the Protestant message they espoused.

The board wanted to grow its congregations in Mexico, but at the same time it respected both informal and formal arrangements with other Protestant denominations not to compete overtly for families, villages, or even regions. From the start the Congregational board thus felt "hemmed in" by the Southern Methodists to the north and the Presbyterians to the south. Eaton ostensibly promoted a nonsectarian philosophy, yet he continually worried that, as Mexico became more accessible by rail, denominational rivalry would strengthen with results "akin to that existing in our Western states and territories."[14] To lay claim to yet open lands, in the early 1880s the board therefore established mission stations in Chihuahua, Batopilas, Guerrero, and Jiménez, while employing native workers and assistants in Hermosillo and throughout the State of Sonora as well as further south in Guadalajara. The American Protestant missions' agreements to divide Mexico so as to avoid competition among themselves resonated with Europe's divisions of foreign territories for colonialism during the Berlin Conference of 1884–85. The board intended to divide and convert.

In September 1882 James and Gertrude Eaton embodied this new religious frontier when they departed from the East Coast with their toddler son, Howard, their new infant of nine weeks, Harry, and Gertrude's sister, Adele Pratt, who had agreed to contribute her labor in exchange for free travel and some worldly experience. An accomplished teacher and pianist at her home in Montclair, Pratt would be especially valuable to a mission needful of her talents, and the Eatons secretly hoped she might stay indefinitely. Bound for Mexico, the extended family carried with it household goods: two suites of bedroom furniture; bookcases and tables; dining room furniture; a cookstove; crockery; glassware; pictures; a sewing machine; canned milk, meats, and fish; cans of kerosene oil; and a piano and small cabinet organ.[15] At the border customs officials inspected, counted, weighed, and taxed these goods, just as Catholic social circles in Chihuahua would soon scrutinize the Eatons' cultural baggage.

When they arrived in Chihuahua City that November the mission-aries confronted a social landscape divided by class and defined by access to education. The vast majority of the lower and middle classes and many of the elites were resistant to Protestant religious beliefs and to breaking the Catholic status quo. Whereas the masses resisted the missionaries' be-liefs, a portion of the upper-middle class recognized the importance of for-eign investment and collaboration in the creation of a stronger Mexico. After staying in a hotel their first month in the city, the Eatons found a suitable room and parlor for a temporary establishment, though they received a curt welcome. The owner attempted to block their rental of the property, to avoid having it be "desecrated by . . . worship." "It would scandalize the whole city," the owner said, for her to "let her house to a Protestant Minis-ter and he the *first* one coming in to introduce another religion."[16] Only after influential Mexicans, including the mayor, interceded did the owner relent and give the Eatons the key to their new home.

By early December 1882 the couple had held their first services with a "handful of people present." Immediately following the service local citi-zens, among them a lawyer, a teacher, and a customshouse agent, asked Pratt to teach them English, and by the end of the month she was teaching language classes five nights a week.[17] Word and intrigue spread quickly, and by Christmas Eve that year, at the first official public service, the Eatons counted more than fifty people in attendance. Despite initially catering to U.S. expatriates, the holiday singing and the organ music drew pass-ersby into their parlor, they claimed, and by the end of the service on Christmas Eve Mexicans comprised half of the assembly.[18]

The early turnout surprised the missionaries, who had heard the "prevailing wisdom" among foreigners that "one must not meddle with the politics or religion in this country, in order to succeed in business." Oc-casional violence and acts of open hostility reminded them not to take early successes for granted. Indeed, ongoing resistance to Protestant expansion frustrated others throughout the country. For example, a Congregational missionary awoke one morning at his station in southern Chihuahua to find a message scrawled on his window: "*Aquí viven los demonios*" (demons live here). "The priests denounced me *publicly* from the pulpit some time ago," he wrote, "and most of the people evidently look upon us as being worse than ordinary criminals." The missionary also described disruptions of his services sufficient to warrant the hiring of a policeman during religious gatherings.[19] As late as 1900, at the Arivechi station in Sonora, "a dynamite cartridge . . . was thrown and exploded on the roof of the house" during a baptism ceremony.[20] Such displays of open, yet anonymous, hostility lasted for decades and kept the Congregational missionaries wary of overt proselytizing and of drawing too much attention to themselves.[21]

The Eatons and others therefore had to find a balance between furthering their mission while respecting tradition and long-held Catholic dogma. Such negotiation informed almost every decision they made. When they rented their first residence and began to circulate socially, James placed an inconspicuous sign in his parlor window advertising the sale of Bibles, tracts, and other religious publications. Locals quickly reprimanded him for his public display of Protestant propaganda, so ostentatious and unbecoming. Even a decade later, as the growing congregation constructed a new, large, and permanent house of worship, Eaton requested that a cross *not* adorn the chapel top for fear of sending a competing message to his Catholic counterparts. Rather, he asked that three crosses be inlayed within the windows of the main entryway.

To help navigate these sensitive terrains—lands governed by strict patriarchal codes in both sacred and secular realms—Eaton determined that the success of the board's mission depended on women and families, both foreign and Mexican. After only four months in Chihuahua he wrote to his superiors in Boston, "Especially is it becoming clear to me that we must attempt educational work for *girls,* if we are to secure any of the future *mothers* of this priest-ridden community."[22] Pratt, in addition to her other duties of teaching English and a Sunday school class to American children, began teaching six girls at "a reputable young *ladies'* school" one hour each morning. By May 1883 the Eatons had started a Spanish hymn service. "A large number of Mexicans were persuaded to enter and take seats," glowed Eaton in his report, "among them some respectable ladies, while many more stood in the open court, and a throng was before the two front windows." With this early adaptation to services in both languages, Eaton recognized he needed to become proficient in Spanish and began taking private lessons from Guadalupe Benitez, the principal of the local girls' school.[23] In June he began preaching in Spanish.

Despite their early achievements, the missionaries struggled to maintain their spirits as tragedy loomed over their household. Beginning in March 1883 their infant, Harry, weakened suddenly and became thin. At eleven months of age the baby weighed only 13.5 pounds, far below normal range. In late June, Gertrude moved with her son to a "shady river-side to obtain better air than the city could afford." For ten days they kept watch and fretted over the baby's survival. Anxiety tested both Eatons' resolve. They felt overwhelmed by their devotion to the mission's early success and their first priority of caring for their child. At the mission they were needed for Spanish and English services, prayer groups, Sunday schools, and sales of religious tracts; yet worrying over their defenseless child nearly incapacitated the couple. James questioned his ability to withstand the burdens of fatherhood. He wrote to administrators that he would abandon the American chapel and preach only in Spanish. "I know not how long I can work on at this present rate without breaking down," he wrote. "If I cannot have helpers, I should prefer letting go my hold before the break-down." Gertrude, fully occupied caring for Harry, lamented not being able to meet her own commitment. "If I were only free," she said, "I could start a women's meeting at once." Her husband added, "We do *so much need* a lady missionary who can go into the homes of these comparatively secluded wives and daughters." The Eatons begged for assistance while their personal lives revolved around the care of Harry.[24] They asked for another missionary to live with them, and "amongst the very desirable 'points' and 'qualifications' of an associate," wrote James, was "the possession of a *wife.*"[25]

The urgency in their petitions for assistance conveys the gravity of the family's position. They were socially isolated in a foreign land, physically worn from evangelical duties, and mentally anguished by the condition of their baby. By September Harry had lost another two pounds. Eaton himself suffered a "break-down," dropping 15 percent of his own bodyweight, forcing him to close the chapel temporarily. Mother and child moved again, to a guest house on the property of a Mexican parishioner, in the hope that fresher air would alleviate the baby's condition. When this proved unhelpful the family decided to return for a time to James's native Wisconsin as a last hope for the young child. But nothing could save him. On September 9, 1883, Eaton wrote, "Early this morning before the dawn, our little one fell asleep with a smile, and is safe with the Good Shepherd. . . . His life, though so brief and full of pain, has, as we can plainly see, been the Providential occasion for influencing the careers of others to a remarkable degree."[26] However virtuous, the Eatons could not avoid the pain and anxiety they felt after a year of watching their infant suffer. James soon lost feeling in his legs below the knees. A doctor in Wisconsin diagnosed his condition as "nervous prostration," the result of a flare-up of a previous malarial infection. But James could not deny the likelihood that his incapacitation resulted from the pain of losing his son.[27]

The deaths of Harry Eaton and Nada Burnham (see chapter 2), separated by thirteen years, highlight a key difference between the Burnhams' experiences in Southern Rhodesia and the Eatons' in Chihuahua. In the Burnhams' case, the extreme distance of family members from home and their location in a war-torn region forced them to withstand the pangs of death in Rhodesia. Circumstances required them to bury their beloved Nada in a land far from home, and, indeed, Grandmother Burnham in southern California did not learn of young Nada's death for two weeks. By contrast, the Eatons lived in a region connected by rail to the United States. While they wrote of the culture as if it were entirely foreign and removed from the comforts of home, they could be in their native country in less than twelve hours at any given moment. Their ability to return to Wisconsin for the death of Harry and to bury him in such a meaningful place to them illustrates one of the attractions that many people saw to living in the Mexican North in the age of railroad extension.

The Eatons attempted to recover emotionally and spiritually with family in the Midwest for a few weeks, but a tough question lingered: would they return to Mexico? They had yet to convert a single Mexican to the Protestant faith. What's more, October had passed, and Gertrude's sister,

Adele Pratt, had left the mission station after fulfilling her obligation of a year's service. Pratt had provided emotional support and almost single-handedly had taught Sunday school and English classes during the past year. Despite her and the Eatons' efforts, their work, much less their pres-ence, was not desired by the native population. James and Gertrude thus faced the reality of returning to their Mexican home without their late infant, without the assistance of Pratt, and without a welcoming community. An empty house and a heavy workload awaited their return in Chihuahua. "I do dread the effect on Mrs. Eaton's system of a return to our desolate home," James confided to the board's secretary in Boston, "where almost everything will remind her of her absent sister and lost little one. But this danger will not become much less through delay."[28] Ever committed to their cause, James and Gertrude mustered the conviction to return to the Mexi-can mission.

They arrived to hear some surprisingly good news, a flicker of hope. Their friend and housekeeper, Antonia Carrasco, informed the Eatons that she had been holding conversations with a local couple, Felipe and Anto-nia Hernández, who had renounced their Catholic adherence and sought new lives in the Congregational Church (fig. 9).[29] On Sunday, November 18, 1883, Eaton baptized the couple. During the ceremony he encouraged those unable to speak Spanish to shake hands with the couple as a gesture of con-gratulations. "What was my surprise and delight afterwards," he wrote, "to see nearly *every one* whether church member or not, shaking hands with these Mexicans (whose seats were by the door) as they passed out of the chapel. It gave proof of a friendliness of feeling toward the work in charge of the Board, which augurs well for the future."[30] The first breakthrough for the Eatons therefore came thanks to the care and effort of Antonia Carrasco, the local housekeeper, who had not only spoken with the Hernán-dez couple but also sold a number of Bibles during the Eatons' absence. Antonia and her husband, Sabrino, now lived in the house with the missionaries.[31]

The absence of her sister forced Gertrude Eaton, like her husband, to maintain a hectic schedule. In addition to mothering her boy, Howard, Gertrude, "brave heart and indefatigable worker," took over teaching

Figure 9.   Antonia and Felipe Hernández.
Eaton, *Life Under Two Flags*, 133.

English and Sunday school. At the same time, the couple hoped to receive
an additional missionary, a young woman from Chicago, "just the right person with a fresh, young heart to love, and lead into a better life, Mexico's
neglected women and needy youth." In early 1884 the couple waited for
someone to relieve Gertrude of some of her duties, while James went on
tours to neighboring cities—150 miles by rail, 60 by coach—to spread the
word, sell Bibles, and cultivate future relations in the region.[32]

Meanwhile, the connection between Gertrude Eaton and Antonia
Carrasco supported a growing Protestant community in Chihuahua. The
pair went to a neighbor's house every day to read the Bible with local
women.[33] Their first convert, Felipe Hernández, accompanied the women

and hauled a portable organ on his shoulder. Eaton remarked to his superiors that their success depended on the link between Gertrude and Antonia, for their shared gender and their different nationalities. Antonia's eyes sparkled when she told of her experiences, wrote James, "and through being a native gains access to houses and hearts where Mrs. Eaton could not accomplish anything." The historian Peggy Pascoe has explored Protestants' reliance on "native helpers" in other contexts, calling them "living proof of the transforming power of female moral authority" and noting how missionaries "lavished attention" on them. This certainly holds true for the case in Mexico, and the Eatons' mission especially shows how assistants sustained the mission in pragmatic ways. Native helpers made Bible readings, Sunday school classes, and English lessons possible, and they enabled the growth of the Protestant mission in Chihuahua. That May, the Eatons converted and baptized three teenagers and students from Gertrude's Sunday school classes. In July nine adults, seven of whom were from the mission's women's meetings, declared their intent to convert.[34]

Though their early successes gave them hope and a muted sense of accomplishment, the Protestant message the Eatons disseminated, along with its accompanying cultural ideologies, was not accepted blindly. Converts did not abandon traditional beliefs for a foreign ideal; rather, as one scholar has shown, they benefited through adopted communities, technologies, and education that provided "a material and spiritual scaffolding" for their own values, drawing on a long history of egalitarian movements.[35] The brand of Protestantism, capitalism, and education demonstrated and offered by the Eatons therefore became a platform for initial converts like Felipe Hernández.

With their growing success, it seems, the personal toll on the couple only intensified. James Eaton's appeals for assistance sharpened: "Let there be sent us *reinforcements,* and that *speedily.*" Otherwise, "please release me that I may either join any Presbyterian brethren or return to a pastorate in the U.S."[36] Gertrude soldiered through her sadness while James began to fail. Numbness in his legs returned, and the chief surgeon of the Mexican Central Railway advised the missionary to leave Chihuahua for a few months of rest. Eaton returned to Beloit College, his alma mater in

Wisconsin, where his brother served as president. Gertrude continued their work in Chihuahua, even translating services to Mexican parishioners through her newly acquired Spanish. After the first services, her dear friend Antonia Carrasco "took me into her arms, and cried and laughed and hugged & kissed me all in one," she wrote to her husband from Mexico.[37] Gertrude's successes still could not soften the demands of her physical and emotional well-being. She wrote of "benumbed spiritual sensibilities," feeling "humiliated" at the "triumph of the physical over the spiritual." Longing for the strictures of a domestic life, and one not spent traveling door-to-door, Gertrude begged her husband, "Oh! James, *do* bring back a lady missionary, if she is anywhere to be found!"[38] Not long after sending this plea to her husband, Gertrude, in consultation with another board missionary in Mexico, left the Chihuahua site alone to return to New Jersey for rest and to visit her mother.

The executives on the Prudential Committee of the ABCFM in Boston heeded the Eatons' calls for additional help. They attempted to hire seven single women to move to Mexico, but for various reasons none ultimately went to the mission station. The committee did, however, reinforce the southern station of Parral by contracting another married couple, Alden and Myra Case, who had been working with the Lakota Indians since 1881. The Cases left for Chihuahua in October 1884.[39] Eaton had first met Case in the United States in August and praised him in his reports, arguing that his colleague's heritage as "a native of the old West" qualified him for the job. His "experience of church organizing and building on the frontier" gave him "immediate and positive value for our purposes."[40]

The addition of the Cases expanded the board's presence in Parral, but it did little to alleviate the growing pains the Eatons suffered in Chihuahua City. That winter, out of desperation, they made arrangements for the return of Gertrude's sister for three months. Pratt offered some respite, but by February the growing congregation forced the Eatons to look for a new location for their expanding enterprises. They made an agreement with Francisco Espinoza, the fellow parishioner who had allowed Gertrude to stay at his place two years previously while caring for their late son. Espinoza and the Eatons would build a new house, to be used as a chapel, on his property. It was to be thirty feet long, twenty-two feet wide, and six-teen feet high and was to be built of twelve thousand adobe bricks.[41] The new building, divided into two rooms, marked a major step forward for the Eatons' visions of influence and allowed for a new component to their mission: education.

As the Chihuahua mission of the ABCFM gained traction, other religious migrants fled to Mexico for very different reasons. Mormon colonists moved south in response to the Edmunds Act of 1882, which had outlawed polygamy in the United States, and they initially considered settling in the Yaqui Valley of Sonora. In December 1884 Brigham Young Jr. and seven others journeyed to the mouth of the Yaqui River. Forging upstream against the advice of the Sonoran secretary of state, the Mormons received "a kindly welcome from a race of Indians whose war-like reputation had spread terror throughout northern Mexico."[42] According to the colonist Thomas Cottam Romney, anti-Mormon agitators had spread rumors that the group wanted to ally themselves with the Yaquis to provoke war against the United States. After this development—and perhaps also due to their inability to convert any Yaquis—church leaders decided it "inopportune to attempt colonization."[43] Romney and his followers continued to western Chihuahua. The establishment of twelve Mormon colonies throughout the state was, in fact, the second Mormon exodus to Mexico. The first, in 1847, had been the epic journey to what would become the Territory of Utah, but was then, in fact, part of Mexico. Most Mormons stayed there, but in light of the Edmunds Act many felt it necessary to seek refuge in Mexican lands a second time, "primarily from persecution." In addition, wrote Romney, "it was a call of the West—that great free, open country of endless plains and rugged mountains—the call which had gripped scores of brave and adventurous frontiersmen before them and gave them courage to brook the lurking dangers of the great unknown."[44]

The Eatons were not initially aware of the Mormon colonies, but as time passed they learned of their presence. Neither would have social interactions with the other; the nearest Mormon colony was more than two hundred miles away. The Eatons may have shared experiences with the Mormon exiles by bringing a non-Catholic religious ideology into Mexico,

but their motivations differed greatly, the former being intent on proselytizing to and converting their neighbors and the latter on fleeing perceived
threats in the United States. Both, though, considered Mexico an extension of a U.S. frontier, and they each felt isolated south of the border.

Solitude soon gave way as the Eatons built their mission to include
educational facilities, setting aside a room adjoining the hall of worship to
be used four evenings a week as a night school for adults, where twelve residents began learning to read and write.[45] Gertrude held meetings for a
dozen women to study the Bible, and she also convened a weekly get-
together for five women called the Willing Workers. These women volun-
teered in the mission's schools, helped with religious services, and went
door-to-door to spread the gospel. On Saturdays the church building was
transformed into an industrial school for thirty-two students in three
classes. There, women made garments and warm underwear for distribu-
tion to the destitute. Girls learned patchwork and quilting. Boys made
scrapbooks, picture frames, and other household goods. The Eatons considered the school a means to "teach habits of industry" while providing
clothes for the poor and "incubating religious truth."[46] And for the first
time, students of the ABCFM mission in Chihuahua could feel—through
the physical objects they made—the material results of newfound allegiances and ideologies. The work of Gertrude and the connections with
Mexican women and the Willing Workers made this all possible. In September 1885 Eaton himself acknowledged as much, writing that his wife's
work was "at the spiritual center of this station."[47]

Connections between women sustained the Mexican mission and its
commitment to education. In the summer of 1889 the mission added a new
boarding school, El Colegio Chihuahuense, with an initial enrollment of
four students. The lack of instructional assistance continued to hamper the
Eatons; Gertrude served as a temporary teacher and boarding director for
nearly two years. One of the first instructors at the day school, Mary Dunning, recalled, "The morning I arrived and on going into Mrs. Eaton's dining room saw the four girls at their breakfast," she wrote. "They constituted
the boarding school in its beginning. Mrs. Eaton had come from her home
with all her household to be with them till some one could care for them.

They did their own washing, ironing, cooking, in fact all their own work outside of school hours." Gertrude managed the school until the Eatons coaxed a teacher to come north from the Parral Station.[48]

Over the next several years total enrollment in the two schools grew. Girls from the surrounding countryside and some from neighboring states attended to receive an education unavailable to their parents. In 1890, 51 of the 57 students were female. By 1895, of the 95 total pupils 67 were girls.[49] Such gender imbalance remained generally consistent at the ABCFM's sites beyond Chihuahua in Mexico, which also established boarding schools exclusively for girls. The emphasis on female education can be explained by two factors: Mexican families likely preferred to send their daughters to a school that could prepare them to be teachers, an overwhelmingly female profession; and the board itself sought to expand its sphere of influence through girls, as evidenced by Eaton's quip about securing the "future mothers of this priest-ridden community."[50] In the ABCFM's annual tabular reports, in fact, columns separated students as well as members of the congregation by gender, giving totals, for example, of 63 church members in 1890, "Of Whom are Women" numbering 40.[51] The Eatons' gendered strategy and ecclesiastical determination began to cultivate a notable Protestant community in Chihuahua.[52] Church memberships, total contributions, and Mexican participation as workers in the mission grew substantially between 1890 and 1905. Sunday school attendance steadily grew as well, from 50 attendees in 1885 to 95 in 1890 and 125 in 1895.

In addition to converting believers from Catholicism to Protestantism and providing education, the Eatons funneled the ABCFM's philosophy of progressive reform into Chihuahua. They stressed sobriety and the avoidance of vices they felt were counterproductive to an enlightened life. Teachers in El Colegio Chihuahuense reinforced notions of cleanliness by emphasizing hygiene, asking pupils to greet their teachers each morning by saying "Yo vengo limpio" (I come clean).[53] The statement referred to the students' grooming habits, which protected the board's workers and parishioners from everyday threats of disease and contagion. The missionaries knew about these dangers all

Table 1. Growth of the Chihuahua Station of the ABCFM, 1890–1905

	U.S. Workers	Mex. Workers	Members	Contributions
1890	3	3	63	$233.61
1895	4	3	112	$292.53
1900	4	10	323	$2,564.00
1905	4	11	442	$7,064.00

Source: ABCFM Annual Reports.

too well. In 1885 one of their paid staff fell ill from smallpox while resid-ing at the mission station. The illness forced the Eatons to leave the property and move in with their neighbor Francisco Espinoza once again, where, two years earlier, Gertrude and James "[had] watched by our dying child."[54]

Clean of body, clean of mind. This dictum especially informed mis-sionaries in Mexico and on other global frontiers. In the case of Southern Rhodesia, the missionary and imperial encounter in the nineteenth century, when Frederick Burnham worked his dreams (see chapter 2), gave way to exogenous cultural habits and beliefs in twentieth-century Zimbabwe. The historian Timothy Burke has shown how an organization based in New York, the Jeanes Teachers, imparted cultural beliefs about cleanliness and hygiene through the commodification of everyday objects like soap and shampoo. Burke unpacks the ways in which imposed notions of cleanliness and the creation of needs worked in collusion with colonial authorities and missionary schools in the conquest of Zimbabwe. Similarly, the novelist Tsitsi Dangarembga's *Nervous Conditions* explores the clash of cultures and how, for her protagonist, Tambu, imperial subjectivity and the allure of modern comforts came to be intertwined by ostensibly innocuous items like the toothbrush, Vaseline, and the bathtub.[55] In Chihuahua the teachers' emphasis on cleanliness grew not only from concerns for their own health but also from deep-seated ideas of cultural supremacy and Mexican so-cial backwardness. They felt surrounded by vice. "Some days a decided improvement can be seen," wrote the school's director, "but there are many others when bull-fighters, circus-riders and '*carretas*' [races] seem to occupy the entire ground, till one's heart fails her at the thought of conquering such territory."[56]

The urge to suppress such *cultura mexicana* did not drive the Eatons, but it was a natural consequence of the religious and cultural dogma they practiced. Their influence broadened in the middle 1880s, when they began building a larger mission complex. However unintentionally, the Eatons replicated the vice-to-virtue practice of the colonial Spanish (who covered Aztec temples with Roman Catholic churches) when they purchased the old Zaragoza Theater to rebuild it into a sacred space. In the 1860s and 1870s the theater had been used for stage entertainment and billiards, once also housing a drinking saloon, a gaming room, and a cockfighting pit, which Eaton immediately covered after leasing the property. The gaming room turned into a library, of sorts, and what was once a den of vice was transformed into a space of worship. The only hitch in the board's plan was that the mission could not choose its neighbors. Across the street, Eaton begrudgingly recalled, was "a notorious house kept by American women. The sounds of revelry which in the early evening issued through its open windows were extremely disturbing to our worshiping congregation; so that even on the hottest nights of summer we were obliged to close our own windows on that side."[57]

Everyday life settled somewhat with the added space provided by the old theater, and the mission's influence, via native Mexican assistants, began to thrive in the city and state. Since 1884 Eaton had trained a native preacher, Francisco Padierna, a former cobbler who had served with Methodists and Presbyterians in Zacatecas and Durango. Working out of Parral for the Congregationalists, Padierna accomplished much with less effort. He established a Sunday school and preached in a private house. He sold subscriptions to religious texts and soon had twenty-three believers. Padierna's success impressed Eaton, yet the native preacher's former employers warned that Padierna could only "be useful under surveillance."[58] Eaton remained skeptical of the Presbyterians' claims (they raised questions about Padierna only *after* he joined the Congregationalists), and he employed Padierna in Chihuahua City for two summers before sending him off to Cusihuiriachi in the mountains with a "two-box load of books balanced across the back of an ass."[59] Padierna made great strides for the Congregationalists in western Chihuahua.

Other locals found opportunities for personal gain in the growing competition between Protestant branches. By October 1885 the Methodists augmented their presence in the North by establishing a mission in Chihuahua City, thus ending the divine division of Mexico established earlier in the decade. Eaton heard the news from a colleague in El Paso, and he quickly wrote to Boston, "We have cried 'Wolf' two or three times already, but this looks like the real animal!"[60] Within a few months half of the board's registered church members in Chihuahua had absconded for the Methodists, and Eaton admitted, in a rare burst of sarcasm, to experiencing the first "delights of denominationalism."[61]

In January 1886 one such "delight" startled the missionary, when he discovered the newest native preacher, Rosindo del Valle, secretly working as an informant for other denominations. Eaton received a letter from the Southern Methodist missionary of Durango, who wanted to avoid such nefarious relations. The letter enclosed del Valle's eight-page report, "the basest treachery, being a confidential report of all the details and inside facts relating to our mission which could possibly be of use to the S. Methodists, at the same time distorted to suit his purposes." Del Valle purportedly sought to improve his standing among foreign missionaries by delivering recruits to competing denominations. He, like others, Eaton replied, "suffered from the vanity and arrogance of this product of denominational rivalry and lavish use of foreign money, leading to parasitism & hypocrisy."[62] Del Valle's "treason" rankled Eaton, and it demonstrates how Mexicans could actively benefit from the Americans' presence. While annual reports and letters to religious superiors tabulated church members, baptisms, and Sunday school attendance, such materials could not divulge the depth of religious conviction or the true success of conversion. Acceptance of Protestantism could indicate genuine belief as much as it could a desire for educational advancement and class mobility. In other words, Mexicans converted on their own terms, a fact that generally eludes the written record. How can historians measure true belief?

Those who chose conversion risked social isolation, and the reper-
cussions could be severe. Antonia Carrasco and Felipe and Antonia
Hernández had to suffer the consequences of their faith. Soon after
Carrasco's employment with the Eatons, a priest referred to her as the "Tail
of the Protestants" and urged followers to refuse her entrance "into their
houses or to touch any books with New York printed on them."[63] Other
attendees of the Eatons' services had stones thrown at them or were ostra-
cized by their families.[64] A change of spiritual belief could provoke retri-
bution and material consequences. Far from being mere receptacles of
Protestant ideology, those who converted had to measure and calculate the
risks and benefits that their decision would bring.

The next few years marked a deeper Congregational entrenchment in
Chihuahua society. In February 1886 the board hired an additional teacher
to work at the day school.[65] Two years later more than thirty students en-
rolled (only five coming from American homes). As a result, the Eatons began
to shift their attention away from the recruitment of women to that of Mexican workers.[66] For the first time, after a period of constant adjustments, the
mission exhibited institutional strength. This—the result of the Eatons, their
Mexican workers, and the strategy of working through female networks—
became codified by the building of a new, permanent house of worship.

The consecration of Templo La Trinidad in November 1892 marked a
defining point in the Eatons' professional and personal lives. Its construction and the objects in its hall told the story of a mission defined by the borderlands. The chairs on the chancel and the communion table were made to
order in New York and supplied by a former congregation in Montclair, New
Jersey. The wooden, six-foot-high wainscoting was made of Texas pine. Beneath the church tower, a plaque dedicated the building to Gertrude Eaton's
late mother, who had sent supplies from the Montclair congregation to her
daughter in Chihuahua. English ivy grew beside the memorial plaque and
up the interior of the tower, once planted at the Montclair church and later
transported to Mexico. At the dedication ceremony the flags of England,
Germany, Mexico, and the United States hung behind the pulpit.[67]

The origins of these objects hinted at the church's international foundations. Not hamstrung by nationality, the ABCFM's mission in Mexico

valued spirituality over statehood insofar as it drew upon a global network of missions to impart what it believed to be true and eternal. Conversely, this network facilitated human prejudices as easily as it did the sacraments. While the Eatons prepared to celebrate the opening of La Trinidad, ABCFM executives met in Chicago. Representatives from around the world gathered for the annual conference, where missionaries from China, India, Sri Lanka, the Pacific Islands, Japan, Turkey, and Africa would crisscross with those from Mexico. A report from the American Zulu Mission, for example, sought transnational assistance and lessons from the American West to address its own challenges. "Thousands of coolies have been imported from Asia," the report stated, "God forbid that we should have the American spirit of Asiatic exclusion! But God has sent us to disciple a nation. . . . The results achieved among the Freedmen and American Indians and in the Lovedale system of South Africa spur our wish to see more done here in this direction. The future of a race is in the balance."[68] In another statement at the conference one attendee used language that would have appealed to all present: "Ignorance, superstition, and bigotry are encountered, and there is not seemingly the readiness for the gospel which cheers the workers in heathen lands." This attendee spoke not of the ABCFM's presence among the Zulu but of the Mexican mission and others in "Nominally Papal Lands."[69]

As their ecclesiastical superiors gathered to the north, swapping global generalities, the Eatons celebrated the opening of La Trinidad. After a decade of piecemeal struggle they now celebrated a bright future. "Congratulations poured in upon us from all nationalities and our cup of joy was full," James wrote to his mother in Wisconsin. "Gertrude and I could not stop talking about it before midnight, when we finally made up our minds to go to bed, but I was awake again at four o'clock."[70] The Eatons had yet another reason to celebrate: Gertrude had given birth to their third child, Dorothy, the previous year. And so on that night in November 1892, where Gertrude and James Eaton once felt emptiness, they now found joy. Nine years earlier they had returned to Chihuahua, after the death of their son Harry and after the departure of Gertrude's sister, to a land that barely welcomed them. The Templo La Trinidad and the cries of a new baby now

Figure 10.   The Eaton household in Chihuahua: *(front row, left to right)* Howard, Katherine (his wife), Dorothy, Gertrude, and Mary Long; *(back row, center)*
James. The unidentified men were likely Mexican pastors or assistants with the
ABCFM's schools in Chihuahua. An onlooker, out of focus on the far right, re-
minds viewers of the gated, relatively privileged world the Eatons struggled to
escape in order to disperse their Protestant message. Image courtesy of the
Family of Dorothy Eaton McGinty.

were ample proof of their progress. It made them proud, for example, to
be able to point to their church from the railroad line when talking with
fellow passengers.[71] Where the Eatons had faced ostracism and isolation,
they now lived with and among their Mexican parishioners. They had a
permanent place in Chihuahua, their adopted home land.

For the next ten years the Congregational influence grew, but the
overall numbers of Protestants in all of Mexico remained low (fig. 10). The
prevalence of the Catholic Church in the countryside continued to ob-
struct many reformist inroads. As late as 1896 Minister of Foreign Affairs Matías Romero estimated Protestant missionizing to "have succeeded
very poorly." Only 63 Protestant houses of worship existed in Mexico,

compared to 8,763 Catholic churches.[72] Nevertheless, the Eatons personified a borderlands mission. They often returned to the United States via
the railroad connection in El Paso. Both spouses occasionally attended
the annual national board conferences. They visited family in Wisconsin,
New Jersey, and California. They gave lectures and sought medical care
north of the border. Life seemed to progress through the early 1900s, when,
starting in 1902, they sensed a shift in the reception of their mission, not
for its message but for its perceived nationality.

Nationalist Response, International Neighbors

As Episcopalians and Baptists established missions in Chihuahua City, and
the American presence became more pronounced, some Mexican Protestants hesitated to be seen as "traitors to their country" and beholden to the
missionaries. James Eaton remarked that members of his congregation
sometimes wavered because they viewed capitalists as "intent upon the
absorption of this country, if not of its territory, at least of its material resources and commercial enterprises."[73] Beginning in 1902 a new Independent Mexican Church sought to spread a Protestant message through shared
nationalist networks. While the independent movement never posed a threat
to the Eatons' work, it did call their attention to a rising nationalism among
their parishioners.

Following this subtle challenge to their religious legitimacy, a series
of events tested the missionaries' resolve yet again. In March 1904 Eaton's
mother, Catherine, died at her home in Beloit, Wisconsin, at a point in time
when he had to officiate the funerals of two American children who had
succumbed to scarlet fever. "The circumstances . . . were so extremely
painful that I was almost prostrated," he noted. The following month Dorothy Eaton, now thirteen years old, developed a nervous disease, a "light
form of chorea" called "St. Vitus's dance" that caused her limbs to shake.
To relieve the anxiety of the teenager, James and Gertrude decided to remove their daughter from the mission temporarily. James wrote to the board
explaining the necessity of relocating Dorothy, "especially since she sym-
pathizes so fully with all phases of the mission work, and feels the drain

upon her vitality, which is caused by the poverty, sin and suffering which cannot be hidden from her." [74]

James then commented that Gertrude looked "much worn" from the entire situation. Perhaps she, on witnessing her husband's sadness over the passing of his mother, relived the pain caused by her own mother's death in 1886. Maybe worrying over the diminished health of Dorothy forced Gertrude to revisit the futile effort to save Harry in 1883. While no evidence identifies the exact source of her anxieties, something began to debilitate Gertrude in late 1903, and her disillusionment weighed heavily on her husband's mind. By 1904 she was nearly incapacitated.

The Eatons turned to their friends for support, and in this they had a fortuitous turn of events. In October 1903 a new development reenergized their hopes for the mission. South of the Eatons a colony of Boers from South Africa had been established at the Hacienda Santa Rosalía. These fair-skinned colonists, of Dutch and French Huguenot descent, renewed James Eaton's faith in his work at a time when it had been waning. The new arrivals lifted his spirits; he felt personally connected to them, given their status as outsiders to the region, and he felt religiously close to the colony, which adhered to the Dutch Reformed Church, for their shared Protestant roots. Furthermore, James used the arrival of the newcomers as a way to build bonds with other foreigners in Mexico, to take Gertrude beyond the confines of their mission, to enjoy the countryside and hope the fresh (though not necessarily cool) air would benefit his wife's present ills.

Additionally, Eaton noted, he realized the colony could help his mission's ecclesiastical agenda. Until then, the ABCFM in Boston had relied on American parishioners, but it desperately wanted to include and to potentially convert more Mexican families. "Does not this Boer Colony make an appeal to the Board?" Eaton wrote to an administrator. "They cannot object that the Boers are American citizens. And the Boers will employ many Mexicans, besides coming into business relations with the people in general."[75] His superiors agreed. They, too, saw the potential "[to] establish among [the Boer colonists] thorough-going Christian institutions in order to reach the Mexicans."[76] The news elated Eaton. Though the Boer exiles could not cure Gertrude's condition, the Eatons became

key witnesses to a Gilded Age frontier that connected southern Africa with
the U.S.–Mexican borderlands. Not only did Boer–missionary neighbors
connect in Chihuahua; they shared common networks with individuals
who would later vie for souls, land, and control in neighboring Sonora's
Yaqui Valley.

When social calls alone did not alleviate Gertrude's suffering, James
sought medical treatment for her. He consulted his son and religious elders
before accompanying her to the Clifton Springs Sanitarium in New York,
a health facility catering to mental and physical recuperation based on
relaxation, religious devotion, and treatment through baths and saunas.
Clifton Springs treated neither contagious diseases nor psychological
problems directly but offered to allow "those who are sick or tired . . . [to]
come at any time throughout the year, and amid cheerful surroundings and
under the care of doctors, . . . be restored to health and thus to a full en-
joyment of the activities of life."[77] The medical care for Gertrude at Clifton Springs and the family's careful observation of her afterward disrupted
all sense of normalcy. Gertrude's symptoms quickly worsened and included
"nervous and wakeful" fits of depression, a wish to go to an insane asylum,
and talk of suicide.[78] Doctors performed some type of procedure in early
August 1904 and by December declared her sufficiently healthy to leave
Clifton Springs. Her doctor "thought she had reached about normal mental
state," yet he noted she became "somewhat disturbed by the thought of returning to Mexico."[79] Knowing the stress that missionary life placed on its
workers, an official of the ABCFM wrote to James, "I hope you will be able
to stand between her and the Mexicans. . . . She must be carefully defended
from the strain and burden of the work and I am sure you and your son will
fully realize that."[80]

James and the ABCFM therefore had to make a difficult decision:
what was best for Gertrude? They and her male doctors did ask for her
thoughts on relocation—though they chose for her to return to Mexico—
but the letters between Eaton and board officials in Boston make it clear
the men surrounding her did not entirely trust her present state of mind.
Nor did she trust them. Once in Chihuahua, in February 1905, James wrote
to the board, "It is very difficult to write about Mrs. Eaton, because she has

forbidden me to mention her in letters or conversation, and watches me like a cat, nosing amongst my . . . papers. Just after my last to you was finished, she demanded to be allowed to read it, though she was in another part of the house during the writing of it. And after I got the letter out of the house, she searched my letter-book for the usual copy." As a result of her surveillance James did not write a duplicate and wrote only before breakfast: "I hear her getting up now, and know not at what moment she may come in upon for I cannot close my door, much less lock it, without exciting her suspicions and displeasing her."[81]

These letters document a concerned husband and his spiritual elders seeking the best care possible for his wife and their employee, but on a deeper level the writings simultaneously show how patriarchy forced a structure upon the lives and futures of female missionaries. The illness of Gertrude Eaton—whether anxiety, depression, or another mental health malady—thus demonstrates the interest that the ABCFM (and other organizations) had in the health of its missionaries, in addition to how female missionaries were situated within a gendered world.

Cases like Gertrude's were common. For decades the ABCFM had kept tabs on its missionaries' health, especially when service exposed the workers to tropical climes and prevalent infectious diseases. Letters from the field constantly reported the mental and physical health of the missionaries, which constituted the single largest investment of the various mission boards. Those in charge of the balance sheets naturally sought to minimize lost resources through illness or abandonment of the field. In a joint study several boards attempted to quantitatively measure the effects of poor health on the turnover of missionaries. "Less than ten per cent of the energy in the gasoline fed to the automobile engine is actually transformed into a forward motion of the car; the rest is lost in friction or in the exhaust," the study said. "How many cents of each missionary dollar are lost in such things as friction between incompatible personalities, physical exhaustion or the failure to elicit from the missionary candidate a history of previous nervous breakdown?"[82] Between 1900 and 1928 "functional nervous" conditions—and into this fuzzy category we may include James and Gertrude Eaton's health challenges—constituted the vast majority of illnesses (29 percent) that caused missionaries to abandon the field, a rate higher than tuberculosis, cancer, fever, malaria, and dysentery combined.[83]

If women served the critical role of getting behind locked doors to preach to native women and children otherwise unreachable by male missionaries, then the various boards had an added interest in assuring good health among their women.[84] On the importance of taking vacation from the field to ensure continued health, one doctor remarked, "If these considerations are just for missionaries in general, they are even more cogent in the case of married women missionaries. They have probably been bearing a threefold burden—climate, work, and family; it would be poor economy indeed, both for the society and the individual, if these ladies were not sent home without hesitation at the end of each term of service."[85] These sentiments led some doctors to recommend draconian physical exams of women headed to the field, including a full examination of the uterus, internal organs via the rectum, and a mental health screening.[86]

When health problems arose among Protestant workers in the field, the board typically granted leave for recovery, as it did for Gertrude's stay at Clifton Springs and as it had for James's temporary paralysis after the loss of Harry. In Gertrude's case, however, the board, her husband, and her doctors all thought she would recover most quickly by *going back* to Mexico. On the return trip via the Mexican Central, James recalled, Gertrude "went to the car door at least three times in the attempt to find a way of escape." After arriving in Chihuahua, James began to make arrangements to send Gertrude—apparently willingly—to a mental institution in his native Wisconsin. Otherwise, her suffering might cause instability in their teenage daughter, Dorothy, if not others.[87]

Gertrude's illness confused the Eaton family and doctors in the 1900s, and historians today have even less chance of understanding it. Given the schedule of her life in Mexico and the strains upon missionaries that the ABCFM recognized, though, her contemporaries empathized with her struggles and never seemed to cast her as a victim of female hysteria, then a common diagnosis. But when Gertrude again spoke of ending her life, James finally decided he could not provide the care she needed to recover. The family prepared for her departure on February 11, 1905. "She packed her trunk yesterday," wrote James, "and breakfasted early this morning, had our hand luggage in a stack before the door, and were about to walk out, when it became necessary to take leave of our son. But when she said to him, cheerfully, 'Goodbye for a little while,' the poor fellow broke down, and that upset it all. For she said, with a quaver in her voice, 'I cannot leave a boy crying,' and sat down immovable."[88] The Eatons decided, in response to young Howard's grief, that Gertrude should stay in Mexico a while longer, come what may.

Gertrude's suffering frustrated and saddened her family in part because she demonstrated a consistent desire to escape the confines of house and home in Mexico. Over the next week she tried to escape six more times, each attempt frustrated by the reality of the immense journey awaiting her.[89] Like other previous "escapes," these appear not to have been driven by a genuine will to abandon her family.[90] For the next month the Eatons kept a closer watch on their matriarch—the center of the mission, in James's words—while simultaneously trying to further their congregational work. Gertrude did receive visitors on occasion. She took walks, and she rested. At the end of February she appeared much improved and attended Sunday services in time to hear James read from the gospel of Matthew: "And he touched her hand, and the fever left her; and she arose and ministered unto him. . . . And they besought him that they might only touch the border of his garment; and as many touched were made whole."[91] The Bible verse captured James's wishes and his wife's centrality to their work. Gertrude continued to improve despite claiming she had "no faith and no feeling and no love"; and she no longer prayed.[92] By the summer months of 1905 the Eatons decided that Gertrude, while improved, should visit her sister in San Francisco. Dorothy accompanied her mother to California and attended school there.

In spite of the Eatons' personal travails and stagnated growth at the North Mexico mission, it maintained levels of involvement, especially by native preachers. Members of this essential cohort worked in Batopilas (Isabel Balderas), Ciudad Camargo (Felipe Hernández), El Paso (José Ibáñez), Ciudad Guerrero (Jesús Valencia), and Chihuahua City (Jesús Nava). Church membership flattened, but the Colegio Chihuahuense grew

Table 2. Growth of the Chihuahua Station of the ABCFM, 1906–1908

	U.S. Workers	Mex. Workers	Members	Contributions
1906	6	8	459	$4,100.00
1907	4	9	461	$3,866.00
1908	5	8?	458	$4,675.00

Source: ABCFM Annual Reports.

to support future generations of the mission, from an initial enrollment of 62 students in 1887 to 205 in 1909.[93] During this time the Eatons took leave from the mission to visit family and ease their stress. Gertrude's mental health appears to have improved. She worked at the mission and engaged in speaking tours throughout the United States and Mexico, laboring "for, and by, the women with greater activity than at any other time since she partially regained her health."[94]

The Eatons and their congregation, by 1909, had fought against social ostracism and indifference to become an established presence in the city and state of Chihuahua. Personally, they also recreated an American childhood experience for their son and daughter, when not traveling back to the United States. Their daily routines, however, began to be affected by the strains of nationalism via the Independent Mexican Church and, they perceived, antiforeign sentiment. Political agitation against President Porfirio Díaz frayed the edges of binational religious cooperation, and, with the breakout of the Mexican Revolution in 1910, the mission started by the Eatons transformed into one principally maintained by their Mexican preachers and parishioners. The Revolution unsettled the peace once taken for granted, and the Eatons—along with thousands of other U.S. citizens and foreigners—fled north across the border.

Ongoing conflict in Mexico disrupted the effectiveness of Protestant missions. Lives and property, while not threatened acutely, became more exposed to xenophobic flares between 1910 and 1914. To reassess the strength of all missions, several Protestant boards convened in 1914 in Cincinnati.[95] This conference resulted in the redistribution of properties and zones of influence. Congregationalists, Southern Baptists, Methodists, and Presbyterians once again agreed on new ground rules for the division of Mexico. As a result, the Eatons' La Trinidad and El Colegio Chihuahuense were transferred to the Methodists; Congregational missionaries thereafter focused their efforts in Guadalajara.[96] The church and the congregation the Eatons and their native ministers like Felipe and Antonia Hernández labored to create—to cover up cockfighting pits, convert souls, and free minds—closed in 1919. Mary Long, the Eatons' colleague and teacher at El Colegio for so many years, finished packing boxes and removing decorative touches from the property. She felt melancholy at the thought that "the voice of the little children in the home had long since departed, and the place began to look strange and *triste*."[97] She closed the doors and turned the keys over to the mission's new Methodist replacements.

Historians of religion in Mexico have investigated the tie between expanding Protestant ideology and the breakout of revolution. While converts often came from the laboring classes, the new religious ideology did not solely account for social movements to upend the Porfiriato. Mexican involvement with the Eatons and other Protestant missions did prove "advantageous during all phases of the Revolution," the historian Deborah Baldwin has noted.[98] The ABCFM's mission supports such a correlation. Given the trials of the Eatons in establishing a presence in Chihuahua City, the slow growth in the first ten years of the mission's establishment, and the increasing hostility toward American workers in the state, it seems that Protestant ideology did not *inspire* social revolution, but that Mexican revolutionaries used the new religious framework to support their own cause. If anything, Protestantism prepared larger portions of Mexican liberal social circles to be receptive to rebellion once it arrived. The ABCFM's teachings had consequences reaching far beyond the Mexican Revolution.[99]

The key to disseminating Protestantism, as the history of the Congregational mission to Chihuahua makes clear, was the targeting and employing of women throughout the countryside. Gertrude and James Eaton achieved much through gendered networks: their Willing Workers, their daily door-to-door walks and women's gatherings, Gertrude's close friendship with

Antonia Carrasco, their conversion of and collaboration with Felipe and Antonia Hernández, their boarding school for girls, and their encouragement of female graduates of the Colegio Chihuahuense to teach in the countryside.[100]

But these limited successes cost the Eatons dearly. Mission work demanded great sacrifices. Isolated in Catholic Mexico, far from family yet connected by rail, the Eatons struggled to carry their burdens when little Harry died in 1893. The isolation Gertrude experienced, her support of the mission notwithstanding, echoed the pain that Blanche Burnham felt when her daughter, Nada, died in Southern Rhodesia while Frederick was away fighting for the Crown and his dreams (see chapter 2). In their parallel situations, Gertrude and Blanche might have found solace in each other's stories. They were virtual neighbors in the borderlands after 1900, traveling between the Mexican North and southern California. Similarly, both matriarchs as well as James Eaton appear to have struggled with anxiety or depression that grew from the stresses of their calling and nearly cost them their lives.

As the Eatons struggled to overcome their personal limitations in the pursuit of something larger, they relied on social networks for solidarity. By 1904 this included several of the Mexican workers and converts from the mission, and it also included exiles from the former Boer Republics, whose own reasons for locating in the Mexican North aligned with James Eaton's in April 1882, as he rode the rails to the "end of track." The Boer neighbors needed a perceived frontier, close enough to the United States to take advantage of opening markets but distant enough, and therefore less costly, to make the venture possible. Their history reveals just as much as the Eatons' how these two regions shared parallel histories of frontier development. These neighbors, unusual at first glance, had left southern Africa to drift along common Gilded Age frontiers, landing in Chihuahua.

FOUR

Boers Without Borders

South African Colonization in Chihuahua and New Mexico

IN OCTOBER 1903, NEAR THE LOW POINT of James and Gertrude Eaton's religious work in Chihuahua, a new development gave them cause for hope: fellow foreigners were moving near them to establish an agricultural colony. Though neither Americans nor missionaries, the presence of non-Mexicans—in this case Boers from southern Africa—improved the Eatons' outlook on their mission work.[1] During the previous year the colony's founders, Willem Snyman and Benjamin Viljoen, had toured the world in search of a new home for their families and friends. The Boers had recently suffered defeat by the British Empire in the South African War (1899–1902). Their republics annexed, their families destitute, and their lands devastated, hundreds if not thousands sought refuge in lands beyond southern Africa, in other developing frontiers.[2] In Mexico they examined lands in several states, where elites welcomed them at every turn.

In a visit to Uruapan, Michoacán, in late 1902 a *New York Times* correspondent covered what appeared to be a rally of Porfirian proportions. An "exquisite sunset" cast hues of orange across the train depot, the journalist noted, while a brass band warmed its mouthpieces expectantly.[3] Hundreds of citizens waited for Snyman and other special guests as they watched a private Pullman car roll to a stop. To secure the best contract possible, Snyman traveled with and sought advice from Americans sympathetic to the Boer cause: Marshall Bond, an American mining expert, and Edward Reeve Merritt, a wealthy financier, cousin to President Theodore Roosevelt and assistant secretary of the Union Trust Company of New York.[4] Mexican officials under President Porfirio Díaz courted the Boers at many stops on the tour, a "princely pilgrimage of unparalleled luxury."[5] When Snyman stepped from the train in Uruapan, his companion wrote, "For a moment we thought we were going to be lynched, when up went a mighty cry of '*Viva Boeros! Viva General!*'" Snyman addressed the crowd, which "went wild" and "hoisted him upon the shoulders of a lot of men, and, amidst screaming and cheering, he was carried to a reserved streetcar."[6] Alongside Snyman's coach "rode caballeros dressed in silver and gold embroidered hats and clothes." Further behind ran "thousands" of Indians and peones.[7]

The scene had all the hallmarks of Porfirian Mexico. The excesses of the elite stood in sharp relief to the poverty of the masses. Officials spared no expense in recruiting these potential colonists. Previously, when the immigrants had toured lands in the Yaqui Valley of Sonora, officials hurried to arrange a musical welcome and excursions to promote "all that they could see" in the state.[8] Despite the warm receptions in Michoacán and Sonora, the Boers did not settle in either state, choosing instead lands near the Eatons in Chihuahua, an agricultural region of great promise and recently connected by rail to markets in the United States. In exchange for tax concessions and low-interest loans, Snyman and Viljoen agreed to relocate fifty families within three years.[9]

The Boers landed in Chihuahua after two decades of intensifying development by foreign capital. With the construction of key railroad trunk lines in the 1880s, as happened in the West, trains facilitated the entrenchment of American finance in the borderlands, and they powered a new era of capitalist expansion. Irrigation expertise, companies, and ditches multiplied. American mine owners recruited investments to the region. These linear networks of rails, irrigation ditches, and mineral veins connected the borderlands in unprecedented ways. Many people sought glittering riches. Some dreamed of new beginnings. Others fled oppression. Immigrants imbued the landscape with hope of a distinctly western variety.

The Boers settled in northern Mexico in large part owing to its recent development and connection to American markets (fig. 11). U.S. economic influence south of the border and the Mexican populations on both sides of it created similar environments for the everyday life of an

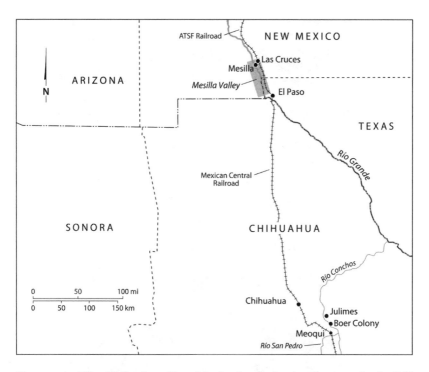

Figure 11.   The Chihuahua–New Mexico borderlands. Cartography by Bill Nelson.

agricultural colony. Between 1880 and the beginning of the Mexican Revolution in 1910 farmers could just as easily produce for the market on either side of the line. They had preferred to locate in the West (and some considered Texas, at first), but between the higher start-up costs north of the border and the financial incentives they would receive south of it, the choice became clear.[10] Destitute, the colonists chose the less developed region, one whose government offered support for settlement, one that recruited earnest if impoverished colonists.

Viljoen, Snyman, and their countrymen traveled on strong historical currents that had been well established in the borderlands since the 1880s (fig. 12), especially in the northern Mexican border states. Between 1881 and 1911 U.S. exports to Mexico grew from eleven to sixty-one million dollars.[11] As in the U.S. West, booster materials attempted to entice immigrants and

Figure 12.   The founders of the Boer colony in Mexico: Benjamin Viljoen (*left*) and Willem Snyman (*right*). *Congregationalist and Christian World*, December 2, 1905.

investors to lesser known areas. For the first time, portions of the Mexican
North, like the U.S. Southwest, appeared potentially profitable owing to irrigation agriculture. The Boer colony, however, faced a tougher challenge
than any corporation or investment group. The Boers had to place families
on Mexican lands and thrive as a transplanted community. Relocation

would break some family bonds and forge others, and the Boer colonization of Chihuahua also would test the viability of booster promises and romanticized frontiers. Having chosen exile over political domination in southern Africa, these emigrants sought simplicity and stability, a stark contrast to other imperial adventurers in Mexico and, indeed, in southern Africa.

The South African War and Exile

Although Snyman surely enjoyed his tours of the countryside and the tremendous *vivas* in his honor, above all else he and his countrymen sought stable ground after nearly two decades of political upheaval. In 1886 vast quantities of gold had been discovered along the Witwatersrand River in southern Africa, in the heart of the Transvaal, one of the two independent Boer Republics.[12] The resulting mineral rush placed immense pressures on the Transvaal government. British subjects from the Cape Colony, like the mining magnate and politician Cecil Rhodes, worked with engineers and experts from the United States and elsewhere to develop southern African resources. Fortune seekers from all over the world rushed to the region in search of potential riches, and the influx of foreigners strained the Boer government. In an attempt to retain authority over their lands, legislators and President Paul Kruger refused foreigners the right to vote. This in turn provoked a conflict with the British government in the Cape Colony, which defended the rights of its citizens to have fair representation. The Transvaal thus placed itself in a precarious position. It relied on the British- and American-led mining industries for the development of its natural resources, and yet this very necessity undermined the Transvaal's ability to maintain its hold on power. England's Cape Colony coveted the mineral wealth in Boer lands and sought any opportunity to strengthen its claims to southern African riches. When a group of Americans and some five hundred Cape colonists attempted a coup to topple the Boer government of the Transvaal between 1895 and 1896, an action known as the infamous Jameson Raid, relations between Britons and Boers in southern Africa eroded. War soon erupted in response to what many viewed as a "flagrant outburst of British imperialism."[13]

The South African War thus illustrated the limited prospects of small-scale independent agriculturalists faced with industrial capitalist development.[14] Completely overpowered, the Boers suffered defeats and clung to independence by resorting to commando raids. This tenacity earned the admiration of anti-imperialist leagues around the world, and Boer generals like Viljoen—portrayed as patriots fighting for liberty and survival—rose to global fame. In response to the nagging threat of Boer raids, the British field marshal Lord Kitchener instituted a "scorched earth policy that imperial troops and Afrikaner commandos had been accustomed to using against Africans."[15] British soldiers forced Boer women and children into concentration camps, where an estimated twenty-eight thousand people perished.[16]

The war left deep wounds in its victims and veterans, and descendants of the Boer colonists still recall how it affected their extended families. Viljoen spent several months as a prisoner of war at St. Helena. The British exploited his capture in the press and, according to one descendant, mistreated their prized catch. Other family members tell of how Snyman's two-year-old niece Martha died in a concentration camp. Martha's older sister, Marie, later wrote in a memoir that "a sergeant came to the pup tent we were living in and brought a little black coffin and we went by cab to the cemetery and buried her. There was no one to pray over her grave, but my mother and I sang an old Dutch hymn, 'Praise God in Joy and Sorrow.'" Marie would help to bury up to fourteen children a day when measles passed through the camp.[17] Descendants of the colonists also shared stories of the British tying small children to rooftops and leaving them "baking in the hot sun, no food, no water, to die."[18] The camps were horrific, and the persistence of these oral histories gives evidence to how deeply the war seared the colonists' souls.

After the war Snyman emigrated from British South Africa with Viljoen and several families, "exiled forever." Watching Cape Town's iconic Table Mountain fade over the horizon, Viljoen reminisced: "Two hundred years ago my forefathers [landed at] the Cape of Good Hope. . . . Here was their descendant, two hundred years later, driven from the land they explored and made out of a roaming wilderness into a beautiful country."[19]

However sentimental, Viljoen's statements obscure a longer and darker history of Boer and British colonialism in southern Africa, one which had dispossessed Khoisan, Nguni, and other indigenous peoples. As Viljoen sailed away from his former home land, the British South Africa Company tightened its grip on Matabeleland and Mashonaland, continuing this process. Viewed through the grand sweep of southern African history, the Boer dispossessors had become the dispossessed.

The embattled Boers faced two wars: one with the military at home and another with the overseas press. The South African War had captured the imaginations of newspaper writers, who portrayed it as either the necessary march of the British Empire to bring civilization to a barbarous white race or the struggle of freedom-loving farmers against the tyrannous John Bull. In southern New Mexico, for example, an article from the *Rio Grande Republican* claimed that Boer "personal habits . . . would shame an Apache Indian. . . . Their underclothing is seldom changed, indeed apparently never till it falls to pieces."[20] Foreign newspaper correspondents such as Rudyard Kipling, Arthur Conan Doyle, Mark Twain, Douglas Blackburn, and Winston Churchill popularized the war, and front pages around the world carried headlines daily from the battlefields. Those who participated or observed key battles, as did Viljoen, often wrote books about their experiences. Others showed stereopticon images of the war to foreign audiences. Some veterans published their memoirs even before the war's end.[21]

In the United States the Boers had an audience sympathetic to their cause among Irish and German immigrants disaffected by Great Britain, "the robber nation of the world, coveting the possession of the earth in violation of the moral law."[22] Because of anti-imperial sentiment during the war, political alliances strained between the United States and England. A large number of Americans sympathized with the failed Boer "war of independence," so much so that a congressional subcommittee on foreign affairs considered issuing a statement in support of the Republics.[23] Pro-Boer activists, alarmed by the blatant British power play, looked beyond their own nation's imperialism to form support leagues and to rally Congress to action.[24] "It is a fight to control South Africa," claimed Senator

William Mason of Illinois, "and the only way England could do it was to threaten, bulldoze, browbeat, and interfere with the Dutchman until, out of sheer humiliation and desperation, he was driven to fight."[25] President Kruger himself often appealed to "the great American nation, who had more than 100 years ago to fight the same British nation to secure their liberty, [and who] will know how to sympathize with a little sister republic, though faraway, which has now to fight a mighty power to maintain its independence."[26] Active fund-raising efforts thrived on public meetings, held in venues like the Grand Central Palace in New York, "elaborately decorated with the American colors interspersed with the colors of the Boers and of the Orange Free State."[27] Eight thousand supporters attended the meeting, organized by the New York Committee to Aid the United Republics of South Africa.[28]

One of the more inventive public relations efforts of Boer sympathizers began at a "school boys' pro-Boer rally" in Philadelphia in April 1900. James Smith, a teenage "messenger boy," left the stage at the rally to begin his own trek. Smith departed to cross the Atlantic and deliver "a message of encouragement from 22,000 of the pupils of Philadelphia's schools to President Paul Kruger of the South African Republic."[29] A Philadelphia journalist accompanied the "flaxen-haired, ruddycheeked" Jimmie on his trip. When he returned five months later, the boy said, "It was a great trip, all right, and I guess I won't never [*sic*] forget it." He met Kruger, who "patted him on the head" and gave his thanks for the moral support. Beneath this story's human interest ran a coordinated effort to promote the Boer cause through the press. Supporters outside southern Africa implemented an impressive public relations strategy to appeal to worldwide audiences.

Unbeknownst to Jimmie, though, his efforts were too little, too late. His time with Kruger happened to be the last moment of the president's time in Pretoria before fleeing for safety. Richard Harding Davis, who was present at the meeting, explained: "The message had been sent by the boys with a man [Kruger] who, at the time it was written, was fighting victoriously for a cause with which they were in sympathy. But it arrived when the cause was a lost one, and so it seemed as though their sympathy was meant for the man himself, because he had lost. . . . [T]he picture made by the Boer President, and the . . . messenger boy staggering under his great roll of signatures, was a pathetic and curious one."[30] In reality, the signatures of thousands of American schoolchildren, if a sweet gesture, mattered little. The support Kruger most needed—guns, munitions, and international recognition—never officially came from the United States.

As prolonged battles and raids destroyed Boer soldiers and families, some men, desperate, swapped the battlefield for the stage and began performing a romanticized version of the war for international audiences. In 1901 twelve veterans performed with William "Buffalo Bill" Cody, "every one of them [with] one or more wounds to exhibit."[31] American audiences saw the Boers as rough, untamed frontiersmen, a perspective reinforced by their appearances in Wild West shows. Their positive reception in much of the country came from the ability to appeal to audiences through the signs and symbols of a romantic, masculine, frontier showmanship.

While these performances of Boer resistance wooed some Americans, veterans also traveled to the United States to speak directly to audiences, to promote their cause and support emigration from South Africa. By 1902, while the British held General Viljoen captive at St. Helena, Snyman toured the lecture circuit throughout the United States. Among his stops were New York, where the Boer anthem opened an evening's presentation and where Snyman led the 1901 St. Patrick's Day Parade; Boston, where Snyman sat as a guest on the speaker's platform of the Massachusetts State Senate, where he debated citizenship with a British historian at Harvard, and where eight hundred attendees cheered his claim that the "Boers will not be conquered any more than the Americans were"; the eastern states; Chicago; Colorado Springs; and San Francisco, where he met with the Transvaal League.[32] When Viljoen was released from prison, he joined the circuit. Both of these men impressed audiences and earned them reputations as historical showmen working for the benefit of their people. They collected contributions for the Boer Relief Fund to assist the destitute families who sought a new life free from the English Crown.

Viljoen also appealed to audiences outside the United States as he toured to support his countrymen. Speaking through an interpreter in

Mexico City early in 1903, he told his audience that his warm reception assured him "that even in this far-away land there are many hearts that beat warmly for my nation, whose freedom has been taken from her. It may be but a small satisfaction, but to me it is like the sweet dew of the early morn, which freshens the withered, and suffering flowers of the prairie."[33] Viljoen then presented material polished from months of delivery: a brief history of the Boers of South Africa, followed by tales from the battlefield, which were often infused with humor and melancholy. Persuasive and charming, Viljoen won over audiences by proclaiming a conviction for nothing more than truth in an age of anti-Boer slander. He claimed to "endeavor to be impartial because I have no motive in view, other than to let the truth be known."[34] Viljoen's and Snyman's speeches swayed audiences in part owing to their gestures to authenticity. Audiences were moved by seeing the veterans in person, these much-maligned Boers, as they told of their past and of their hopes and fears; these were not the same degenerate folks portrayed as dirty villains with unkempt skivvies. The two veterans leveraged their minor celebrity status to support not only their cause before the war's end but also emigration thereafter.

In Mexico the Boers especially charmed audiences because of the nation's simultaneous growth and instability brought on by capitalist development, by imperialist rhetoric from the north, and by rising Mexican nationalism. Wartime South Africa provided fodder for critics of President Díaz's modernization ideology and his welcoming of foreign ownership and immigration. One journalist in Mexico City, for example, lamented the loss of the Boer Republics, glorified their cause, and placed blame on the uitlanders, foreigners who developed Boer mines but were restricted from voting. The lesson for the nation was clear, said the editorial: "If the immigrant blends into the dough of our nation, we will have increased national strength, but if the immigrant clings to an independent social circle and has eyes fixed on his home land, it will have raised a formidable danger. The problem is inevitable: immigration strengthens, like in the United States, or immigration brings the loss of the state, as in the Transvaal."[35] The discussion about citizens and Uitlanders resonated in Mexico, particularly in the North, where the eyes of the imperial Uncle Sam coveted

Mexican riches, where early railroad lines linked to continental routes north of the border, and where the transactions between foreign investment and local elites polarized classes.[36]

Once the war ended, Snyman's and Viljoen's speeches shifted away from informing about the war to supporting Boer immigration plans to North America. Toward this end, Viljoen and other renowned rebels had an electrifying idea: to assemble their own troupe for a Wild West show, a spectacle not of cowboys and Indians but of the South African War, for the upcoming St. Louis World's Fair in 1904. With the backing of Frank Fillis, a London-born circus manager and "the Barnum of South Africa," the St. Louis spectacle would give the generals a chance to capitalize on their wartime fame more than lecture circuits or book contracts could.[37] Viljoen organized to go to St. Louis to perform a wartime frontier, while Snyman trekked to Chihuahua to establish roots in the new colony.

Romance in St. Louis and the Imperial Western

The "Boer War Spectacle" at the St. Louis World's Fair, said one attendee, was "the grandest spectacle ever produced in America," where "you have your ears pounded and your heart wrung dry."[38] Then secretary of war and, later, President William Howard Taft remarked that "never before had he experienced the thrills of warfare in such a manner as in the performance he had just witnessed."[39] Although the show's profits did not meet expectations, the romanticized visions of war created a ready audience for two of Viljoen's books, which he promoted after each show: *My Reminiscences of the Anglo–Boer War*, a memoir, and *Under the Vierkleur: Romance of a Lost Cause*, a novel.[40] Viljoen thus attempted to cash in on his considerable fame. He had become somewhat of a media darling for his resistance to imperial forces in South Africa (as had the American scout, Burnham, in the field), for his striking presence, for his bravery and indulgence in the dramatic, and for his love of attention.

Having practiced journalism before the war, Viljoen infused both *My Reminiscences* and *Under the Vierkleur* (the "four-colored" flag of the Transvaal Republics) with a sense of reportage and melodramatic flair.[41] He attempted to convey to American audiences the plight of his countrymen, who had been so slandered by the British press and, as a result, by others around the world. "My only and conscientious desire, when I commenced this work," he wrote, "was to place on record a small picture of the life and character of my people, overshadowed by war though I had to draw it, and to try to do some little further justice to a nation so sadly misunderstood and so long maligned."[42] To do so, Viljoen steeped his writings in adventure and romance. His prose fit within a subgenre that might be called the imperial western, a decidedly redundant phrase uniting frontiers and the British Empire, referring to works written during the late nineteenth and early twentieth centuries. His style had ready purchase among readers, who expected a Boer man to fit the image of a rough frontiersman. Including nonfiction and fiction alike, these works mixed elements of war, adventure, love, social Darwinism and racial otherness, masculinity, and, most important, a romancing of the western frontier. While Viljoen claimed to approach his wartime subject as objectively as possible, he sought via the imperial western to sway his readers to the Boer cause. He leveraged western tropes: desperate nighttime escapes on horseback; an endearing connection to his steed mixed with distrust of indigenous peoples; the fury of combat; the taciturn search for unrequited love; the plight of Boer women; and plenty of horses, guns, and open prairies.[43]

Such symbols operated in a transnational circuit of romanticized frontiers, building on Roosevelt's Rough Rider ethos and the tradition of Wild West shows.[44] In the early 1900s, in fact, President Roosevelt had befriended the Boer immigrants and even challenged Snyman to a shoot-out.[45] Their shared values in strength, sport, honor, and duty—in a word, masculinity—made them brothers in a global network of quasi-frontiersmen-showmen unique to the early 1900s.[46] Two weeks after the gun contest, none other than Rudyard Kipling wrote, "The Boer cattle breeders of the high veldt had been training themselves by outdoor life, rough riding and gun practice for a defence of their country so effective and withal so economical as to challenge the wonder and admiration of the world."[47] These global networks of masculinity did not culminate in shows only for Americans' consumption. At the same time Viljoen performed in the Boer War

Spectacle in St. Louis, the comedian and showman Will Rogers, the "Cherokee Kid," learned his roping skills and horsemanship in South Africa, performing for Texas Jack's Wild West Show and Circus near Johannesburg.[48]

Viljoen's memoir and his novel, as imperial westerns, implicitly lament a vanishing frontier. Each, as the novel's subtitle makes clear, is a "romance of a lost cause." Viljoen turned to this genre several times throughout his life.[49] Written while in exile, *Under the Vierkleur* follows Danie, a young conscript in the Boer forces, as he is captured in war, escapes imprisonment, impersonates a British officer to avoid recapture, revisits his home land, and searches for his long-lost love, Bettie. He encounters loss everywhere, especially at Bettie's home at Blaauwkop, abandoned when she and her mother were taken away to be imprisoned. "There were left no traces of the neat, clipped hedges that had enclosed the garden and bordered the paths," the narrator observes. "The once bright and blooming beds had long been choked and overgrown with the grass and weeds of the veldt. Their sites were alone indicated by a few hardy perennial blossoms that still managed to struggle through the tangled mass around them. Danie turned and walked out to the road, his eyes blinded by tears. He could look no longer on the grave of Blaauwkop."[50] Danie discovers his own mother and two sisters in a concentration camp.[51] He notices their fragility: "Dressed in such poor mourning as they had been able to collect, [they] sat despondently on their rough, unmattressed cots. Their faces were browned by the long camp life; but otherwise how changed!"[52]

If images of isolation and loss define the novel, patriarchal notions of gender undergird its structure. Flowers and gardens decay when the women are away, just as the women appear to be wilting—emaciated, skinny—in the rigid confines of the concentration camp. The separation of Danie and Bettie, of man and woman, becomes a necessary but destructive aspect of war, in Viljoen's telling, but their reunion proves inevitable. Bettie's home "had rerisen from its ashes," and its "gardens grew again, and their flowers bloomed about its walls and doors. . . . Then with a great cry of love he drove his spurs into his horse's flanks, and dashed down the well-remembered road to the home of his beloved, the treasury of his happiness."[53] Viljoen described the world he craved. His own extended family suffered in the concentration camps over a two-year-stay. Viljoen himself would not see most of his relatives for months or years at a time. Births and deaths passed unknown, unrecognized, without ceremony. And after his capture at Lydenburg in January 1902, British forces sent him into exile at St. Helena with other prisoners of war; such isolation suffuses his novel's text, a roman-à-clef of emotional truth that follows Danie wandering through changing, apocalyptic landscapes. A young frontiersman, instilled with older, Boer values, watches his world slip away. Turner's closing frontier echoed across the South African landscape.

The readership that made the imperial western genre possible was a product of intersecting historical forces: steam travel, expanding U.S. and European geographies, the pursuit of mineral resources, the incorporation of heretofore remote populations, a booming genre of dime novels, and anxiety over a closing American frontier.[54] These global circuits of people and texts created an imperial strain of jingoism and patriarchy, but they also afforded mobility to a new generation of women who more forcefully pursued suffrage and progressive reform.[55] In contrast to the restrictive roles afforded them in the imperial western genre, women began to explore, change, and travel their own routes to personal and professional fulfillment. One such woman, May Belfort, an Irish-English actress and vaudeville singer, was empowered by her mobility and typified a new female cosmopolitanism. She worked in Paris in the 1890s, where the French painter Henri Toulouse-Lautrec captured her performances on canvas. She sang and danced in Russia and throughout England, South Africa, and the United States. Known for her bawdy, salacious repertoire, Belfort became a minor stage celebrity on three sides of the Atlantic. On a fortuitous day in 1903 she boarded a steamship for Cape Town and met a certain Boer general, a soldier-turned-celebrity with piercing blue eyes, a "manly man."[56] She later recalled, "I think it was really settled on that trip; those sea voyages, you know, have many such affairs to answer for."[57]

Belfort was traveling from Southampton to Johannesburg to perform a series of shows; Viljoen sailed the same route, albeit briefly, to make arrangements in South Africa for the Boer War Spectacle and to prepare friends and family for immigration to Mexico. Over the previous year he had lectured in and toured New York, Boston, Kansas City, Hermosillo, and Mexico City. He raised funds for the show and his compatriots. Onboard a ship for eighteen days, Belfort and Viljoen consummated their affair. After arriving in South Africa, smitten with love, Viljoen and Belfort saw each other frequently. He taught her to sing songs in Afrikaans. They had their photo taken together and placed it in a heart-shaped frame. When the couple returned to London in November 1903—Belfort for a performance at the Palace Theater, Viljoen on his way to the St. Louis World's Fair—they disembarked an engaged couple.[58] They spent a magical couple of weeks together. When Viljoen sent off the proofs of *Under the Vierkleur* that year, he asked that the illustrator use Belfort's image as Bettie, surveying the open veldt.[59] Viljoen and Belfort set a February wedding date. By the time of his arrival in St. Louis, the *London Daily Express* had broken the story. "Yes, it is quite true," Belfort confirmed, "though we had no intention of making the news public just yet."[60] Suddenly, a spotlight shined on their hidden romance and caught Viljoen unaware.

Try as he might, something was keeping this gallant war hero from galloping off with his fiancée over the horizon and reveling in amorous bliss: his wife of fourteen years, Helena Els Viljoen, and their three children. For reasons that remain unclear, Helena chose to stay in South Africa while the general emigrated (with a son following him later). One can only speculate about the reasons the family divided, but it appears Helena did not know of her husband's ties to Belfort when he sailed from Cape Town. Days after the engagement news broke, Helena sued for divorce.[61] The general, by then a public figure, reeled from the controversy. Just before Christmas, in 1903, he wrote to Belfort, "I am sorry, yes, doubly so, that you should have been taken in by that newspaper man. I fear I am ruined. The divorce lawyers refuse to take my case unless I deny in toto that I contemplate marriage."[62] Meanwhile, Viljoen rebuffed rumors of his engagement in the press.[63] He claimed that "dissimilar tastes" precipitated his divorce suit.[64] However intentionally, Viljoen began to sacrifice his newfound vaudevillian love for the benefit of the Boer War Spectacle and its support of himself, his family, and potentially hundreds of his compatriots. He tried to keep Belfort at a distance. In February 1904, on the eve of dining with President Roosevelt,

Viljoen wrote again, "I am unable, according to best advice, to proceed with my divorce suit until this company is fixed up and the newspaper story has blown over."[65] Later that fall the romantic overtures in his letters faded: "As my obligations are simply outrageous it would be folly for any sane person to make promises and drag a woman into ties which would never bring happiness. I will, of course, be glad to see you again. But, my dear girl, the day of marriage with me is past forever."[66] Belfort sensed a change in her beau. She suspected another woman. She was right.

In January 1905 the livid Belfort stormed into Chicago, where Viljoen was working with a traveling version of the Boer War Spectacle. She surprised the general on a street outside the Chicago Coliseum. Newspapers reported her asking, "What do you mean by your scurrilous letter to me? Have you acted toward me as a man would toward a woman?" Belfort then "snatched a heavy rawhide whip from the folds of her skirt and struck him a cutting blow upon the arm. Gen. Viljoen retreated before a shower of blows, the woman following him."[67] " 'Take that! and that! and that!' cried the enraged beauty, each exclamation accompanied by a stinging cut of the rawhide whip. . . . 'Now go to your new love, whoever she is, but you will never forget this whipping,' cried Miss Belfort, after which she walked away, leaving the general in the midst of a group of interested spectators" (fig. 13).[68]

Notwithstanding the embellishment of these stories—reported in smaller daily newspapers hundreds of miles from the scene and all but ignored by the *Chicago Tribune*—the fact remains that Belfort journeyed to Chicago and administered a liberal horsewhipping to a hero, a "manly man."[69] Belfort felt cheated not only because Viljoen canceled the wedding but also because, in her mind, the tone of his letter broke an unspoken code of gender relations. Her tongue- and whip-lashing inverted gender norms— hence the appeal and humor of the news story—and ruptured the romance of Viljoen's frontier on a street in Chicago. Belfort was no Bettie. Appalled at the breaking of patriarchal codes, Viljoen "refused to discuss" the incident, "saying that the notoriety was distasteful to him."[70] For the first time the Boer War hero's public scandal could possibly threaten his and his countrymen's ability to establish a new colony in the United States. He

Figure 13.   May Belfort whips General
Viljoen. "General Viljoen Is Horsewhipped," *Richmond Planet*, February
25, 1905, 2.

disassociated himself from the Boer War Spectacle (likely in the interests
of the show) and began lecturing of his own accord.[71] And Viljoen then
married another, newer belle, Myrtle Dickason Lowden, an American di-
vorcée he had met in St. Louis.

Reality in Chihuahua

As Viljoen wooed audiences, Snyman tried to ground an imagined Boer
colony. Mexico appealed to the Boers because of the landscape's familiarity and promise. They focused on eighty-three thousand acres at the confluence of the San Pedro and Conchos Rivers in Chihuahua, a landscape
that reminded them, to some degree, of home (fig. 14).[72] The region had

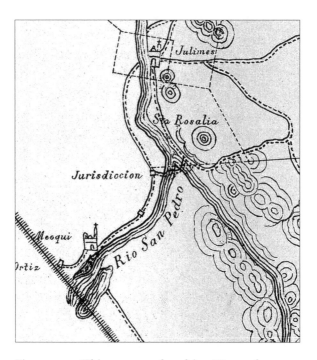

Figure 14.   This map, produced in 1884, underscores
the importance of the railroad connection to the Hacienda Santa Rosalía. The Boer colony would establish itself near the "Sta" in Santa Rosalia. Detail of "Mapa del
canton Meoqui, estado de Chihuahua / . . . levantado en
tres copias por el ingo. civil nombrado para ello C. A. Q.
Wingo" (1884). Beinecke Rare Book and Manuscript Library, Yale University.

undergone a significant reorientation during the last fifty years. When U.S.
Commissioner John Russell Bartlett passed through this area as part of
his boundary survey of 1853 he noted its isolation. On the nearby town of
Santa Cruz, Bartlett wrote, "I did not observe a good-looking house in it.
Men, women, and children crowded to the doors as we passed, attracted
by the cracking of the whips and yells of the teamsters, and seemed to eye
us with as much curiosity as though they had never seen a [wagon] train
before."[73] By the time the Boers arrived, though, Chihuahua and the

broader region had entered a golden age of development and economic boom.[74] Railroads facilitated the growth of the cattle industry on both sides of the border, and agriculturalists saw northern Mexico as an extension of American markets.[75] The Mexican Central established a stop at Estación Ortíz, only ten miles away. Whatever produce the region grew, it could easily be sold to markets north or south of the international boundary.

Snyman, in agreement with Viljoen, purchased the land in Chihuahua by securing a loan of fifty thousand pesos from the Mexican government and a personal loan of three times that amount from Enrique Creel, a two-time governor of Chihuahua and one of the wealthiest men in the nation.[76] Implicit in the contract was the necessity to work out a sharecropping agreement with the fifty-five resident Mexican peones that had lived on the lands, or nearby, for generations. In the fields, the Boers and the Mexican workers subdivided the lands into thirty parcels of between twenty-five and sixty acres each. The locals then sharecropped their portion of lands and gave their South African hacendados half of the harvest.[77] Although immense to the colonists, the 130-square-mile territory was smaller than forty other landholdings in Chihuahua in the early 1900s.[78] Multimillion-acre estates dwarfed the Boer enterprise. Still a respectable size, the colony's lands benefited from the adjacent Conchos River. This filled irrigation ditches, running the length of the property, but the river also left them prone to floods from heavy rains.

The colony began at a time when regional elites partnered to varying degrees with immigrants and foreign investors to strengthen the state's ties to national and international commerce. The capital's population of thirty thousand relied on newly built rail connections to Mexico City and to the United States and beyond. Reflecting this reach, the main newspaper, *El Correo de Chihuahua*, advertised bourgeois items in Spanish while also providing information on the city's German academy and the operations of local Methodist and Congregational services. The weekly paper often reported on railroad developments as much as it did on U.S. imperialism in the Philippines, immigration, and the prevalence of foreign influences, once noting, "There are times when you go out in these glorious streets and you find so much English spoken and so much Chinese, that you'd think you were in California itself."[79]

In this same article the author tells an insightful joke: "A gringo arrives at a factory and says, 'I wish to have some cloth for shirts.' Nobody answers. The man repeats his question a little more loudly, and the same thing happens. Desperate, chewing his tobacco and spitting, he asks, pointing to a sign on the window, '*No intende foura decir* English Spoken? *No hablar ingles aqui?*' [Don't you understand that outside it says "English Spoken"? Don't you speak English here?]. A worker replies, '*Dice* English Spoken *porque lo hablan los marchantes. Nosotros no sabemos ni jota*' [It says English Spoken because the owners speak it, but we (workers) don't know the first thing]. The man leaves, thinking to himself, 'Of course, not all that glitters is gold.'" More allegory than humor, the joke is packed with meanings that expose the everyday world of Chihuahua. First, it pokes fun at the crass, tobacco-spitting American for assuming all store workers speak English and also for butchering his spoken Spanish. Second, it shows the deeper divisions between the Chihuahua elite, often cultured and well versed in English if not French, and the laboring classes. And, third, the cowboy's realization that "not all that glitters is gold" exposes the reality of many foreign investors in the region, who are there chasing profits and gilded dreams. The Boer colonists, who sought stability, fit in a strange, wide middle ground between American dream–chasers and everyday laborers.

For Snyman, May 1903 bloomed with expectation. His sturdy fingers clutched the earth once again, after combat, after exile, after lecture tours and incessant handshakes. For the first time in years he felt free. He hunted on horseback for three weeks in the region, "one of the finest trips" of his life. "We were out entirely away from towns and cities in the free open country," he told one reporter, "and in a picturesque environment on mountain and plain that made one's heart beat exultantly and the blood course more rapidly through the veins."[80] Snyman felt younger for it, his "face wreathed in smiles." Years of uncertainty and strife gave way to the pleasure of knowing he was securing land for his people. "It's all right," he acknowledged, with a whiff of exuberance.[81] That May, Snyman prepared the land for his countrymen and family, soon to follow in piecemeal fashion. He broke ground, planted corn and wheat, purchased angora goats, and irrigated his fields. The newfound freedom, however, must have paled in comparison to the anticipation of reuniting with his wife and six children, who had lived in concentration camps for two years and whom he had not seen for four.

Snyman's family was one of four Boer families to establish this new home at the Hacienda Santa Rosalía—in poverty, with few possessions, and with dilapidated buildings. Only the family Bible and his certificate as a Freemason made the transatlantic voyage, he claimed. Inside their house nothing adorned the walls save a small piece of paper—a target with holes in the bull's-eye—a souvenir from Snyman's 1902 shooting challenge with President Roosevelt.[82] Near the main house, remnants of a chapel broke the horizon. The adobe and stone walls still supported crossbeams, but wind whipped through the roofless and floorless structure.[83]

None of the Boers spoke Spanish, and this separated the colonists from the *campesinos* nearby. Some colonists spoke only Afrikaans and struggled with English. Early attempts to integrate culturally inevitably led to polyglot phrases in Afrikaans, Spanish, and English, such as, "*Keer die maranas daar*, and *ponga* them back in the *kraal*" (Stop those pigs, and put them back in the pen).[84] Initially, it seemed as if the colonists would work and live closely with their Mexican neighbors. Snyman had arranged with Governor Creel to build and staff a school for local children.[85]

As devout members of the Dutch Reformed Church, the colonists must have felt culturally and religiously isolated in the Catholic countryside. To their good fortune, James and Gertrude Eaton lived in Chihuahua City, along the Mexican Central line fifty miles distant. The Eatons often visited the Hacienda Santa Rosalía while riding rounds throughout the state, and soon the Snymans made the long journey to attend services in the city. Three of the Snyman children joined the Colegio Chihuahuense and were members of Gertrude Eaton's Sunday school classes. Thus Congregational beliefs and the Boers' adherence to the Dutch Reformed Church produced a tight friendship forged through a spiritual lingua franca. When not attending services in Chihuahua, the colonists gathered at Snyman's house on Sundays for "the old fashioned Boer home religious service." Snyman's father-in-law led prayers and hymnal readings with "beautiful,

simple faith." Communal singing in Afrikaans followed "in that old fashioned style of fifty or more years ago." The Boers led fairly isolated lives,
not associating with their Mexican neighbors because of linguistic differences, and meeting with closer friends by way of rail networks to the
north. They were often secluded by choice as much as by location.[86]

As we have seen, the Eatons likewise struggled to create community.
So when the Eatons and Snymans became neighbors they connected on
many levels. In October 1904 the Snymans stayed with the missionaries in
Chihuahua while Willem lectured at the church's social hall, explaining
South African current events and describing the war and the infamous concentration camps. In a report sent to his superior Eaton recalled how Snyman's wife, Sarah, "sat with the tears coursing silently down her cheeks."[87]
Soon the two families had become close enough friends that Eaton lobbied
the ABCFM to assign a Dutch-speaking missionary to locate on the Boer
colony's premises.[88] The letters he sent to the board's central office in Boston are one of the only sources to offer a glimpse into daily life on the Boer
colony and to explain why, notwithstanding its early success, it would fail
after just two years.

Despite their isolation and poverty, the colonists did not wish to recede into anonymity and become small-time peasants engaged in subsistence farming. They intended to produce for the market, which made them
appealing to Governor Luis Terrazas and his son-in-law, Enrique Creel.
To the Terrazas-Creel political and economic regime, the Boers would have
a modernizing influence in the region and produce more goods for the market and regional mining industries.[89] To the Boers, the support of Terrazas
and Creel made their colonization scheme possible. At last the immigrants
could begin anew. Creel's assistance endeared him to the Snyman family
to such an extent that the firstborn child at the colony, a son of Johanna
Snyman and Johan Viljoen, was named Enrique Creel Viljoen.

The first full year of the colony, 1904, challenged Snyman's optimism.
Flooding of the San Pedro and Conchos Rivers destroyed all the corn,
wheat, and seven hundred young fruit trees the colonists had planted. The
great flood of 1904, which wiped out much of the region, is remembered in
a *corrido,* or a Mexican folk ballad about historical events. It tells of cows,

mules, horses, and dogs drowning, of garlic bulbs and lettuce heads floating downstream, and of the people's struggle to recover. One Chihuahuan
recalled how farmers "were left without a harvest, without animals, without homes. But you know how we are in the country. With sadness and tears
in our eyes, we'll start again to hoe the ground now and in the future."[90]
After the waters subsided a team of four Boers and fifty-five Mexicans
cleaned the silt out of the fourteen-mile-long irrigation canal within eleven
days.[91] Something soured that year, though, and several American newspapers reported that the colonists would rely only on themselves for labor,
their "experience with the Mexicans the first year prov[ing] that class of
labor unreliable and unsatisfactory."[92] One article written in Chihuahua
depicts a more hostile situation: "[The] native peones on the property are
being gotten off as these Boers propose doing their own work."[93]

While labor relations became strained in the fields, the women did
continue to employ domestic servants. One article alluded to tensions when
it explained that the Boer women had "sufficiently mastered" Spanish to
"tell their servants what to do and how to do it."[94] Such brief glimpses into
the cultural climate at the Hacienda Santa Rosalía expose a complicated, if
not fraught, relationship with neighboring families. Separated by language,
culture, and religion, the Snymans and Viljoens kept Mexican labor at a
distance in the fields as well as in the domestic realm. Race and labor relations slowed intercultural exchanges; only one Snyman child was born to a
native Mexican.

Like the Eatons, the Boers never associated closely with the Mormon
colonists, owing in part to geography and timing. The latter were hundreds
of miles removed, and they had established their colonies twenty years earlier. Yet, unlike the Eatons, the South African emigrants did share two
significant traits with the Mormons. First, members of both groups saw
themselves not as colonists but as exiles, seemingly oppressed, acted upon,
and described in the passive voice—"hunted like wild beasts" or "driven
from the land." Each would be described as "men without a country."[95]
Second, published memoirs and records from both groups evoke tensions
around a foreigner / native binary. One Mormon colonist wrote, "We loved
our dark neighbors, we shouldn't do otherwise for we were in *their* country."[96]

The Boers also had a difficult time adjusting to the idea of being regarded as Mexicans. These two similarities characterize the two groups generally, but slight variations distinguished them from each other, of course. For example, the Mormons would adopt over time their own kind of *Mexicanidad*, celebrating national holidays and feeling patriotic toward the state.[97] Still, one senses in Mormon memoirs that the colonists never found an answer to the question of complete social acculturation, and the author of one of them argued that they were genetically different from Mexicans— not from racial superiority, he claimed, but "from a feeling that groups of people having different social standards, resulting from radically different environments, will have more enduring friendships for one another if they do not become too intimate."[98] In other words, they supported the claim of being "separate but equal," an idea codified in U.S. law in *Plessy v. Ferguson* (1896) as much as it would justify South African apartheid after 1948. Beneath the writings of the Mormons and Boers in Mexico, one gets a strong whiff of cultural superiority; they felt inherently different from, if not above, their Mexican neighbors.

As the Snymans and their neighbors in Chihuahua established the colony that first year, Viljoen and some 200 fellow Boers, 150 British soldiers, and 40 Africans recreated the South African War at the 1904 World's Fair in St. Louis.[99] The performance was not without controversy. Many in the media criticized the Boers for "selling out," cashing in on their wartime fame in a crass materialistic fashion. At a time when Viljoen, his collaborators in the show, and his partners in the colony depended on positive public relations, Viljoen's marital scandal threatened to halt advances in supporting the Boer cause. By then, however, Snyman and his family had rooted themselves enough in the Mexican North that the colony had a solid foundation, one that could weather a personal controversy three thousand miles away.

By August 1905 the colony appeared to be thriving. Snyman's eldest brother, his eldest son, and Viljoen, his parents, his son, five siblings, and their children all arrived at Santa Rosalía that month, bringing the total to nearly twenty-five families. With no import tax on farm implements, colonists purchased equipment from Texas to produce larger yields, including a thirty-horsepower engine capable of pulling ten plows.[100] Corn and wheat fields and fruit orchards all yielded in abundance. The Boers and other farmers produced and profited from the biggest harvest and economic boom in Chihuahua history.[101] In late August newspapers reported the colony to be prospering and its land to be rich and "brought to a high state of cultivation."[102]

No sooner had life begun to flourish for the displaced families, though, than the colony suddenly collapsed in October 1905. Oral histories among the descendants imply that the colonists abandoned the lands when they discovered that government officials had taken it illegally from resident peones.[103] Contemporary newspapers in the United States and Mexico reported that the colony failed owing to the settlers' inability to "acquire clear titles to their farms and [while being] harassed by a series of embarrassments."[104] Another reporter wrote that "monetary difficulties" caused the failure.[105] In the press Viljoen blamed it on the inability to clear individual titles to the land. The truth, however, centered around a disagreement between Snyman and Viljoen on how the colony should secure its lands.

In 1902 the cofounders had agreed to split equally the potential profits and losses of the colony and to divide equally the title to lands acquired.[106] They thus embarked on a communal venture. On arriving at the colony from St. Louis, however, Viljoen refused to improve or work the land unless "title deeds for the individual allotments be made out for himself and his relatives."[107] Until that point all land had been common property, and although Snyman alone signed the contract with Creel and the federal government, the agreement "carefully guard[ed] the personal interests of all the colonists."[108] In an attempt to assuage Viljoen's concerns, and at Snyman's request, Creel proposed "to have a committee of a dozen of Chihuahua's best citizens named to look after the interests of the colonists, in order to satisfy Viljoen that there was no danger from the possible deaths of the chief creditors, or even from some change of good will on their part." Viljoen, the prouder of the two Boers, apparently declined. Eaton, the nearby Protestant missionary, noted that "Mr. Creel stands by Snyman, and Gen. Viljoen has withdrawn." Eaton felt Viljoen had acted unjustly toward Snyman and the colony, and a friend in common, the editor of the

Chihuahua Enterprise, thought Viljoen had been "injured by flattery from those who admired his military prowess, and that he who managed the 'Boer War Exhibition' at St. Louis, wanted to be the manager of the colony."[109] Whatever the reason, Viljoen and his relatives and those Snymans married to Viljoens abandoned the colony and moved north to the United States.[110] Only Snyman and his immediate family remained in Mexico.

Snyman confided to his closest confidant, James Eaton, that he felt "like collapsing," the strain "almost above my strength; more so as this colony was started by myself with the feeling, Here I stand a chance to help my fellow countrymen this side of the ocean; and I am bitterly disappointed. . . . I feel that I have to show now more than ever, with the help of God, my honesty of purpose, and do what is right, now lending an ear to wrong." Still, when Eaton visited Snyman at home, he recalled, "Snyman told me of the outcome of his 'eight years' of attempting to live for ideals— loss and suffering and criticism; and how he could not sleep at night, after a hard day's work in the field, because of his 'worry.' "[111]

The split between Snyman and Viljoen produced a moment of evaluation and, as a result, the best view into the relations between the colonists and their Mexican neighbors. In October 1905 the governor of Chihuahua sent a representative, the well-known historian José María Ponce de León, to evaluate the state of the colony. His report, recorded in the *Periódico Oficial*, documented tensions at the colony. Many of the Mexicans threatened to leave the hacienda because of disagreements on the apportionment of waters between the Boer canals and their fields. The governor's emissary assured the *campesinos* that they could take their complaints directly to the governor should any further dispute arise. The agreement appeared to work. Many of the descendants of the Mexicans who signed the pact remain on hacienda lands today, long after the disappearance of all colonists.[112] When the Viljoens left, Snyman moved to a small portion of his properties and sold the large estate to a German immigrant and scientific agriculturalist, Pablo Hoffmann, who once worked for the Departamento de Fomento in Mexico City. Hoffmann renegotiated the contract with the government, which instituted the Hacienda de Humboldt in 1905.[113]

Personal dynamics evidently played a role in the fracturing of the colony, one patriarch remaining on the site, the other migrating north. Snyman and Viljoen would later bicker in the press about South African affairs, and while their families would be forever connected through interlocking marriages, the two patriarchs preferred to keep their distance from each other.[114] They seemed to fit the description of their ancestors as "fractious frontiersmen."[115] Indeed, one Snyman descendant recalls his grandfather referring to the Viljoens as "weak tea."[116] Looking beyond personality clashes, the fundamental issue of land divided the colony. Viljoen and the Boers knew the importance of securing individual title. That the British had shattered their autonomy in South Africa only highlighted the point. They were, after all, "without a country." Like countless immigrants before them, the Boers sought new lands beyond British control.

Immigrants and the Mesilla Valley

Lured by the promises of irrigation agriculture and pushed by social divisions, Viljoen abandoned Chihuahua and led most of the Boer colonists north to the Mesilla Valley of New Mexico, the easternmost portion of the Gadsden Purchase of 1853. Acquired to allow for a southern transcontinental railroad route and as a buffer against indigenous raids, the added territory attracted increased investments, land offices, boosters, and eventually immigrants. Unlike other regions of the U.S. West, American immigration did not immediately follow acquisition, and this was so for two reasons. First, Native American resistance destabilized the Southwest until the surrender of Geronimo in 1886. And second, southern New Mexico did not immediately receive a large rush of immigrants, because farmland required larger investments and uncommon expertise in irrigation agriculture. Once the U.S. military established a stronger presence in the region, emigrants from the eastern United States and from other countries could justify the risk of moving to this unknown land. Perhaps of greater influence than booster materials, medical doctors in the East and Midwest urged patients with respiratory and rheumatic illnesses to move to the dry, warm climate.

As part of the last territorial addition to the contiguous forty-eight states, the Mesilla Valley became characterized as a frontier region of "sun, silence, and adobe" and "the United States which is *not* United States."[117] By the late 1880s pamphlets glorified the valley as New Mexico's Garden of Eden or the American Nile Valley.[118] In stark contrast to such glowing assessments, one longtime resident found instead an "interminable sandy waste, gloomily dotted with mesquite, sagebrush, grama, and the like."[119] With the slow arrival of immigrants in the valley and in all of southern New Mexico, a region once governed from the south, a new history began to be written. Politicians attached lands formerly belonging to Mexico to the U.S. body politic. Writers and, more important, immigrants began to perform the everyday actions of acquisition in the new territories, through words and plows.[120] In the 1890s and 1900s opponents of Arizona and New Mexican statehood, which included much of the eastern United States, viewed the territories similarly to how U.S. politicians understood the Philippines and other imperial possessions.[121] Their semantic choices labeled the region as strange and often drew on colonial rhetoric to describe life "in darkest New Mexico."[122] The acquisition of the Southwest exemplified the opposing currents of territorial expansion and cultural homogeneity.

To others, notably those with investments in the territory, the region overflowed with promise, if not water. "The lights and shades of valley and plain," waxed one brochure, "the rich verdure, the fields of waving grain and alfalfa, the luscious fruits of orchard and vineyard, beautiful to behold in the ever present sunshine, are inspiring indeed, and no man can view them, and take note of the truly diversified character of the resources that abound without concluding that there is as yet a country truly undiscovered."[123] The narrative tone adhered to the romantic tradition of booster materials in the American West.

These publications and their representative organizations sought to capitalize on idealized descriptions of their locations to potential immigrants, but reality seldom aligned with such Edenic visions. In contrast to the "rich verdure" of the Mesilla Valley, for example, Edith Nicholl, a British immigrant, described her isolation in a landscape of vast, dusty nothingness. She wrote, "A huge wall of sand, without end or beginning, roared steadily along . . . wiping out our sky and mountains. Across the street men, invisible to one another, shouted vaguely, like hailing and separated ships in storm or fog."[124] Born in England in 1853, Nicholl grew up in the heart of the British Empire. Her father had been master of University College, Oxford, and dean of Westminster, overseeing Queen Victoria's Golden Jubilee Service and King Edward VII's coronation.[125] Her brother-in-law served as a colonial administrator in Rhodesia and for the British South Africa Company in the early 1900s. Nicholl moved to the Mesilla Valley from Virginia with her husband, an asthmatic doctor in search of an environment conducive to improving his health. She gained some notoriety for a memoir, *Observations of a Ranchwoman*, which described a reality—and the author's prejudice against Mexican Americans—far from the romantic ink of promotional brochures. Her vision of her neighbors as a lesser race exemplified many, but not all, of the immigrant views at the time, be they from the heart of the British Empire, from the Transvaal, or from the U.S. East Coast.

Though Doña Ana County had belonged politically to the United States for fifty years when the Boer settlers arrived, immigrants were sparse in its Mesilla Valley. Mexican families and their first-generation descendants constituted the cultural majority. In 1900, in the farming community of La Mesa, the new home of Viljoen, 77 percent of the 460 residents did not speak English. Of the town's 84 families, 71 of them self-identified as Mexican, 11 as white, and 2 as having mixed ancestry. Farming sustained the vast majority of the residents: 77 families labored on or owned farms or handled livestock, 2 worked as merchants, 2 manufactured brooms, 1 mined, 1 peddled goods, and 1 weaved baskets. Of the settler minority, 13 adults claiming to be white came from the South, 7 from the Midwest, 4 from overseas, and 1 from the Northeast.[126]

These statistics show that while most Boer immigrants moved from Mexico to the United States, they did not find life in the Mesilla Valley to be radically different from that at the Hacienda Santa Rosalía. In both locations irrigation channels fed fields not far removed from a larger urban center: the hacienda was located sixty miles from Chihuahua City, while La Mesa was twenty miles from Las Cruces and thirty miles from El Paso.

All of these cities had cultured elites and offered opportunities to escape from rural isolation. And each region put the minority settlers in direct contact with Mexicans and Mexican Americans who primarily spoke Spanish. While the Boers had previously expressed a preference for settling in the United States, it is unclear exactly why La Mesa was a more attractive option for Viljoen. Perhaps he believed in the reclamation literature and thought that purchasing land in southern New Mexico would produce higher profits than Chihuahua. It is likely that, though some claimed Chihuahua to be like "California itself," the Boers had difficulty navigating the dominant Mexican culture in Chihuahua and that the strengthening Anglo elite of southern New Mexico created an environment more to their liking. Before long, local developers would use Viljoen's image to promote the region through imperial overtures to the Nile's fertility in Egypt.

In the Mesilla Valley of 1905, seen through the colonists' eyes, rocky outcroppings resembled southern African *kopjes*. Alfalfa fields looked like the veldt of the Transvaal. Viljoen and his compatriots viewed the landscape, whether dusty or verdant, through their own geographies and experiences. Viljoen himself extolled the promise and virtues of irrigation in reclaiming a region from the desert. In the same spirit as promotional materials published by the New Mexico Immigration Bureau, immigrants like Viljoen's countrymen and others like Nicholl each presented romanticized versions of their own Mesilla Valley.

No evidence maintains that Nicholl and the Viljoens knew each other closely, but their proximity and circulation in the same social circles would have certainly made them acquaintances. Their residences in southern New Mexico overlapped, as did their racial prejudices. And while these two characters came from opposing political worlds that had fought a gruesome war in southern Africa, evidence as to their views on race shows how they ordered their Darwinist worlds. Viljoen complained of the "La Mesa Mexicans" and their "songs when they are drunk and sitting on [a neighbor's] ditch bank in little groups and pretend to immitate [*sic*] [opera legend Enrico] Caruso!" During a visit to Germany he felt cheated out of his money and wrote that "mexicans [*sic*] and Bunco men in Juarez" had lessons "to learn if they wish to get in the same street with [these] parasites."[127] Such thoughts, recorded in a private journal, give a much sharper tone to the showman's rhetoric than one would hear before an audience. Nicholl similarly derided her neighbors, seeing them as "unsupported by intelligence" and speaking "the lingo of the imbecile."[128]

These sentiments, far too common at this place and time, expose the everyday nature of cultural imperialism. Like Viljoen, Nicholl subscribed to social Darwinism and saw the acquisition of the Southwest by the United States as a step toward civilization for the resident Mexicans and Mexican Americans. The irony is that Nicholl and Viljoen, as British and Boer immigrants themselves, should be viewed as agents of American cultural imperialism. They were as different as two people could be—in national origin, language, education, class, and gender—but they shared one important exception: the lighter color of their skin. Like horses, prairies, guns, and romance, racial ideology traveled along with immigrants on steamers in the Gilded Age.

Early immigrants may have classified the region as "not of the United States," but southern New Mexico, principally Mesilla and Las Cruces, had burgeoning cultural and educational institutions and a rising middle class in the late nineteenth century. In 1888 citizens established Las Cruces College and merged it the following year with the New Mexico College of Agriculture and Mechanic Arts, a land-grant institution made possible by the Morrill Act of 1862. The new college fostered the early careers of many Mexican Americans and immigrants alike. Fabián García, a Chihuahua transplant, became a noted scientist experimenting with strains of the chili pepper. García was naturalized as a U.S. citizen in 1889 and graduated with the first class of students from the college. The examples of García and numerous others, like the successful merchant Demetrio Chávez of Mesilla (see chapter 1), belie the race- and class-based perspectives that arrived all too often with immigrants and others holding social Darwinist views. And these biases determined to a great extent the social networks in which the Boers, like others, circulated. Descendants today recall a warm relationship between the colonists and their Mexican-American field hands, but very little evidence corroborates these claims.

Judging by documents held by descendants and the "Social Notes" contained in the *El Paso Herald*, Viljoen and his relatives spent much of their time with fellow "American Boers" and within a white, middle-class community comprised of fellow immigrants and New Mexicans with reasonably modest means but of limited social reach. Viljoen's closest friends, for example, were Harry Hannum, with whom he established a real estate business, and the lawyer Herbert Holt. The three men participated in several fraternal organizations such as the Aztec Lodge, the Modern Woodmen of America, and the Masonic Lodge in El Paso. For agricultural support, many of the colonists' neighbors joined the Western Mesilla Valley Farmers' Union. By all measures the Viljoens and Snymans who moved north of the border became actively involved in the community. Between 1910 and 1920 the *El Paso Herald* mentioned Boer colonists more than 310 times in news articles and social notes. The stories in the *Herald* included the usual petty squabbles over local politics, for example, when Viljoen and others left the Republican Party to become progressives supporting the failed candidacy of Theodore Roosevelt in 1912.[129] Their overwhelming presence in local newspapers therefore indicates that they became culturally ensconced in the community while maintaining a sense of their South African origins.

Myrtle Viljoen and Boer and local women between Las Cruces and El Paso formed equally tight bonds, as evidenced by the formation of the "H5 Club," or Hunger Five Club, a dining group of close friends: Myrtle Viljoen, Abba Lynn, Olive Richard, Maud Hannum, and Annie Stettmund. Though the club itself demonstrates a clear segregation of self-perceived whites from Mexican Americans, there is no question the women's group gave these settlers the social outlet they desired, living as they did in an agricultural community. When the club bid farewell to the Viljoens as they left on a three-month trip to Germany, for example, the H-Fivers created a comic book of sorts to poke fun at the travelers, who faced certain seasickness on their transatlantic voyage.[130] "I have a new job, gee, but it's a snap," the book has Myrtle saying on one page. "Feeding the fish from 3 a.m. 'til 3 p.m., then from 3 p.m. 'til 3 a.m. All I have to do is open my mouth, me [*sic*] stomach does the rest." The sheer quantity of men's appearances in

the *El Paso Herald* and the quality (or depth) of feeling found in the women's
H5 booklet testify to the social inculcation of the settlers into their comfortable middle-class lives north of the border. After 1909 many of them
acquired citizenship.

It could have been fulfilling enough: this comfortable life of newfound stability built on the rewards of hard work in alfalfa agriculture,
the close-knit ties of a small community, and their protection as U.S.
citizens under the law. Viljoen especially, as the "man without a country" who had been exiled to St. Helena as a prisoner of war, might have
been satisfied. In the Mesilla Valley he tried to stow away his gunpow-
der days and become a regular citizen. He participated in local and state
politics, irrigated fields, established a real estate business, and took on,
as one paper reported, the "humdrum occupation selling two-cent stamps"
as "fourth-class postmaster" of Chamberino.[131] He attended several international irrigation conferences, served on agricultural panels with a
former governor, and even considered running for customs agent at El
Paso. Viljoen and his fellow expatriates also led Fourth of July parades
in Las Cruces, carrying both the American and Boer Republics' flags.
"If the shadows of past greatness sometimes haunt him," opined the
Washington Times in 1907, "he banishes regret" in his wife's "sympathetic arms."[132]

It could all have been enough, but it was not. The memories of wartime heroism nagged the Boer veteran, and enticed his ego, calling for the
return of the decorated general, galloping to the defense of liberty cloaked
in romantic righteousness.

The Boer General, the American Scout,
and the Mexican Revolution

While the colonists established themselves in Mesilla Valley civic life after
1905, political agitation began to unsettle Mexico and the borderlands, a
process thirty years in the making. Ever since the late nineteenth century
President Porfirio Díaz and his supporters had recruited foreign investment to bring, in the president's official motto, Progress and Order to the

nation. Increased investment transformed regional and national econo-
mies and created a burgeoning middle class, but it did so at the expense of
social cohesion. Dissent spread among peasant laborers in the countryside and among liberal reformers in regional cities. These developing
dissidents, unevenly distributed by region, by motive, and by class, were
responding in part to abysmal working conditions, a widening gap between the wealthy elite and the starving masses, a lack of civil services,
and a captive press. Opposition groups emerged in the early 1900s, among
them the radical Partido Liberal Mexicano (PLM) and the more moderate
Anti-Reelectionist Party of Francisco Madero. These resistance movements attempted to evade the president's control by forging connections
and migrating across the international border and throughout the United
States. The cities of St. Louis, San Antonio, El Paso, and Los Angeles
formed an informal circuit of resistance to the Porfiriato. Railroad lines
typified the connections between American capital and Mexican development, but these same routes enabled the transmission of revolutionary
ideas, leaders, and soldiers.[133]

Political opposition flourished throughout the early 1900s, and high
politics responded by cracking down on dissidents while maintaining a rosy
image of binational cooperation. In 1909 Presidents Taft and Díaz carefully
orchestrated a series of meetings between El Paso and Ciudad Juárez.[134]
A number of regional and national celebrities and politicians attended the
gala affairs. John Hays Hammond, a classmate of Taft's at Yale and a heavy
investor in Sonora, featured prominently among the visitors, and Hammond
arranged for his colleague and fellow investor Frederick Russell Burnham
to handle security for the president. Burnham, in fact, earned a footnote
in the historical record when he stopped an assassination attempt on Taft's
life. Little is known of the would-be assailant carrying a hidden gun, but
the attempted strike underscored the unstable world of cross-border politics. At the Taft–Díaz meeting, peace was inextricably bound with the bran-
dishing of guns. Political and capital security depended on the threat of
violence. Burnham, the adventurer who had killed a religious leader in
Matabeleland, earned hero status once again, but this time as the man who
foiled an attempt on a leader's life.

Viljoen also went to the binational meeting in 1909. He could no longer subdue his attraction to the spotlight or his military showmanship.
Shadows of greatness haunted him. After taking the oath of allegiance for
U.S. citizenship that year and attending the Taft–Díaz rendezvous, Viljoen
began to emerge on the fringes of New Mexican and national politics. By
1911, with social unrest rumbling in Mexico, he sought to insert himself into
international affairs. He traveled to San Antonio to offer his assistance as a
military advisor to Madero, the leader of a nascent rebellion.[135] Viljoen's
reasons for joining the Revolution are not known. Perhaps he felt slighted
following his dispute with the Díaz political machine over control of the
lands of the failed Boer colony. Perhaps his glory days of wartime heroism
enticed him to leave sleepy La Mesa and take action. Whatever the reason
or combination of factors, Viljoen devoted himself fully to Madero, placing a newfound loyalty to the Mexican Revolution even before his Boer
nationalism.

Thus formed one of the stranger political couples of its day. For Viljoen, fighting alongside Madero would give him a taste of his former glory
in the Transvaal. For Madero, having a Boer general renowned for his experience in anti-imperial guerrilla warfare certainly appealed to the Mexican revolutionary. The scion of a wealthy family in Coahuila, Madero knew
little of military affairs. Educated in Paris and Berkeley, a believer in spiritual mediums, and a manager of his family's numerous irrigation and factory enterprises, Madero would have been more familiar with the philosophy
of Auguste Comte than with the fog of war. Although his center-left ideology appealed to a broad swath of Mexicans by 1910, he needed Viljoen and
a corps of foreign fighters to achieve on the battlefield what he could realize only ideologically.

In May 1911 Madero relied on mercenaries and Mexicans alike, including his family, other dissenting elites such as Pascual Orozco and
Venustiano Carranza, social bandits and rebels like Francisco "Pancho"
Villa, and foreign military men. Together, the group attacked Ciudad Juárez,
just across the Rio Grande from El Paso. Despite Madero's shaky military
legs, within a few days the city fell. Suddenly, the isolated attack with such
grandiose aims—a rebellion that had seemed so unlikely to succeed—turned

into a legitimate threat to Díaz's power. By the end of the month Díaz had resigned his office, bringing a new reality as well as a larger revolution to Mexico. Viljoen basked in a rekindled spotlight more intense than regional or even national politics.

The quick and stinging defeat of Porfirismo left many of the deposed president's allies in positions of power. While the dictator may have fallen, his cronies quickly attempted to forge alliances with or disrupt revolutionaries new to the national scene. Not long after the taking of Ciudad Juárez, politicians loyal to Díaz made clandestine appeals to Viljoen to betray Madero, to disclose the leader's location and travel schedule in hopes of launching a coup. They did so by appealing to Boer nationalism, sending another expatriate, the son of a rich Transvaal family whom Viljoen had met in the South African War.[136] Rather than conspire for personal gain, Viljoen disclosed the plot to his leader. "I do not know why," Viljoen said, "but [the emissary] seems to have taken it for granted that I, being a Boer, of the same country as himself, would join with him in betraying Mr. Madero into the hands of his enemies of a free, peaceful and prosperous Mexico."[137] This single act settled Viljoen's realigning allegiance in a fluid historical era and geography. As a former Boer general and rebel and now a U.S. citizen and proponent of a free Mexico, Viljoen shifted his loyalties from those of an anti-imperial guerrilla warrior to those of an agent of Mexican state-building.

The Revolution tested individuals' loyalties while it simultaneously redefined the priorities of the larger Mexican nation. No longer would the government prioritize foreign investments at the expense of its citizens, one of the many abuses Madero had identified as symptomatic of Díaz's absolute power. When Madero first made his case against the old regime by publishing his tract *La sucesión presidencial* (1908), he focused on this question in part by discussing the plight of the Yaqui Indians of Sonora and the campaigns of ethnic cleansing and indentured servitude—more radical dissidents called it slavery—that had almost destroyed the tribe entirely.[138] Knowledge of these atrocities began to disseminate throughout the world; foreign critics of Díaz, labor activists, and revolutionaries alike could and did hold up the Yaqui example, one among many, to justify political change.

When the Revolution succeeded, Madero therefore felt the need to bring lasting peace to the Yaqui Valley. On June 1, the day after Díaz fled Mexico for Spain, Madero addressed Yaqui soldiers in Ciudad Juárez: "Have faith in us, I tell you. Return to your homes; wait there for the return of your dispossessed friends and wait, too, so that soon, as circumstances allow, we will share with you the lands that I have offered."[139] If the problems of Sonora had been caused by the absolute power of Díaz, according to Madero's earlier proclamations, then the republic should be able to incorporate indigenous Yaquis into the national body politic under a democratic administration. In theory, indigenous peoples in Mexico should no longer suffer from the abuses of an administration wed to foreign capital.

To attain peace Madero turned to a trusted ally, one who had faced down imperial powers to defend his own territory, one who understood the threat posed by foreign capital. In July 1911 Madero and his wife, Sara, invited Benjamin and Myrtle Viljoen to their residence in Mexico City. The "alfalfa growing fighter" had intended to lend his services to the president-elect only until the end of the Revolution and then "[to] return to his task of border building and field flooding" in the Mesilla Valley.[140] But Madero asked Viljoen to serve in the new government as peace commissioner to the Yaqui Indians. "I knew nothing of Yaqui Indians," Viljoen later wrote, but Madero's request surely inflated the general's ego. "Before I knew what had happened," he went on, "I was a duly commissioned peace envoy . . . , a thing which scores of others before me had failed to accomplish and which for over a hundred years had baffled the Mexican government and the Mexican army."[141]

Viljoen thus became involved in a historical process that had driven development for decades in the U.S.–Mexican borderlands. The story of his commission to attain peace with the Yaqui Indians reveals how the borderlands became interlocked in larger processes of capitalist development and indigenous resistance at the end of the nineteenth century and the first decades of the twentieth. This process responded to the push by the United States for mineral resources and the domination of foreign markets. While several movements had resisted these developments (for example, Mexican workers struck against the American-owned Cananea Consolidated Copper Company in 1906) the history of the Yaqui resistance in Sonora—the Yaquis' incorporation into American interests, their transformation into romantic symbols in western literature, and ultimately their rejection of industrial agriculture—constitutes the turning point of this Gilded Age frontier.

FIVE

Frontier in the Borderlands

The Yaqui Peace Conference of 1911

SOME THOUGHT HIS MISSION SUICIDAL. In early December 1911 Benjamin Viljoen mounted his horse at Cruz de Piedra, an administrative station in Sonora's fertile Yaqui Valley three hundred miles south of Tucson. Viljoen and a translator prepared to ride into the Bacatete Mountains, the renowned stronghold of the Yaqui Indians, or Yoemem, to hold a conference with rebel leaders. His station sat along a branch of the Southern Pacific Railroad that cut diagonally through the valley. The rail lines separated the Bacatete to the northeast from fertile lands and the eight traditional pueblos to the southwest (fig. 15). At the same time these lines split indigenous territory, they captured the attention of investors from southern California and facilitated capitalist development. As a result, the Yaquis had sought refuge for years in the mountains, raiding local haciendas owned by Mexicans and Americans and taking food and provisions in commando-style raids. Viljoen knew nothing about the region and the deep roots of Yaqui sovereignty but nevertheless believed he could bring about a lasting peace.[1]

Ever since American investors connected this region by rail to southern Arizona, the Yoemem had faced immense pressure to relinquish their lands for industrial irrigation projects. By late 1911, though the Revolution had deposed Porfirio Díaz and challenged his blind faith in foreign capital, most Yaquis remained deeply skeptical of, if not hostile to, the new administration's agenda. President Francisco Madero, like all leaders of Mexico before him, inherited a dilemma on the Sonoran frontier, a region essential to the national economy. How could the new government satisfy

147

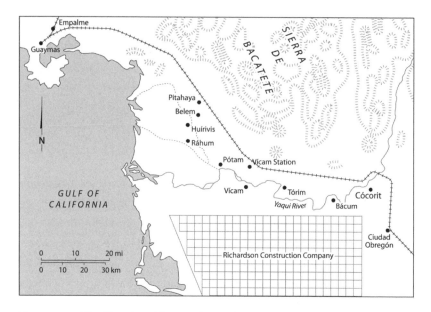

Figure 15.   The Yaqui pueblos as of 1947. Cartography by Bill Nelson, based on
Spicer, *Potam*, fig. 3.

indigenous territorial claims while simultaneously maintaining industrial
agriculture on Yaqui lands? After 1890 the failure to find an answer to this
question had resulted in encroachment on Yaqui lands and livelihoods, and
this, in turn, sparked Yoeme "depredations" against valley farmers and the
Richardson Construction Company (RCC), a large-scale irrigation company backed by American investors.

Viljoen therefore had a perilous mission as Madero's peace commissioner to the Yoemem: to ride into the traditional lands and broker a treaty
between rebelling indigenous factions, Mexican and American settlers
on their lands, and a weak federal government. His ascent echoes the exploits of Frederick Burnham in Southern Rhodesia, who had scaled the
Matobo Hills in search of an indigenous leader inciting rebellion (see
chapter 2). While their missions differed in nature—Viljoen aimed to negotiate peace, Burnham to execute a spiritual leader—the impetus behind
both adventurers was the same: to remove the last native resistance to the
large-scale development of indigenous lands.

In fact, this tie between these frontiers involved a similar cast of characters. In the 1890s Burnham and the American mining engineer John Hays Hammond worked with Cecil Rhodes and the British South Africa Company to exploit mineral wealth near Johannesburg and in Southern Rhodesia; in the 1900s Burnham, Hammond, and Haggard all invested in the RCC. Other figures entered and exited these borderlands as well. The Boer settlers inhabited both southern Africa and northern Mexico; indeed, they had considered purchasing Yaqui lands before settling in Chihuahua. And Viljoen himself crisscrossed these regions as a military expert, defending Boer nationalism, on the one hand, and serving the Mexican state to dispossess indigenous Yaquis, on the other. Though these men and their families were well traveled, their way of understanding adventure, investments, frontier life, and indigenous populations filtered through a consistent lens, one that equated Ndebele resistance to imperial advancement in southern Africa with Yaqui resistance to capitalist development in Sonora. One can only speculate how self-assured Viljoen or Burnham or Hammond felt when rough riding on separate continents, but these men never questioned the superiority of their worldviews.

Viljoen's peace mission signaled the closing of this Gilded Age frontier. The history of his negotiations with the Yaqui, and vice versa, is emblematic of capitalist networks and indigenous resistance in northern Mexico. Whereas adventure capitalism and the British Empire profoundly altered Matabeleland and Mashonaland in Southern Rhodesia in the 1890s, the history of the Sonoran borderlands of the 1910s shows how resistance among the Yoemem and Mexican revolutionaries, shaped by rising nationalism, sapped the strength of cross-border enterprises.

This chapter examines this past by placing archival evidence in conversation with Yaqui oral histories. While state archives can document when violence erupted and how the government responded, they cannot explain how the Yoemem remained unified despite their internal political divisions. Viljoen and his superiors struggled to disentangle faithful laborers from rebel Yaquis. They attempted to physically separate the two groups by creating passbooks and distributing white peace flags to loyalists. Having little access to Yoeme internal dynamics, they could not understand how deeply these two factions were intertwined. Oral histories collected in 2012, together with previously published *testimonios*, add a new perspective of the past and suggest how the Yoemem pushed back against a long history of persecution. This oral record touts the strength of Yaqui soldiers who fought for their territory, but it also conveys the centrality of women and families in times of great suffering. These stories supplement official records in the state archives to show how this global frontier came to a close in Sonora.

The American Frontier, *la Frontera del Norte*, and Indigenous Home Lands

As he prepared to ride into the mountains Viljoen claimed that local residents feared for his life. "Why should the Yaquis kill me?" Viljoen asked in defiance. "I am not a Mexican, and if they do kill me they know they would only aggravate things for themselves."[2] Naiveté and a false sense of security complemented the Boer commissioner's confidence, bolstered by his fame from the late South African War. His saddlebags stuffed with provisions, Viljoen, equally brimming with bravado, left his station in search of the rebel natives. In particular he wanted to locate the renowned but elusive leader of the resistance, José María Sibalaume. The commissioner and his translator headed "straight for the black, forbidding-looking Bacatete Mountains," he later recalled, "with their towering peaks and hidden nooks, where the mysterious Yaqui nation for many generations past held sway."

Viljoen relied on stock adjectives from adventure fiction, such as "black, forbidding-looking," "hidden," and "mysterious," to paint the region in the same broad strokes that imperial adventure fiction writers had used for decades. Haggard, the adventure novelist and doyen of this genre, and Burnham, the American scout and imperial cowboy, had both invested in lands in the Yaqui Valley, replicating their previous interests in Southern Rhodesia. Indeed, Burnham worked near Empalme, Sonora, employed by the RCC, the main company with landholdings in the Yaqui Valley. Viljoen, Burnham, and Haggard trafficked in the tropes of adventure fiction and used them to describe frontiers in Africa and the borderlands, but the

Yoemem, like the Ndebele and Shona of Southern Rhodesia, possessed a far richer culture and history than frontier texts portrayed.[3]

For millennia the Uto-Aztecan peoples had inhabited northwestern Mexico and had negotiated with numerous external political powers: the Spanish starting in the sixteenth century, the Apache and Comanche through the seventeenth and eighteenth centuries, the Mexican state after 1821, the French during the 1860s, and large-scale American capitalists after 1880. The Yaqui cosmology that developed from this history incorporated indigenous ideologies with Catholic traditions. Political negotiations followed an equally hybrid trajectory.[4] Rather than "hidden" and "mysterious," Yaqui culture by 1911 was complex, robust, and dynamic, one that maintained itself through conversations—and sometimes battles—with others holding ulterior motives. The importance placed on the natural world led to an intimate Yoeme awareness of the environment, interactive ecosystems, plants, animals, and flowers, all of which informed their social, religious, and medicinal practices. For instance, the deer dancer, the most recognized cultural icon outside of the tribe and one central to Yaqui identity, merges hunter and prey in the figure of the performer, blindfolded, donning a decorated deer head, dancing with hand and leg rattles to imitate the animal's movements and to celebrate the hunt. Given the significance of the environment to Yaqui culture and daily life, one can easily assume that Yoemem living in the Bacatete Mountains would have been keenly aware of outsiders, whether guests or intruders, approaching their settlements in the sierras.

They must have been intrigued, then, upon hearing hooves in the distance and encountering not a deer prancing through the underbrush but a yori, an outsider, a fair-skinned man on horseback clodhopping through indigenous landscapes, wearing a khaki slouch hat, speaking a peculiar language, unsure of his destination, and utterly reliant on native goodwill to secure a meeting with leaders of the resistance. However strange or exotic the Yaquis may have appeared to Viljoen, he must have afforded a spectacle to indigenous eyes and ears. Just as Viljoen conformed Yoeme complexities into a martial worldview, the Yaquis ignored equally all national and racial complexities in the person of the peace commissioner, disregarding his transnational roots and fitting him into their own cultural compartments. The Yaquis defined him through a binary system of belonging. Not of the Yoemem, he was therefore an outsider, a yori. In this way Viljoen differed little from others, Americans and Mexicans alike, who had interests in Yaqui lands. The dimensions of Viljoen's heritage flattened with each step of his horse as he approached the recalcitrant rebels in the mountains.

For centuries the Yoemem had resisted foreign pressures on their lands and waters. Ever since their first encounters with Jesuit missionaries on Spain's northwestern frontier the Yaquis had defended their tribal sovereignty in a remarkably effective dual strategy of resistance and cooperation.[5] Their religion, incorporating Catholic ideology and indigenous practices, and their celebration of the eight sacred pueblos—a Jesuit introduction—symbolized the Yoeme ability to adopt, adapt, develop, and refine their self-identity through centuries of colonization and attempted conquest. Between 1876 and 1900 their defiance of Díaz's positivist ideology of *progreso* embarrassed the federal government, which, along with Sonoran state officials, had attempted to solve the "Yaqui problem" with intensified campaigns to vanquish rebels. American and foreign investment and Mexico's desire to transform Sonora therefore threatened the Yaquis' cultural survival.

The earliest attempt by Americans to promote large-scale development of the Yaqui River leveraged irrigation expertise from the American West as well as from family ties. Walter Logan, a prominent New York attorney and self-proclaimed "apostle of irrigation," joined his brother to invest in Carlos Conant's Sonora and Sinaloa Irrigation Company (SSIC). The company acquired lands in 1890 and assembled a borderlands business, guided by builders experienced in the U.S. Southwest. Their chief engineer, for example, had already worked in Colorado Springs and the Pecos Valley in New Mexico, served as Colorado's first state engineer in the middle 1880s, and surveyed the artesian basin as chief engineer of the U.S. Geological Survey under John Wesley Powell.[6] Other associates combined experience in the Southwest with Northeastern capital.[7] By 1905 the company had moved more than 1.3 million cubic meters of earth, and the Yaqui Valley began to transform from subsistence farming to industrial agriculture. Yet owing to the challenges of the local environment and a lack of sufficient financial backing, Logan and Conant could not sustain the enterprise.[8] The SSIC went bankrupt, and its lands were acquired by the RCC, headed by wealthy entrepreneurs from southern California. This second push for development of the Yaqui River soon attracted investors who looked in all corners of the earth for new frontiers, whether the Yukon, Africa, or Mexico. The globe-trotting mining engineer Hammond recruited capital and used his connections as an advisor to Guggenheim interests throughout northern Mexico. He and his associates, with experience in southern Africa, felt confident they knew how to handle indigenous resistance while carving out a slice of territory for development.

As Americans became increasingly invested in Sonoran enterprises after 1890, evidence of a romanticized western past emerged in newspapers, dime novels, fiction, and corporate propaganda. Caricatures of Yaquis proliferated in these cultural productions, and their increasing presence in this literature attests to a process of cultural encounter that was sweeping more generally through the U.S. Southwest and into Mexico. For example, business promoters claimed that progress had either pacified warring Indians or was leading to their imminent extinction. Boosters rhetorically cleared the land of rebellion. When the SSIC promoted investment in Sonora, its pamphlets misrepresented Díaz's campaigns to ethnically cleanse the Yaqui delta. Logan and the SSIC obscured the Yaqui presence entirely in an 1894 pamphlet. "Old jealousies are dying away," reads the eighteen-page sales pitch. The "Anglo-Saxon and the Latin, the Puritan, the Californian and the Mexican all belong to the great brotherhood of man. American settlers in Mexico will find a very different state of affairs there now from what they have been accustomed to read of in the books."[9] The only appearance of the Yoemem comes in the pamphlet's appendix, where Logan substituted contemporary, warring Yaquis with a snapshot of their "naturally docile" ancestors.[10] In reality, three months before the printing of Logan's booklet, the Mexican government had begun an aggressive plan of surveillance, mapping, and military action against the Yaquis. Heightened indigenous persecution coincided with American investment in the region. Within ten years Mexican federal troops gathered the Yoemem and deported most to Yucatán and to the Valle Nacional in the South.[11] The promoters of such Sonoran development schemes justified their actions by pointing to the proclaimed backwardness of the Yaqui people.

Travelers in the region similarly relied on tired caricatures from the western past, where natives purportedly faced extinction. An Irish-Canadian priest wrote in 1907 of the "romance and weird fascination which belong to immense solitudes and untenanted wilds" and of how such landscapes and their Yaqui residents were "fading away and, in a few years, will be as if they were not." These visions borrowed directly from a Turnerian perspective which cast the Yaquis as the "last of the fighting tribes" and "a most serious menace to the progress and development of central and southern Sonora."[12] Extinction narratives existed in part because of Díaz's persecution of the Yoemen, and such stories therefore exculpated, even justified, the twin processes of development and dispossession. They engendered a particular way of seeing Mexico, with its underdeveloped land and latent mineral wealth.[13] Authors' obsessions with Yaqui ferocity and near extinction repeated the western genre's representations of Indians, as demonstrated earlier. In particular, the insistent focus on indigenous eyes and the aggressive silence they exuded aligned with other colonial literatures. The silence behind the eyes of colonized subjects bore witness to the outrages of colonialism. They unsettled the colonizers' consciences and provided a subaltern challenge to colonial authority.[14] This same obsession with the dark, silent eyes of the Yaquis—found in much tourist material from Mexico—brings into focus the historical continuities between northern Mexico of the late nineteenth century and other colonial sites around the world.[15]

In stark contrast to the fantasy of western literature and folklore, capitalists and the Mexican state actually lauded and relied on Yaqui labor, whom authors described as the "arms of the state" and the "bearers of heavy burdens, the builders of railways, the boatmen, and porters of the land."[16] Dependence on Yaqui workers, though, caught the state government and local agriculturalists in a bind. The more land and labor officials needed, the more they attempted to control Yaqui settlement and the more the Yoemem rebelled. In fact, as recent historical work has argued, the Yoemem had long maintained their own position vis-à-vis the Mexican government and did not fit neatly into a paradigm of resistance/acceptance to modernity. From earliest contacts with Spanish and Mexican administrations, writes the historian Raphael Folsom, "the Yaquis carried knowledge of the outside world, experience dealing politically with outsiders, and a carefully preserved yet flexible native culture." Such a "flexible . . . culture" thwarted the dreams and plans of western expansionists in the Yaqui Valley and an "uncomprehending Mexican state."[17]

Few people experienced the perils of misreading the Yaqui Indians and Sonora's dependence on indigenous labor more than Governor José María Maytorena, both as a politician and as an owner of several large haciendas.[18] In times of peace the Maytorena family profited from cheap labor and enjoyed a half-hearted reputation as "guardians of the Yaqui Indians." But when politics unsettled the region, Yaquis traversed and targeted the central Maytorena property, La Misa, which lay between the fertile valley and indigenous strongholds in the mountains.[19] Given the Maytorenas' dependence on cheap labor, they generally opposed military persecution of native rebels, but the Yaqui resistance had embarrassed the Díaz government for decades. In previous years, during the Porfiriato, the governor had relinquished hope of solving this riddle, writing in 1902, "I hold the secret conviction that the only effective means of putting an end to the depredations of the Yaquis is, if not their extermination, then their elimination as a special factor in the territory of the state."[20] In 1903 the government began to implement his proscription. It began shipping hundreds of men, women, and children to the South to serve in the military, to work as indebted peones or slaves, and to support a booming industry on henequen plantations, one dominated by American business interests. In 1907 an American mining engineer witnessed the ethnic cleansing. "They were ragged, dirty, barefooted, emaciated, weary and tired," he wrote, "and all were walking and herded along by an equal or larger number of mounted soldiers heavily armed and with belts filled with cartridges crisscrossing their shoulders and around their waists. Never to be forgotten is that picture, and the facial expressions of hopelessness, suffering, fear—the agony of despair." One young man wore "a chain which allowed steps of about eighteen inches. The chain led up front and around his neck, while his arms and hands were tightly bound behind his back. A look of abject humiliation did not hide the fierce, burning hatred of his captivity and his captors."[21]

Property holders were not ignorant of these scenes. In 1908 Burnham, Hammond, and Harry Payne Whitney bought into the RCC's holdings in the Yaqui Valley. Burnham had convinced the other investors to front a million dollars for the creation of a land company, which Burnham would manage on site.[22] His letters home to his wife, Blanche, from this era and the photos in his archived papers capture at best an indifference to the ethnic cleansing linked to his investments. While the letters report the potential successes of the land company, several photographs from the era show the "arrival of Yaqui women and children in Guaymas, en route to death in Yucatan" as well as "putting the Yaqui women on the trains for Guaymas" and "children sent away to die in Yucatan."[23] Burnham, or "He-Who-Sees-in-the-Dark," blinded himself to the sights before him lest they disrupt his quest for wealth. By 1909, as Díaz's policies and the Sonoran military decimated the Yoemem, Burnham ignored the ties between capitalist development and dispossession. He reported to his wife only that "several other things look well but the water is still far away from our settlers however the feeling in valley is hopeful in spite of failure to market melons & all that."[24]

Other agents of expansion had failed to make inroads with the Yaquis. While the missionaries James and Gertrude Eaton attained limited success in the first decade of the twentieth century with middle-class Mexicans in Chihuahua, their religious colleagues in Sonora remained on the margins of the Yaqui pueblos. The Sonoran out-station of the American Board of Commissioners for Foreign Missions, headquartered in Hermosillo, sat a hundred miles from the pueblos and had meager resources to fund mission expeditions. In 1906 a survey of the state noted that although Yaquis had not been overtly hostile to Protestant missionaries, they had not received any.[25] Soon Díaz's campaign of ethnic cleansing had minimized sufficient resistance such that the board considered locating a person in the Yaqui Valley expressly for the benefit of American settlers. "This valley was infested by the Yaqui Indians," wrote the Sonoran minister Horace Wagner, "but there are very few now."[26] In the absence of active local missionaries like the Eatons, the board never made inroads with potential indigenous converts. Despite this early failure Wagner continued to aspire to starting a nationwide conversation, writing, "I often wonder whether the American people realize that the U.S. has more territory that formerly belonged to Mexico than what Mexico possesses now. We Americans got that cheap at the last and I think we might at least begin to pay some interest on the gains accumulated from that acquired territory to educate some seven million *MexicanAmericanIndians* [*sic*], and evangelize the country as a whole."[27] The Yaqui Indians, like the Mexican Revolution writ large, would soon demonstrate that grand plans like Burnham's and Wagner's would falter. The Yoemem and their deportations would be impossible to ignore with the arrival of another yori from the North.

Images of the deportations, which Burnham witnessed but looked beyond, *did* catch the attention of labor activists in the United States, especially among Mexican expatriates in Los Angeles. Leaders of the socialist Partido Liberal Mexicano (PLM) leveraged Yaqui abuse to shame the Díaz administration. They recruited the American muckraking journalist John Kenneth Turner to tour plantations, disguised as a potential investor, and to interview owners and officials. His series of articles in 1908, compiled as *Barbarous Mexico* the following year, embarrassed the Díaz regime and forewarned American readers of an impending revolution.[28] Turner's text caused a sensation on both sides of the border. Díaz's acolytes rushed their own books to press, offering "the true" version of current affairs in Mexico. In the United States socialists such as Eugene V. Debs and reformers like William Jennings Bryan mined Turner's text for talking points on progressive reform.[29] Writing for an American readership, Turner lamented, "Over and over again I have compared in my mind the condition of the slaves of Yucatan with what I have read of the slaves of our southern states before the Civil War. And always the result has been in favor of the black man. . . . The Yaquis are exiles. They are dying in a strange land, they are dying faster, and they are dying alone, away from their families, for every Yaqui family sent to Yucatan is broken up on the way. Husbands and wives are torn apart and babes are taken from their mothers' breasts."[30]

Turner's depiction of helpless babies being snatched away while suckling at a mother's breast resonates with powerful Yaqui imagery in oral histories. (It is unclear whether Turner himself witnessed such atrocities or appropriated the story from Yaquis; his version and Yaqui oral history both draw from the power of myth and metaphor.) In oral history interviews, many Yaquis today either repeated or recognized this story, how, in the words of Santiago Matuz, "con el seno ahogaban a sus niños" (some women suffocated their children against their breast).[31] The story Matuz told also appeared in another form in 1994, which recalled how Herminia Estrella López and other women constantly migrated, "hiding ourselves at the feet of the peaks to not be seen by the enemies. . . . In several instances, when women carried small babies, they suffocated them against their breast so the cries would not divulge our location and they would kill us all."[32] Another version, told by two interview subjects together, relates breastfeeding to moments of political awareness. The first said, "From childhood, the mother prepares the baby, such that she prepares the child to be leery of the yori. If she is breast-feeding and she sees a yori, she says, 'Look out! Careful! There is a yori!'" The second interjected, "She sees the yori and she takes the breast away." The first continued, "'Careful! He will hurt you!'"[33] This example effectively takes past aggressions against the Yaquis and reframes them as a contemporary indigenous response: the politicization of Yoeme youth through the strength of maternal bonds. The breastfeeding image thereby has come to symbolize the resistance. In the prefatory notes to a Yaqui testimonio, the main female character is introduced as one who "breast-fed dignity to her babies so they would defend their inherited territory with their blood."[34] The scholars Nancy Rose Hunt and Ann Laura Stoler have explored themes tangential to this in other colonial settings, addressing the intimacy of power and the struggle over women's breast-feeding and reproductive cycles.[35]

Turner used this intimate and powerful imagery to press his socialist cause. "American capitalists support Diaz because they are looking to Diaz to keep Mexican labor always cheap," he wrote. "And they are looking to Mexican cheap labor to help them break the back of organized labor in the United States, both by transferring a part of their capital to Mexico and by importing a part of Mexico's laborers into this country."[36] *Barbarous Mexico*'s mission was to foster dissent through propaganda, and Turner's agenda may have warped his observations or sensationalized them. Nevertheless, state abuses of the Yoemem solidified international opposition to the Díaz regime.

Revolutionaries exploited the symbolic importance of making overtures to the oppressed Yaquis, and they equally hoped the Yoemem would fight in their ranks as a result. The socialist PLM and Anti-Reelectionists like Madero each courted tribal leaders to assist in overthrowing the government. Known for their recalcitrance and indomitability, Yaqui rebels did maintain some power in determining the scope of revolt in Sonora. Their participation could cripple the Sonoran economy and bolster the revolutionary front. As Madero prepared for revolution, he appealed to Yoeme leaders for support. Some Yaquis accepted his overtures, but most refused to cooperate.[37] Once the Revolution erupted and Madero secured the presidency, he involved Governor Maytorena in an attempt to resolve competing claims to indigenous lands while continuing to benefit from Yaqui labor. Establishing peace in Sonora would legitimize the new administration in powerfully symbolic ways. The path to a more equitable Mexico lay in part through the winding trails of the Bacatete Mountains.

Resilience through *Correría* and Mobility

As with other factions vying for control of the Mexican state, divisions among Yoeme leaders created a fractured political order. Particularly after the assassination in 1887 of their leader, José María Leyva (Cajemé), Yaqui governors of the eight pueblos disagreed on how to maintain autonomy. No single leader fully commanded authority over the entire region. Governors in the valley approached negotiations differently than did more militaristic rebels in the mountains. To outside eyes, the divergence in political philosophy gave the appearance of schisms and weakness, and those new to the region—or armchair critics in Mexico City—thought the solution would be easy: divide and conquer. After all, these known divisions between Yaquis created intense rivalries. *Caujomem*, rebel Yaquis who would not negotiate with state officials and often lived in the mountains, thought all others were *torocoyorim*, or sellouts, Yaquis who worked on farms in the Valley (owned by yorim) and especially those who served in the Mexican military.[38] Though political and geographical divisions naturally undermined cohesion among these Yaqui groups, they were not mutually exclusive. These categories often overlapped within families, tying together rebels in the mountains with farmers in the Valley through extended kin networks. What's more, warring factions in the mountains *relied* on constant runners—through a system of *correría*—to connect them with the pueblos for supplies and information. This organic strategy functioned extremely well in resisting the advances of the Mexican state and its American capitalist allies, who operated on the incorrect assumption that the rebel/sellout split could be used to the government's advantage.

The childhood of a Yaqui girl named Ricarda León Flores exemplifies how the mobility of families worked in tandem with correría between mountains and haciendas (fig. 16). Born into a life of migration in 1905, León Flores was the child of parents who had survived the Mazocoba massacre of 1900 (when hundreds of Yaquis died in armed conflict with the government), deportation to the Valle Nacional, indentured servitude, and a three-year return migration. During the early revolutionary years her family reestablished a home between the Yaqui pueblo of Belém and the tribal stronghold in the Bacatete Mountains. Her family's stories, as recorded and published in 2000, demonstrate that León Flores and her parents suffered through the most intense era of persecution in Yaqui history. "This my mother never forgot, as if running through her blood, from such courage and anger," she said, and then paraphrased her mother: " 'The yorim have always treated us like this,' she would say. 'Ever since arriving to these lands, you see, they sent us to other lands, they have whipped us, they have hung and executed us and still they do not defeat us, because we have stronger beliefs than they.' "[39]

Leading a life marked by migration forced the León Flores family to create home places on the move in inhospitable regions: in slave quarters in the Valle Nacional, in hidden enclaves in the Yaqui Valley, and in the sierras of the Bacatete. There she found her home and her education. "Our school

Figure 16.   Ricarda León Flores (*seated*) with her first cousin,
Manuela. [n.d.] Courtesy of Juan Silverio Jaime León.

was how to defend ourselves, how to shoot a gun, how to climb peaks," she
said. "That is what our elders taught us. For us it was nice, because we were
not yet aware of the danger."[40] Baptized in the Sierra de Bacatete, León Flores
and her mother spent a year in the shelter of the rebel leader Sibalaume between 1909 and 1910, just prior to the arrival of Viljoen as peace commissioner. In her testimonios León Flores recalled the importance of Sibalaume's
"kitchen," the open eating area beneath a shady *ramada*. "[There] we helped

the rest of the women," she remembered her mother saying. The area "was used for serving visitors or for the news scout who arrived every day to notify us of news from the detachments, the general [Sibalaume] was informed of everything that happened, below in the pueblos, the movements of the federales, everything."[41] The migrant kitchen functioned in overlapping ways: the Yaqui women served sustenance while the men learned of the latest military developments. The home places created in the Bacatete inevitably differed from established Yaqui homes in the pueblos. Recent studies have shed light on the roles of women in the domestic sphere, what Kirstin Erickson identifies as the "kernel of Yaqui Society."[42]

Mobility and women's home places sustained Yaqui resistance. In Belem, before and during the Revolution, León Flores and her family cultivated fields. This fed her immediate family and also supported her absent brother, Juan, who moved among Yaqui rebels in the Bacatete range. Fighting alongside Sibalaume, Juan seldom saw his sister despite his frequent trips to the valley. Under cover of night he and other emissaries participated in correría.[43] These types of activities—what officials like Viljoen, Maytorena, and Madero called depredations—sustained the tribe through times of persecution. Stealing horses, killing cattle for meat, stripping settlers of their clothes, and taking away hundreds of bushels of produce were ideologically justified in the eyes of the Yaquis.

In early 1911 such encounters turned violent only when the settlers resisted.[44] As the Revolution continued, the attacks on local ranches intensified, destabilizing the region. Municipalities around the Bacatete Mountains complained of lawlessness. Ranch workers refused to harvest the fields. Townsfolk requested guns and protection from their local and state governments. Many farmers—Mexican, American, and others—soon threatened to leave the valley. By the end of 1912, more than three hundred residents near San Javier petitioned for immediate protection from the government, given the Yaquis' destruction of the towns of San Marcial and San José de Pimas and the haciendas La Cuesta, Agua Caliente, Noria de Pesqueira, Ojo de Agua, Noria de Elías, La Palma, Palos Altos, "and several others, all located to the northeast of the Bacatete."[45] Strong alliances, such as the bond between León Flores and her brother, united the various groups in resistance. Ancestral home lands provided material support for the mountain strongholds, the main source of power to ensure the continuation of Yaqui life in the valley. Like *soldaderas* alongside men in the battlefields, women's work in the valley enabled the Yoemem to survive the early years of revolution.

Previous peace commissions had misread the Yaquis' internal divisions as discrete groups separated by ideology, a mistake Viljoen would also make. Attempts to defuse hostilities had centered on signing treaties with most, but not all, leaders.[46] For example, Yaquis famished during the peak of ethnic cleansing in 1908 survived by slaughtering lowland cattle, stealing horses, abducting yori farmhands, and carrying off provisions to the sierras. Landowners and agriculturalists complained to local officials of "Indian depredations" and asked for guns to protect their properties. The government typically complied with such requests. Furthermore, the authorities tried to make the divisions between caujomem and torocoyorim legible by controlling movement. It issued "passbooks" to track friendlies and enemies as they moved between the mountains and the valley. When officials and Yaquis finally agreed to a peace treaty on January 4, 1909, the government disarmed those amenable to peace and created a special squadron of sixty Yoeme soldiers under the command of Luis Bule.[47] This arrangement appeared to be successful at first, but during the official peace ceremony a gun discharged and startled many Yoemem. Still wary after the Battle of Mazocoba massacre nine years earlier, some fled into the mountains. Though government officials eventually reported news of a signed treaty, by the end of the month signs pointed to a renewed resistance in the sierras. Subsequent tracks made by Yaquis and increasing thefts put ranchers on edge.[48] By June 1911, before the Viljoen appointment, the provisional Revolutionary government therefore had already failed once to attain peace. It seemed all but impossible, but the series of peace conferences between 1909 and 1911 did give Madero a glimmer of hope that most Yoeme governors and leaders preferred to negotiate. He placed these hopes in the hands of a South African Boer-turned-American.

By the time Viljoen ascended into the Bacatete in December 1911, the region was collapsing from dozens, if not hundreds, of violent encounters, thefts, and, in rare cases, murders. From January through September 1911 officials reported twenty-eight incidents, three resulting in fatalities (fig. 17). Yaquis stole cattle or butchered them. They took clothes from witnesses but seldom threatened their safety. They carried off carbines, horses, sacks of corn and wheat, mules, garbanzo beans, cigars, matches, and any of their relatives who were working in the valley.[49] Although these crimes were committed to ensure subsistence, the escalating unrest worried ranchers. In one of the rare instances of outright violence, Yaquis killed two Americans on the Hacienda La Colorada. The Mexican secretary of foreign relations wrote, "The indians justified their actions by claiming that they should have received some lands back after the recent revolution, that they haven't been returned, and some of these belonged to irresponsible buyers, including some Americans."[50] In July Burnham would report home, "The Yaqui question is still to the fore—Yesterday in Guaymas Felippe a Yaqui chief & four of his men came in with arms (rifles) & got into trouble with the guards & were all shot in a pitched battle inside a house. While I do not attach much political import to it, it shows on what a powder magazine we slumber. Today as I write the drums are again throbbing on outskirts of Cócorit."[51]

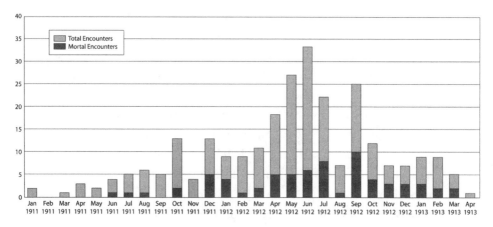

Figure 17.   Compiled from Tomos en Oficialía Mayor, 1911–13, AGES. Graph by Bill Nelson.

In the Sonoran archives, correspondence between Viljoen and Governor Maytorena shows how frequently the administration dealt with (but rarely punished or prevented) the so-called Yaqui depredations during peace negotiations. One-off violent incidents frustrated their calls for peace, and the officials as well as some Yaqui leaders often struggled to interpret news of violence in the valley. The appendix represents the incidents reported in the archives of the executive branch during this period as a way to interpret overall political conditions from the perspective of Yaqui rebels, something that daily correspondence among officials does not divulge. After compiling the events, I separated them based on the type of incident reported: either as thefts/vandalism or as mortal encounters. The resulting data informs figure 17 and makes two important points. First, incidents of bodily harm greatly increased as peace negotiations began in earnest in December 1911, when the Yaqui delegation and Viljoen traveled to Mexico City to meet with Madero; second, violence was an effective tool used by the Yoemem. The different acts of aggression therefore constituted a range of Yaqui responses as much as they presented a robust opposition to the peace conferences.

As the appendix makes clear, thefts continued for the duration of 1911. The threat to all owners of Yaqui lands intensified, not only from indigenous resistance but also from new flare-ups of revolutionary activity. In Sonora's northern frontier, federal troops battled Magonistas (socialists) and insurgents backed by Pascual Orozco in lands near the international border and in neighboring Baja California. In an effort to prevent further revolutionary activities and to defend the northern region, the state government seized arms from its citizens. This left farmers vulnerable to attack, and the Yaquis struck with impunity. In November 1911 a state official reported that Indians near Bácum had stolen twenty cows, horses, and mules and then had gone to the nearby train station, where, in a show of power, they "forced the [manager] to play the phonograph for them; when they departed they told him that they would soon return."[52] Residents petitioned the state government for military protection or the right to form (and arm) local forces. They needed safeguarding from "the parties of Yaqui indians that stalk these towns, who have no other mission than to rob and annihilate the towns, leaving the families exposed to starvation," taking everything, "even including the dressing cabinets."[53] The government denied most petitions for security, citing a lack of funds or other commitments. Some locations, Cruz de Piedra and Pótam, among them, nearly disappeared as settler families emigrated from the volatile region.

Escalating violence continued to destabilize the entire valley. Residents near La Cuesta abandoned their grounds in late June, after Yaquis attacked and held the ranch for more than two months. They took nearly thirty-one hundred bushels of corn and wheat and hundreds of horses and cattle. Four employees died in the struggle. "The insufficiency [of resources] claimed by the State Government to confront these bandits," wrote one worker to the governor, "surely was not credible. . . . I, like others, think [it] was just a ruse to show that American interests could be vulnerable under the futile pretext that it isn't essential to give them special protection. The general public appreciated the destruction of such American property and they forget to ask how it was permitted to happen."[54] This employee's complaint exposes the underlying tensions in Sonora and in much of northern Mexico between hired labor, foreign-owned enterprises, and the government. The state needed to maintain its legitimacy and could no longer coddle American investors or protect residents' properties. Whether or not the government ignored American interests, the attack at the Cuesta property marked a shift in economic relations between investors, residents, and workers. The press criticized Viljoen and the state government for their inability to stop attacks on local properties and residents.[55]

Continued suffering in the Bacatete Mountains and the ease of taking provisions from nearby ranches drove the Yaquis to increase their guerrilla raids in the latter half of 1911. In early July they attacked Leonardo Montaño's hacienda, taking 9 workers, 22 mules, 9 horses, and 150 sacks of garbanzo beans. An additional 150 sacks rotted from moisture because employees refused to work for fear of being killed.[56] Growing unrest not only disrupted agricultural production but also challenged state and national authority. It especially nagged Madero, who had criticized Yaqui exploitation in his revolutionary tract. Something needed to change. By October 1911 thirteen confrontations between Yaquis and hacendados—nearly one every other day, on average—diminished confidence in the Sonoran government. With Orozquistas rebelling in the north, Madero and Maytorena faced civil unrest in the Yaqui Valley from several sides: the Yoemem, peasant farmers, and hacendados alike.

That month, in a clearing near his administrative station, Viljoen had attempted to defuse tensions by convening five hundred Yaquis and their leaders.[57] With a translator and Governor Maytorena at his side, Viljoen composed his thoughts in Afrikaans and spoke in English. He explained his mission to attain peace, speaking for an hour and forty minutes, interrupted only by the translation. What hope did Viljoen—or Maytorena, or anyone—have of sustaining peace with the Yaquis, given that so many envoys had failed before him? He understood, at least in theory, the impasse facing the tribe, an isolated community threatened by a more powerful state. With memories fresh in his mind from the South African War—of his fellow Boers perishing in concentration camps, of the forced relocation of his own family members—Viljoen appealed to the Yaqui struggle for autonomy. He related the "sad story of my own people, and how I was an exile without a country, my country having been stolen from us; how I was there on behalf of the President to restore them to their land, so that they did not fight in vain, and showed them how much better off they were than the Boer people."[58] Such a statement reeks of manipulation, and it also lays bare how identities so easily shifted in the borderlands during the early twentieth century. Many people in fact claimed that the Boers were "lower than an Apache," a dying race vanquished by the British Empire, an impediment removed from the forward march of progress. For a brief time around the dawn of the twentieth century Boers and Yaquis occupied analogous social spaces. They buckled beneath capitalist and imperialist boots. The Boers' social status thus depended on time, place, and perception. Viljoen's hovering between subhuman savage and imperialist extraordinaire—between a backward farmer subjugated by the British and the peace commissioner to the Yaquis—shifted based on his changing relationship to the conjoined processes of development and dispossession in frontier zones.

As Viljoen spoke, he faced many challenges. Governor Maytorena doubted the Yaquis would accept peace unless by force.[59] The Flores Magón brothers and PLM socialists had sent messengers through Yaqui pueblos to "convince our brothers to not believe for any reason the promises" of the government.[60] "Carry on, brothers," they exhorted the Yaquis from afar: "Take all the lands. Take the reins of labor and work for yourselves without acknowledging authorities or bosses."[61] Viljoen knew his opposition and was aware that the immediate past offered few prospects for peace. For several weeks the Yaquis had encountered difficulties in obtaining their biweekly rations from the government at Cruz de Piedra. Owing to the Revolution and the destruction of rail lines, the provision of food proved costly and difficult. "Several of the chiefs," the commissioner later wrote, "told us that they were peacefully inclined and were anxious to settle down, but one of the chiefs, who has quite a following in the mountains, had but little to say and seemed rather sullen."[62] They requested five days to relate the offer for peace to others in the mountains and to convey the reply. Despite his earlier misgivings, Maytorena held out hope that the Revolution and the rise of Madero would soon ease hostilities.

It appeared to work. After speaking to the Yaquis from his wagon, sharing his personal experience and that of the Boer people in the late South African War, Viljoen claimed that many in his audience, "especially elderly Yaquis, wept. Gov. Maytorena said after the meeting that it was the first time in his life that he had seen a Yaqui shed tears. We all expected great things from our conference."[63] Whether the Yaquis produced genuine or crocodile tears, or whether Viljoen's pen spilled its characteristic romantic ink, it did not matter. His perceived breakthrough with the elders collapsed within twenty-four hours. A report arrived that a group of Yaquis had killed four laborers and robbed their camp the night of the conference. "After just dreaming of my weeping reconciled Yaquis of the day before," he wrote, "this telegram was a decided shock."[64] Peace now faced what looked to be insurmountable odds. Factions divided the Yaquis, and agreements reached with one leader were not always honored by others. Antiforeign sentiment grew with each passing month. And Viljoen faced an old enemy: his health. For years the commissioner had suffered from a pulmonary ailment. His breath faltering, Viljoen checked himself into the Sud-Pacífico de México Hospital in Empalme while awaiting word from Yaqui leaders.[65] As he lay prostrate, three more Americans were reported killed.

Socialists in the anarchist newspaper *Regeneración* and the elite loyal to the old regime, that is, Madero's political enemies, smirked with self-righteousness at any sign of failure. By the end of 1911 they had much to critique. Violence had returned to a monthly high of thirteen instances of Yaqui attacks on local farms. More than a third of these included fatalities. The trend does not appear to be random. Spikes in October and December 1911 coincided with months immediately following peace negotiations. While most of the Yaqui governors expressed their interest in working with the government, some recalcitrant Yoemem refused to negotiate. Attacks increasingly targeted not only individual landholdings but also the mechanisms of development: railroad cars, tracks, and telegraph wires. Under the leadership of Sibalaume, rebels raided haciendas in the valley and disrupted all negotiations. Notable peaks in violence around peace discussions indicate that while most of the tribe wished to accommodate the revolutionary government, steadfast loyalists used violence to disrupt any potential move toward peace. One oral history remembers Sibalaume as being "very radical. He never befriended a white man. He did not trust anybody."[66]

Perceived divisions between caujomem and torocoyorim—rebels and sellouts—frustrated any attempts to reach a peace even as they simultaneously gave individual leaders like General Luis Espinosa and Sibalaume the opportunity to exert influence far beyond their direct control. The decentralization of political authority made it nearly impossible for peace commissioners and other state authorities to remain confident that a treaty signed by anything less than all the Yaqui leaders had any chance of lasting. Conferences therefore required many participants. Because some leaders refused to descend from their mountain fastnesses, serious attempts to broker peace had to be expressed directly to the rebels in the higher altitudes of the Bacatete. Once rehabilitated, Viljoen pursued this strategy and embarked on "what was depicted as our perilous journey to the mysterious secret retreat" in the Bacatete.[67] The commissioner and his translator entered deep into the mountains, and, as they did, drums announced their arrival: "Some 2000 armed men arose from either side of the trail and formed a cordon around me and my caravan."[68] Viljoen was hopeful if naïve.

The Peace Conference Amid Intensifying Nationalism

Viljoen's position as peace commissioner during the Revolution exposed Madero to nationalist critiques. Ricardo Flores Magón, his brothers, and PLM loyalists especially attacked Viljoen, whom they saw as meddling in the nation's business merely for personal profit. The PLM targeted the commissioner as one of several "soldiers of fortune who seek to gain for themselves and not for everybody." Flores Magón ended one of his stinging editorials with a curt message for Madero: "Get rid of all that gringo-ness."[69] Flores Magón derided Viljoen and other foreigners partly because Madero was successful in achieving what the PLM never could. And when socialists revolted in Baja California concurrent with Madero's rise to power, the revolutionary leader threatened through the press to send Viljoen and a force of hundreds to take back the peninsula. The implosion of the socialist revolution in Baja California prevented conflict, and it set Viljoen forever in the crosshairs of the PLM and its publications.

The connection between South Africa and Mexico—two states shaped by minerals, foreign investments, immigration, and empire— became personified in the professional relationship between Madero and Viljoen. Each saw himself as a persecuted member of the elite, fighting for national autonomy against overwhelming imperial powers.[70] For others in Mexico, however, such as the PLM, the alliance provoked derision. How could a Boer contribute to a Mexican nationalist movement? Flores Magón berated Viljoen, whom he called "el filibustero," a dead man walking in Yaqui territory. In contrast, Viljoen considered his foreign heritage to be an advantage, an argument with some validity. Perhaps the peace commissioner's heritage could offer enough cultural latitude to allow him to engage in negotiations that included the state, its indigenous populations, and all the factions among these respective groups.

On arriving at a Yoeme camp in the sierras, Viljoen observed the transient world around him. He stayed three days under the *ramada* of Ignacio Mori, living on a makeshift diet of tortillas and black coffee. He noticed an elegant simplicity that kept the stronghold functioning, and he witnessed the Yoeme capacity for continued rebellion. "On a high peak, within plain view of the camping place," a sentinel stood guard, he noted. "[He] possessed a powerful telescope with which the country clear to Guaymas, Cruz de Piedra, could be scanned. They could plainly see ships on the ocean near Guamúchil and the mouth of the Yaqui River. This sentry was constantly changed, and every move was signaled to the tribe by means of rifle shots or the drum." Viljoen appeared to be unsettled by his realization that the Yoeme had a capacity for sustained rebellion. He noted caches of bows, arrows, and an array of guns. Yet the commissioner's mischaracterization of his adversaries as simple persisted. When he met the supreme chief, Sibalaume, Viljoen felt greeted coldly. "He had nothing to say," he wrote, "and left it to me to inform him of my arrival and the object of my mission. He looked down his nose and only grunted."[71] It is clear, though, that the tribe received Viljoen in good faith despite his misgivings. They arranged a *pajco'ola* that night, a festive Yaqui tradition led by men wearing bearded wooden masks who would dance, tell stories, and share cigarettes and drinks, thereby keeping alive "a great deal of the old mythology and point of view toward the universe."[72] They treated him to generous amounts of food, and exchanged weaponry.

The following morning, at a meeting with all the principal governors and rebels—the first of its kind in decades—the leaders made their demands clear: the "removal of all whites, the surrender of all their land and the removal of the Southern Pacific Railroad."[73] The commissioner could not oblige. The RCC and its predecessor, the SSIC, had already developed much of the Yaqui Valley. To concede the entire region would undermine Madero's authority and the fragile peace between tribe, state, and nation. In lieu of an immediate peace pact, Viljoen requested that rebel authorities travel with him to Mexico City to meet directly with President Madero.

Viljoen's memoir of the conference, published as an extended essay in the *Los Angeles Times* four years later, constitutes one of the few—if not

the only—first-person narratives describing the Yaqui stronghold during
the early years of the Revolution. It conveys the resilience of the people
and their adaptation to immense pressures. The Yaquis, as portrayed by
the commissioner, had become exiles in their own country, prey to diseases emanating from a single water source. Viljoen's article also belies the
peace commissioner's ethnocentrism, regardless of his proclaimed sym-
pathies. The stereotypes of savagery, hidden escapes, and silence—"he
looked down his nose and only grunted"—gave a taste of how writers
and folklorists would characterize the Yaquis in years to come. Viljoen, in
other words, operated from the same perspective of cultural supremacy
that informed many western dime novels.

The main Mexican dailies reported on Viljoen's Yaqui delegation as
it traveled first to El Paso and then south to Mexico City via the Mexican
Central Railway, over lines that had been financed with foreign capital and
tracks that had been laid by Mexican, Chinese, and Indian laborers. The
conference with Madero in late December sought to clarify which lands the
government would restore to the Yaquis, whether all nonoccupied lands
or all lands once considered belonging to the tribe, much of them now in
yori hands. An editorialist in *Regeneración* wrote that the struggle over
lands got to "the heart of the Mexican Revolution. The Indians want their
lands, and the Americans are in possession."[74] As the group traveled south,
factions of Yaquis continued raiding in Sonora, straining the credibility of
the peace mission. Governor Maytorena felt compelled to have an editorial
published in *El Correo de Sonora*. The author downplayed the unanimity
of revolt and reaffirmed faith in Viljoen, who acted "with the conciliatory
spirit of a talented, refined, and prudent man who is inspiring confidence
in the Yaquis."[75]

The article made brief mention of another significant detail: Viljoen
had begun the naturalization process to become a Mexican citizen. Conflicting accounts emerged of Viljoen's intentions, but the evidence makes
clear that, with the approval of Madero, the commissioner had filed citizenship papers in Mexican courts merely to defuse criticisms of him as a
foreigner meddling in Mexican affairs.[76] Questions of citizenship extended
beyond the battlefield and government offices, and the debate crystallized

as the Revolution dislodged the Porfiriato. New spaces of civic participation may have opened, but Mexican nationals scrutinized any foreign contribution. The status of Yaquis and of immigrants such as the Boers in the national body politic therefore depended less on ideology than on political circumstance. The Yoemem would need to accept some kind of formal relationship with the federal government in order to reclaim their lands, despite their ultimate desire for self-governance. Viljoen and his translator, Enrique Anaya, born in Arizona, applied to become citizens out of pragmatism rather than any kind of national pride.

The duo traveled to Mexico City with eight Yaqui leaders: Pedro García, Rudesindo Amarillas, General Lino Morales, and Governors José Espinosa, Juan Buenamea, Vincent Moroyoqui, Franco Valencia, and Juan Valencia—but not Luis Espinosa or Sibalaume. Viljoen "tried to win over the eight delegates" while they spent more than two weeks in the capital, yet, he remembered, they "remained cold, distant and often would recognize a great favor or a gift with barely a sickly smile."[77] He attempted to curry favor with the leaders by taking them, at Madero's request, to the canals and floating gardens of Xochimilco. He pointed out that the Yaquis maintained a superior position—retaining their own land—in comparison to the other indigenous peoples struggling to survive. The group eventually met with President Madero, his minister of development, and Vice President José María Pino Suárez. Viljoen wrote that he urged the president to "concede as much as possible," and Madero offered more than fifty thousand acres from the mouth of the Yaqui River to the Bacatete Mountains.[78] The delegates appeared displeased, promising only to report this offer to the rest of the tribe. Several days later Luis Espinosa responded. He did not concede. The Yaquis demanded that all of their lands be returned and that squatters, American or Mexican, be evicted.

Meanwhile, caujomem under Sibalaume continued raiding local ranches and killing residents and settlers near Yaqui lands.[79] They wielded violence as a political tool. A deadlock halted all negotiations. The Yoemem refused to cease hostilities unilaterally before the restitution of their lands, and Madero would not restore lands until the rebels relinquished their arms. Confronted with Porfirian and PLM enemies and a hundred years of history, the commission failed to secure unanimous agreement. The only remaining chance the Madero administration had at achieving a lasting peace would be by doing what no administration before it had been able to do: discern caujomem from torocoyorim, regulate the movements of runners between the groups, and hold multiple leaders to their word while chasing down rebels in the Bacatete Mountains.

Yaqui violence continued through the early months of 1912, and soon the press reported that the state would take up arms against all rebels.[80] Out of desperation, Maytorena and Viljoen implemented various systems of control to minimize damages. They asked Luis Espinosa to relocate to Huírivis, near Cruz de Piedra, "where there is enough room while lands are distributed for the tribe, and as such, the Government can distinguish between friends and enemies and so you can prove your good intentions."[81] Espinosa demurred, and when officials offered to move him to a separate location in the Bacatete, beyond the influence of Sibalaume, he claimed to be too ill to move. Officials also tried to institute a system of "peace flags" signed by the commissioner to regulate movements. Any Yaquis seen descending the mountains without one, Viljoen warned, would be treated as enemies. At the same time, the government found itself having to defend attacks both literal and figurative—from Orozquistas as well as intellectuals—in its negotiations with the Yaquis.[82]

Despite the government's best efforts, attacks on haciendas continued unabated, endangering Sonora's economy. Followers of Sibalaume raided valley haciendas for provisions and to abduct hostages to take into the Bacatete. Officials nevertheless held out hope; certain signs promised change. "According to reports," Viljoen wrote to Maytorena, "it seems as if the tribe is going to change its *generalisimo*. There are many who are against Espinosa and it is likely that General Mori . . . will be tribal chief."[83] The divisions among Yaqui leaders, along with the reported fears of torocoyorim in the valley being taken by Sibalaume's people, likely reflected Viljoen's misinformation more than a legitimate collapse of political leadership and internal displacement.

Considering the strong challenges to Yaqui sovereignty, how did the Yoemem maintain control of their lands? Few records in the Sonoran state archives address this question. Yaquis as a group appear in written records as a raiding nuisance, as a labor source to exploit, or, when revolting, as a challenge to the state. Scant documentary evidence offers a window into the Yoeme perspective, but a growing corpus of oral histories—collected from my interviews and from other published accounts—offers a critical counterbalance to official narratives.[84]

Filial Networks of Resilience

Within the larger tradition of Yaqui mythology and storytelling, a subset of oral histories pertains to the era between 1880 and 1927. Raquel Padilla Ramos has recognized how the Yoemem refer to this period as *aquel entonces,* or "those times," when the Mexican government intensified attacks against them and waged a campaign of ethnic cleansing.[85] Yaqui stories of this period constitute a tradition forged through interactions with yorim, and these oral sources resound in the field of subaltern studies and with the testimonio, a form that excels in amplifying the voices of peasants and indigenous peoples under oppressive regimes. Historians of Latin America, Asia, Africa, and Native America in particular have drawn on the strengths of social history and subaltern studies to counterbalance dominant narratives. While oral histories contain inherent limitations, such as the instability of historical memory and first-person bias, the testimonio can preserve the lived experiences of authors, challenge existing power structures, and expose the blind spots of official narratives.[86] And whereas individual stories about a general time period are less likely to challenge specific historical information like dates, events, and outcomes, shared stories can allow historians to listen to, and to evaluate, indigenous motives and interpretations where official documents fall silent.[87]

Yaqui oral histories of aquel entonces testify to how the state and its soldiers aimed to destroy the filial bonds that maintained Yoeme sovereignty. In the early twentieth century the government specifically targeted Yaqui families and homes in order to seize their fertile home lands. Through this personal struggle, an important strain of narratives codifies the perspectives of women, children, and families. Regardless of the narrator's gender, these themes recur and illuminate how the Yaqui home became a key site of resistance between 1880 and 1927, a dynamic that escaped state officials' attempts to group indigenous peoples into distinct categories of loyalists and rebels.[88] This filial resilience emerges most strikingly in three predominant subtopics: violence, heroism, and kin networks.

Stories of violence against Yaquis, as opposed to aggressions perpetrated by them, challenge many of the romanticizations of fierce Yaqui warriors found in western dime novels. In fact, the violence against and by Yaquis in this era was at times intimate and not exclusive to men. Yoeme legal advisor Cornelio Molina told his grandmother's history, which contributes to "part of what we recognize as open archives to reflect on the persistence of Yaqui life," he said. "It is a narrative of life," he continued with equal parts melancholy and pride.[89] His grandmother, Luisa Flores Espinosa, migrated through the sierras with her family. In an encounter with federal troops, he said in the present tense, her family becomes separated from the others near a branch of a stream. She—then fifteen years old—hides in the nearby brush, silent. In the clearing, "a federal soldier, . . . very tired, sits down and discovers that a woman is facing him. Without time for thought, she had to act," he says, switching to past tense. Doña Luisa and her family "had to kill him with big rocks, with sticks. They killed him and left him there. There they left him . . . and fled." Molina remembered watching his grandmother, in her eighties, tell this story. Tears welled in her eyes. Through his expressions and body language Molina showed he still felt the weight of his grandmother's memories. He, like generations of Yaqui grandchildren before him, grew up hearing these anecdotes. Children gathered around seated elders at night, he recalled fondly. Small fires and family bonds provided warmth. Yaqui grandparents, softened with age, spoke of brutality and survival.

The story of Molina's grandmother constitutes but one violent encounter among many in the minds of contemporary Yaquis. Other oral histories contain far more gruesome details, such as Yaqui bodies left in the sun without burial, bloated and unrecognizable. Stories from slavery in Yucatán form a subset of violent narratives; cultural memories parlay the injustices of *hacendados* branding their Yaqui slaves with the owners' initials or of the whipping of lax workers, the raping of women, and the forced crossbreeding with other indigenous peoples. To punish a second offender, says one informant while raising a clenched fist in the air, an owner would squeeze a half orange above open wounds on the Yaqui's back.[90] These details crackle in contemporary oral histories like echoes of gunfire from centuries past. Some of them, like the example of the squeezed orange, intertwine with the written record to form a feedback loop, and so one cannot assume all stories told today originate in the oral tradition. This narrative interdependency stands as another example of the fusion between Yaqui resistance and accommodation strategies, of indigenous traditions and yori incursions.

Tales of heroism, nonexistent in the archives, abound in the oral tradition. Santiago Matuz, at seventy-two, recounted the story of his relative's bravery fighting federal soldiers. "There was a unit of soldiers surrounding the water," he said. "The Yaquis, in order to drink some [water], they had to fight against the soldiers. . . . Comandante Pedro Matuz arrived there. . . . There were thousands of soldiers that he had to face."[91] Santiago's son, Jesús Matuz, added that the comandante "sold his soul in the *yo'o juara*," a sacred and spiritual realm in Yaqui cosmology. "He wanted to sell his soul . . . in order to kill a thousand soldiers. And if he could reach that number, he would die. And that's what happened to him."[92] Father and son told of the comandante's heroism, an oral history saturated with images and meanings. A Yaqui rebel attacks a formation of government troops to obtain water. The comandante breaks the systematic control of water, of life, by appealing to the *yo'o juara*, a place of spiritual power entirely foreign to the soldiers, and, Jesús says, a realm that predated the arrival of the Spanish. Indigenous cultural memories thus flow from a communal reservoir of resistance against the state. When yori officials restricted access to these cultural reservoirs, Yaqui rebels maintained sovereignty by transecting the state, or breaking its linear efficiencies. They destroyed the lines of development upon which the government depended. This replicates documented history. During Díaz's presidency and the Mexican Revolution, Yaquis resorted to violence to resist incursions: they shot at and derailed passing trains, burned bridges, cut telegraph and telephone wires and poles, disrupted mail service. In the Matuz oral history, Comandante Matuz himself breaks through detachments of soldiers to reach water.

A third theme highlights kin networks—by focusing on their separation—to record the moment of parting between a parent and child. Don "Nacho" Ignacio Ochoa Álvarez of Pótam told of the moment when his father, as a child, unwittingly witnessed authorities take his grandfather to be deported (fig. 18). "They put him in handcuffs . . . and they took him," Álvarez said. His grandfather "said to my father, 'Go, my boy, I will be back soon. I am going to buy some candies for you.'"[93] Another story captured the intrusion of wartime realities on youthful naiveté. Enrique Sanchez shared his grandfather's story of when he was a little boy, returning to his house from playing in the fields. As he lay in a watermelon patch, a neighboring man and woman yell to him, "Run, little boy, they are killing your family back there!"[94] The stories of Sanchez and Álvarez perform the same work: they shock the listener and bring to life the moment of innocence lost. Álvarez's grandfather going off to "buy candies" forces

Figure 18.   Ignacio Ochoa Álvarez. Pótam. Photo by the author, June 2012.

listeners to witness, at an innocent child's expense, the last tender moment between father and son. Listeners therefore become complicit in the horrible reality awaiting the child. If Álvarez's anecdote exerts its power through delayed recognition, Sanchez's story does so through blunt force. In contrasting styles, each of these stories imparts the pain of separation as state power pushed into Yaqui families and social structures.

The effects of the deportation and extermination campaigns during the Porfiriato never appeared in officials' reports, although one chronicler in 1900 did record a number of Yaquis who "precipitated themselves" during the Battle of Mazocoba.[95] Oral histories discussed entire families that committed suicide by jumping off ledges or off slave ships bound for Yucatán. Other stories described the killing of babies by smashing them against tree trunks. Vivid and horrifying, these tales challenge the sanitized perspective offered by state histories and document orally the atrocities not found in contemporary storylines. Oral histories focused on kin networks convey an interpretation of victimhood by individuals, their relatives, and the larger Yaqui family. Relating a story of why his grandmother, Manuela Baumea, walked with a limp, Teodulo Rubio Jusacamea said she took a bullet in the leg while running to escape an ambush. "They walked [through the sierras] without food, sick, with pregnant women. . . . They didn't even have water to drink, [but wanted to] escape, pure and simple, without carrying anything: no clothes, nothing, no guns. They only fought to escape."[96]

Women also embodied the government's intent to break Yaqui lineage and culture. In a moving anecdote about his grandmother's deportation during the 1926 uprising, Teodoro Buitimea Flores, a teacher and coordinator of indigenous education, described why Estación Lencho near Tórim still evoked emotions in him (fig. 19). "In Estación Lencho," he said, "when women were sent [away,] they were taken as spoils of war. There, in that stone edifice. [The soldiers] raped them. No shit. They raped them as many times as they wanted. . . . My grandmother was a spoil of war, and from that my mother was born."[97]

Together, these stories of violence, of heroism, and of kin networks convey the pressures against the Yoemem as well as their modes of resistance. While any one Yaqui oral history might describe a particular moment

Figure 19.   In Tórim, Teodoro Buitimea Flores stands in front of ruins dating
to the Porfiriato. Estación Lencho (not pictured) sits alongside the highway on
the outskirts of town. Photo by the author, June 2012.

in time, it also contributes to a collective record of resilience over a long,
cyclical process of global cultural encounter: with the Spanish Crown, with
the Jesuits, with the Mexican government under Díaz, and with American
capitalists and their collaborators.[98]

Regarding the new Madero administration and the Viljoen peace
commission, the Yoemem therefore confronted a process neither surpris-
ing nor new. Whereas officials like Madero, Maytorena, and Viljoen dealt
with men and appointed leaders, kin networks proved the most potent
weapon in the fight against dispossession. Families broke apart, shifted, and
adapted to both migratory and sedentary lives, but these adjustments had
two consequences. First, family dislocation strained meaningful social ties.
Husbands went away (as related by León Flores in her testimonio), for work
or for war, never to be heard from again; children grew up not knowing their
mothers or fathers. The anthropologist Jane Holden Kelley writes that the
"fact that individuals, especially men, were so interchangeable in fulfilling

basic family roles contributed markedly to the preservation of family cores." Kelley, in her study of four Yaqui women's life histories, calls this trait an "emotional shallowness" that pervades Yaqui society, a coping mechanism and an outgrowth of resistance generations deep.[99] Kelley offers a hypothesis that these shallow emotional bonds developed in response to the widespread social persecution between 1880 and 1920. A second result—the strengthening of the Yaqui *compadrazgo*, or godparent system—enabled families to produce non-kin connections. Introduced by the Jesuits in the seventeenth century, the Yaqui compadrazgo contributed in unique ways to Yoeme ethnic identity.[100] At minimum, the system of godparents and other indirect kinships helped to maintain links with families dispersed over a vast geographical area during a time of intense persecution. For a people struggling against annihilation, the compadrazgo proved invaluable. These two effects influenced individual lives just as they reinforced broader Yaqui social structures.

León Flores's childhood and her brother's participation in correría reveal how women and children survived in makeshift circumstances during the early years of the Revolution. Oral histories about aquel entonces, between 1880 and 1927, equally emphasize family and gendered networks. Of a dozen conversations and oral histories collected in 2012, nearly all of them were from male informants, yet most referred to the roles and the importance of women and families in the years of intense persecution.[101] These networks created deep ties, which yorim only saw as political factions.

The Fallout

Given how filial bonds withstood generations of persecution, the Madero administration had little chance at effecting a lasting peace by trying to separate the distinct, yet interdependent, factions of caujomem and torocoyorim. Neither passbooks nor white flags could make the resistance legible to the government and to those who brokered peace on its behalf. The Yoemem rebelled *and* cooperated, a paradoxical strategy that frustrated state administrators at every turn.

Though Viljoen and Maytorena often decried the fractured Yaqui polity, the Mexican government itself had been surpassingly unreliable. Between 1909 and 1911 the Yoemem signed peace treaties with three separate commissioners representing as many presidents. Indeed, in the early revolutionary years the Mexican governments proved less stable than indigenous internal politics. What hope of peace could have existed if past negotiations taught the Yaquis to distrust officials and if a different commissioner appeared on the horizon with each administration? Caujomem and torocoyorim were not likely to agree with a single outside authority, much less with the multiheaded state they saw in 1911, as revolutionary factions circulated in the instable region.

These pressures established unrealistic parameters on the discussions between the Yoeme leaders, Viljoen, and Madero in Mexico City in December 1911 (figs. 20, 21). All participants agreed on the causes of the impasse, but no unanimous solution emerged among the leaders around the unfurled map in Chapultepec Castle. Any hope of peace perished without the presence of the rebels. Between March and May 1912 caujomem led by Sibalaume and Luis Espinosa attacked many properties and maintained correría. In late May the Yoemem killed Governor Maytorena's nephew and began a campaign of destroying railroad cars and bridges.[102] Viljoen was absent again, recovering a second time from his chronic pulmonary disease, and his good friend and assistant, Comandant W. Malan, a fellow Boer immigrant, assumed the duties as peace commissioner. Weakened by illness and frustration, Viljoen relinquished his duties in July.[103] He relented. Viljoen—the Boer who had lost his country to imperialism, the man who purportedly sympathized with an oppressed people defending their land, and, perhaps most important of all, the famed general— wrote to President Madero and recommended "bullets as an antidote" to the "Yaqui problem."[104] Violence in the valley soared soon thereafter. What began as an important and necessary reform for Madero's presidency succumbed to the weight of the past. In President Madero's first state of the nation address he remained silent on the subject of the Yoemem.

Burnham, charged with security for the RCC in the Yaqui Valley, sensed escalating tensions. Earlier in the year he and Hammond had received

Figure 20.   Benjamin Viljoen (*seated at far right*) escorted a delegation of Yoeme leaders to Mexico City in December 1911. Newspapers, like government officials, seldom photographed or identified individual Yaqui leaders, a practice that has led to historical erasure. To the best of my ability, and with assistance from colleagues as much as the peace commissioner's files, I can tentatively identify the following Yaqui leaders: Rudesindo Amarillas (*middle row, second from left*), Vincent Moroyoqui (*middle row, third from left*), Juan Valencia (*back row, second from left*), Ignacio Mori (*middle row, fourth from left and central figure*), and Lino Morales (*middle row, third from right, wearing black shirt*). This photograph captures ten Yaqui representatives, while the peace commissioner's article in the *San Francisco Chronicle* mentions eight leaders and shows only seven in a related photograph. Clearly, the historical record suffers from silences, a result of the unwillingness of publishers, readers, and writers to understand indigenous politics at an individual level. I hope my best effort here will lead to clarifications, potential corrections, or additional identifications. National Archives and Records Service of South Africa, Pretoria, South Africa.

Figure 21.   Benjamin Viljoen (*to immediate left of man in rocking chair*) with Governor of Sonora José María Maytorena (*fourth from left*), Vice President José María Pino Suárez (*to left of table*), President Francisco Madero (*behind table*), and Yaqui leaders (*at right*). National Archives and Records Service of South Africa, Pretoria, South Africa.

permission from the U.S. government to import one hundred rifles and twenty thousand rounds of ammunition for the protection of settlers. Frightened by the murder of the company's superintendent a few months earlier, Burnham began to put into place drastic measures, what other company officials called "panicky recommendations."[105] The adventurer imported bloodhounds for the purpose of tracking caujomem, who, he claimed that April, "absolutely control this situation."[106] Burnham and Hammond had trained a force of men to shoot rifles along the U.S. East Coast before landing them in Sonora to repulse any attack on the company's properties. With echoes of his position at the sharp edge of capitalist development in Southern Rhodesia, Burnham prepared for a fight. Little did he expect it to come from his own supporters, who balked at the scout's aggressive tactics. Harry Sibbet and other company men feared that reports of Burnham's provisional militia might imperil the business, especially when the news reached Mexico City. The RCC soon requested his resignation. He begrudgingly complied. Burnham wrote to Hammond's son, fuming at Sibbet's cowardice and fear of armed conflict for the sake of progress. "If our little handful of settlers in Rhodesia had abandoned Mashonaland . . . just before the 1st Matabele War," he recalled of his African exploits, "Rhodes could never have raised $40 million in his lifetime. . . . We built this U.S. by sticking. My forbears helped in sticking to Minnesota, Kentucky, Texas, . . . many are *willing* to take *some* risks."[107] Sibbet ordered Burnham to leave the country, escorted if necessary, and the scout mocked his employer as a sham "Colossus." Dejected, Burnham moved north of the border, returning to his wife, defeated by Yaqui rebellion and the Mexican Revolution, though he would never lose his dream of developing the valley.

After Burnham's departure, attacks on haciendas continued, endangering Sonora's economy. In mid-1912 the chief engineer at RCC wrote to the municipal president of Cócorit. The state had denied the company's previous request for protection, and now the company sensed disaster for the upcoming harvest. "The company alone has done and will continue to do all in its power to finish the [harvest]," the engineer wrote, "but if a detachment [of troops] doesn't come immediately and the state suffers a loss of 25% of its agricultural production, [the company] will refuse all responsibility that will befall the state government, from which it has asked for protection."[108] At the time the RCC sent this threat, violence had destabilized the valley at a rate of thirty-three incidents per month.

The increased Yaqui hostilities that compelled Burnham to leave Mexico also contributed to a rising perception of the Madero administration as ineffective. Within a year a coup ousted him from power, placed him in prison, and threatened his life.[109] In an infamous blot on American diplomatic history, U.S. Ambassador Henry Lane Wilson blocked the exile of Madero and former Vice President Pino Suárez. Two days later an assassin's bullets killed both leaders.[110] The fall of Madero influenced national politics, and, in Sonora, it also ended any remaining hope in the short term for the recognition of Yaqui sovereignty.[111] While the Yoemem had failed to evict all yorim from their lands, to remove the Sud-Pacífico de México, and to close all military outposts among the eight pueblos, the divisions between caujomem and torocoyorim and the inability to reach an understanding with Viljoen and Madero assured sovereignty for the foreseeable future. The Revolution had resisted, and the Yoemem endured the strengthening grip of American capital in the borderlands.

Pushed out of Mexico, Burnham kept working in the borderlands from his home base in southern California. He never stopped coveting the Yaqui Valley. He often wrote to friends and acquaintances, sure that political stability might enable him to resume work with the RCC. After 1917 and the adoption of the new constitution in Mexico, Burnham recognized that his frontier visions were fading. "It was my intention to repeat my work in Africa," he wrote to Haggard, a fellow investor in the Yaqui lands, "and find the lost cities and buried treasure. For twelve years this search has continued. When my own hand which held the torch grew weak, it was passed to another and another."[112]

Like the Burnhams, Viljoen and his wife, Myrtle, relocated to southern California after his Sonoran adventure. For a time, the Viljoens, Burnhams, and Eatons all lived within a 12-mile radius of each other around Pasadena, unfamiliar with the others' contributing roles in this borderland history. Neither Benjamin Viljoen nor Frederick Burnham garnered the attention he once demanded on the battlefield or in his romancing of the frontier between southern Africa and the U.S.–Mexican borderlands. Each turned to the symbolic, to rhetorical flourishes of the pen: Burnham to his first memoir and Viljoen to a romance script about Madero's courting of his wife, Sara Pérez, and of American capital. Yaqui sovereignty had defeated them in Sonora—their Gilded Age frontier now tarnished and closed—but each adventurer clung to his typewriter, determined to reenact the pageantry of the past.

Epilogue

WHEN THE 1911 CONFERENCE BETWEEN the Yoemem and the first revolutionary regime failed in Mexico City, the peace commissioner and former Boer general, Benjamin Viljoen, could only watch as violence destabilized the region. Landowners like Frederick Burnham, Rider Haggard, and other American and Mexican investors questioned the security of their land titles. Throughout 1912 increased violence and personal health issues pushed the commissioner out of his job and back north of the border. Indeed, by 1913 administrators of the Sud-Pacífico de México Railroad, which transected Yaqui lands, urged residents to seek cover in several train cars. One young American schoolteacher naively wrote about the Yaquis from her railcar, where she lived for weeks, "Nobody knows what their fuss is." It seemed "just like the early days in the states. They murder for the fun of it."[1] Ignorant of the historical dynamics that made her world possible, the teacher soon gave up on her own Sonoran adventure and returned to the Midwest.

Burnham, on the other hand, and his deep-pocketed friend and mining engineer John Hays Hammond refused to budge so easily. Spurred by the scout, Hammond offered, through newspaper reports, to broker peace with the Yaquis. Hammond and Burnham ventured that they could succeed where Viljoen had failed and could protect their investments in the region. They proposed to go "into the mountainous stronghold . . . to pacify that warlike and apparently ungovernable tribe." Whereas Viljoen erroneously assumed that his Boer status would give him an advantage, Hammond held another yori misconception, namely, that "the understanding between him[self] and the Yaquis is so thorough as to obviate the risk of his being injured or killed."[2] He proposed negotiating peace assisted by Burnham, the embodiment of western and imperial dreams. The government ignored their informal offer.

Readers at the time, lacking access to Burnham's inner thoughts, letters, or subsequent memoirs, could not have known how violent his "peace commission" might have been. He had enriched himself and his family by dispossessing Ndebele and Shona in Southern Rhodesia, and, as he did in his African exploits, he now claimed title to indigenous lands in Mexico. Furthermore, as we have seen, Burnham regarded himself and his fellow Anglo-Saxons as a superior people destined to lead the world (see chapter 2). Ironically, the only way their offer would have resulted in peace, it seems clear now, would have been through all-out war against the Yaquis and removal of the *caujomem,* something Viljoen had in fact proposed at the end of his tenure as commissioner (and the same conclusion Porfirio Díaz had reached before them). In this, the Boer general and the American frontier scout, who had fought on opposing sides of the South African War thirteen years earlier, stood on common ground.

The Mexican government may not have responded to his offer, but the scout nonetheless held out hope for the next decade that he might return to untold riches in the Yaqui Valley. It did not happen. The death knell to his and Hammond's Mexican dreams, the revised Constitution of 1917 under President Venustiano Carranza, designated the closing of this Gilded Age frontier. Article 27 of the Constitution sent shockwaves through borderland capital networks. Created to protect Mexico from the rampant foreign investment that had characterized the Porfiriato, Article 27 proclaimed that all Mexican lands and subsoil rights belonged to the nation and that it reserved the right to expropriate properties—even those acquired before 1917—that could otherwise serve the public interest. Article 27 therefore provided the legal framework by which Mexico could shrink the distance between wealthy hacendados and landless peasants.

Those capitalists that foresaw a radical tide approaching Mexican shores attempted to use back channels to exert influence and maintain control of their investments. For example, Harry Chandler, the publisher of the *Los Angeles Times,* owned vast properties along the border. Apparently impressed by Viljoen's collaboration with Madero, Chandler befriended the American Boer and set him "to the task of adjusting tax and other matters" for two companies.[3] While Viljoen knew key players in Mexican politics, federal agents in Washington, D.C., found it odd that a military man would handle tax negotiations. They sensed the scheming of a cross-border raid. When news of the Viljoen–Chandler link became known, the U.S. government charged the two men and others of conspiring to incite a coup in Baja California for the purposes of annexing it to the United States.

Details of the alleged coup demonstrate the murky legal tactics that American capitalists used to protect property in Mexico. The charges centered around a payment of five thousand dollars made from Viljoen to the former governor of Baja California. According to the U.S. government, the payment provided funding for the stockpiling of arms near the border, which would enable the former governor to return to power.[4] With insufficient evidence, the government dropped the case after 1917. Historians to date have questioned Chandler's role in the alleged revolt but judged him innocent, as well.[5] New evidence, however, strengthens the link between Chandler, Viljoen, capitalists, and revolutionary activity. A message from Viljoen to Chandler's lawyer shows that Viljoen had received a telegraph from his previous superior, Governor José María Maytorena of Sonora: "Your kind message received relating to expedition to California, if the case arises[,] important information given by you will be made use of."[6] It would appear, based on this, that Chandler's link to Viljoen went beyond financial matters. More than likely, Chandler used Viljoen not for a raid on Baja California but to support a particular revolutionary faction; Chandler's ranches could thereby cease tax payments to multiple revolutionary groups.[7] In a single year his companies had paid more than a million dollars in taxes and duties to "a gang of robbers that are masquerading as a Government in Mexico."[8] Viljoen, who once worked for nominal peace on behalf of Maytorena, now allegedly conspired so that his associates might retain control of their lands.

Beyond the question of culpability, the government's case against Chandler, Viljoen, and others signified a shift, with tightening restrictions from the American side, away from the free rein of capital in this global frontier. From Mexico, the case exposes the messiness of cross-border business in a time of revolution. Gone were the safe old days of Don Porfirio, whose affinity for foreign investments induced golden visions and rejuvenated American dreams. The strength of ties between elites gave way to revolutionary realities in a bordered land.[9] The Revolution had posed new questions for the region, forcing both nations and capital interests to readjust to a changing political landscape.

The new world invoked by Article 27 prompted other regional investors to take note. In November 1917 many American investors began a secret propaganda campaign funded by Chandler and others.[10] They aimed to influence public opinion by translating newspaper articles critical of the Revolution from Spanish-language publications in Mexico City and feeding them to news outlets in the United States.[11] Their ultimate goal was to provoke the United States to intervene in Mexican affairs, which would have propped up their investments on more stable economic grounds. To do so, these businessmen formed the National Association for the Protection of American Rights in Mexico. Within a year it had three thousand members.

The history of this organization requires a separate study, but its creation in response to Article 27 stands as another sign of the strengthening border. If the biggest and richest players in the United States needed an organization to lobby for the protection of their properties in Mexico, then the region was certainly less promising to individuals with only a pocketful of frontier dreams. Indeed, after 1917, after the dashed hopes of Burnham and the deaths of Viljoen and his compatriot Willem Snyman, after the abandonment of Chihuahua by the Eatons, and after the salience of lost wealth awaiting recovery in Mexico, this particular history came to its conclusion. The rail lines that connected the American Southwest with the Mexican North and the tracks that stretched north from South Africa into Southern Rhodesia lost the glitter of their earlier days.

For indigenous peoples like the Yoemem, with a deeper history on their home lands, leaving the destabilized region was never an option. This was home. It was not an investment opportunity nor an adventure, and the international line could not provide them the safety and security that capitalists, adventurers, and their families enjoyed. Despite internal (yet interdependent) divisions between caujomem and torocoyorim, and even among the various revolutionary factions, the Yoemem continued to maintain their sovereignty. The intrusion of yorim had not subdued the tribe as a whole, but it did disrupt personal lives.

Ricarda León Flores, for example, spent her childhood and, later, motherhood between the Bacatete Mountains of Sonora and the Central Valley near Mexico City. Married in 1918 to Francisco Buitimea Matuz, she led a stable life for a short time until political instability returned in 1926, when the federal government renewed hostilities against the Yaquis. The opportunity to move among the Bacatete Mountains again appealed to her and caused old feelings to resurface. The thought of the sierras, Léon Flores said, "inspired me to keep living and to fight to see my first child born."[12] The couple and four other families fled to the same locations she remembered from her childhood, "and there remained only rubble and ashes of the house we once had," she remembered. "Soldiers had burned it during the last campaign against the Yaquis."[13] By migrating, this time while pregnant, in response to government intrusions into the valley, she and her husband repeated the experiences of her parents and previous Yoeme generations. Messengers soon warned of active battles nearby. This time the men separated from the women, the former to fight and the latter to take shelter. As her husband marched away, León Flores turned and saw him "waving his hat [goodbye] without knowing that he would never see me again. He was lost from my life forever."[14] The goodbye pained her, and soon, "in plain view of the peaks and pursued by soldiers," she walked to a nearby village, where she gave birth to a baby boy.[15] Like her mother, León Flores gave birth beyond the bounds of her home. Her parents had migrated in response to deportation in the battle of Mazocoba; León Flores did so in response to *federales* and revolutionary politics. She had lost her husband to the necessity of survival, but she had contributed to the perseverance of her people.

The lives of León Flores and of Yoeme women in general stand in stark contrast to those of women on other sides of this global frontier. Blanche Burnham, Myrtle Viljoen, and Gertrude Eaton all benefited from increased mobility wherever their spouses ventured. Burnham had joined her husband in Southern Rhodesia and in the Alaskan Yukon, but she also had lived in London while the scout fought in the South African War. Viljoen had accompanied her general to southern Mexico for a prolonged stay with the Maderos, yet she also had read the news of the Yaqui peace commission headed by her husband from the safety of her home in New Mexico's Mesilla Valley. Eaton had worked tirelessly to spread Protestantism alongside her husband in Chihuahua, but when situations with her in-laws arose in Wisconsin she easily hopped aboard the Mexican Central and joined them two days later. These three families drifted along the tide of this global frontier into Mexico; when revolutionary currents pushed back against these Gilded Age dreamers, they washed ashore near Pasadena. León Flores, on the other hand, migrated by foot along Bacatete trails.

Benjamin Viljoen and the Boer emigrants, like other global migrants, present a challenge to conventional histories based in a singular regional context, in ways that León Flores does not. After the Boer immigrants moved to the United States in 1905, Viljoen and his fellow colonists finally reaped the benefits of an established national identity. Those who moved with him felt a strong bond with the United States. Upon receiving U.S. citizenship, with "tears streaming down his bronzed cheeks," Viljoen "made those about him a stirring little speech in which he declared that for seven years he had been 'a man without a country,' and that this was the proudest moment of his life." Viljoen declared that "every 'oom' and 'tante' [uncle and aunt], every man and maid, every boy and girl of them was already loyally American to the core."[16] In making such a statement Viljoen strove for stability after years of dislocation, and an ascribed and accepted national identity helped him achieve this sense of having, finally, a new home. Yet the final years of Viljoen's and Snyman's lives show how nationality often shifted according to local circumstances. In 1912 Viljoen served President Madero and filed papers for naturalization in Mexico.[17] And just two years later, when two other Boer veterans in South Africa attempted to foment rebellion once again, Viljoen stood ready for the call. Writing from El Paso, he declared, "All Boers in this country will rally to the old flag."[18] Snyman, meanwhile, never applied for Mexican citizenship. When the revolutionary

Francisco "Pancho" Villa attacked Snyman's ranch, the Boer sought protection through the British consulate.[19] Privately, Snyman also hoped to
one day serve as a "special representative" of the British government on Mexican affairs.[20] He thus considered expedient circumstances when determining allegiance, once emigrating away from British citizenship in South
Africa while later desiring to serve the Union Jack in Mexico.

   This question of identity maps onto the issue of families' mobility.
Whereas Boer emigrants enjoyed an ability to choose a national identity
depending on circumstances (Boer? South African? Mexican? American?),
the Yaquis maintained a rigid indigenous status. One's ability to move freely
with multiple identity formations often determined one's mobility in the
literal sense, and vice versa.

   As fluid or rigid as nationalities may have been, the U.S.-Mexican
border influenced immigrant and indigenous families alike in profound
ways. Of the Boer descendants in the United States today, only one
remembered anything of the Snyman family that had remained in
Mexico—and this by pure chance. A New Mexican rancher named
George M. "Dogie" Jones recalled his work for the U.S. government in
1948–49. Jones traveled to Guanajuato to inspect cows for hoof and mouth
disease. He and his Mexican collaborator "were driving around the outskirts of León, Guanajuato," Jones said. They were in a military vehicle,
and as they drove down the road "this fellow was standing there, and he
flagged us down. He walked up on my side. I was driving. Of course all
the conversation was in Spanish. And he wanted to know if we could test
his cows. He had a little dairy." The man gave his last name: Snyman.
Jones's Mexican partner struggled to write down the odd last name, and
Jones immediately spelled it out, thinking, "My Lord, way down here in
Guanajuato? Who the heck is this?" The man was Hector Snyman, the son
of Willem and a distant cousin to Jones. "And I'm not kidding you," Jones
said. "[Hector] looked at me, and I got a real weird feeling. He said, 'You've
got to be Doreen's boy.'" Purely by accident, over a brief few days the northern and southern Boers reunited. Hector Snyman invited Jones to his
house and welcomed him "like a son."[21] It was the last time the two branches
would meet.

The border greatly influenced the Yoemem as well. In 1978 the U.S. government officially recognized the Pascua Yaqui Tribe of Arizona. The financial resources that resulted from federal recognition improved the lives of Yaquis in the United States, but those in Mexico had to wage ad hoc campaigns to maintain their sovereignty. In the 1930s the Cárdenas administration passed legislation to protect Yaqui territory (and 50 percent of surface waters), a major advance for the Yoemem, yet in 1952 Mexico built a dam to divert waters away from the pueblos and into the cities of Obregón and Hermosillo. A second dam has now dried up former riverbeds.[22] Giant cement irrigation canals carry water from these two dams, distributing it to other parts of the state.[23] As of this writing, the traditional Yoeme authorities in Sonora are campaigning to prevent the depletion of their natural resources. As in the days of aquel entonces, Yaqui authorities take two simultaneous approaches to these encroachments and group themselves as either *culturalistas*, those willing to work with the government to celebrate Yaqui culture, or as *indigenistas*, those refusing to collaborate owing to the government's appropriation of their resources. The present resounds with the past.

The tangible consequences of this resistance convince both Juan Silverio Jaime León and Cornelio Molina (oral history contributors quoted in chapter 5) that each is following the most effective route to secure water and lands for the Yaquis. Of the interviewees and dozens of Yoeme discussants sharing their knowledge of the past for this book, only Jaime León met me outside of Yaqui sacred lands, perhaps as a matter of convenience; yet his mere presence in a Quality Inn café signals an ability and a willingness to operate beyond the pueblos in an effort to advance the Yoeme cause. His portrait captures an expert of the Yaqui past and present standing in front of large, rectilinear windows reminiscent of a city grid (fig. 22).

Conversely, recent developments make Molina (fig. 23) ever more suspicious of *culturalista* perspectives like Jaime León's. The Sonoran state government, Molina said, has "its routes [into Yaqui sovereignty] well calculated" for future exploitation. Books on Yaqui history line his shelves. A bearded wooden *pajco'ola* mask hangs between a Yaqui flag and a cow skull (painted to represent plumes worn by Yoeme military men), on the left, and Molina's degree in agronomy from the Universi-

Figure 22.   Juan Silverio Jaime León. Ciudad Obregón. Photo by the author, June 2012.

dad de Sonora, specializing in irrigation, on the right. A map in the background identifies the paved routes and rail lines through the state.

These were the routes global capitalists and adventurers traveled, coveting the fertile Yaqui Valley during the Porfiriato and through the early Revolution. They brought with them romanticized ideals of frontiers and empires, and they connected, by virtue of their networks and their ideologies, regions far removed from traditional borderland histories. They attempted to work this frontier for their own livelihood (Boer settlers), for enrichment (Burnham and Hammond) or for personal fulfillment (the Eatons). Few if any of their traces remain in the Yaqui Valley or in Chihuahua. Pablo Hoffmann, whose German grandfather purchased the defunct Boer hacienda, had no idea of its South African past. The Gilded Age dreamers who chased success in the Mexican North left little behind, both in property and in history, after the Revolution. The Eatons prove the exception to this, having built a legacy in the form of a church, La Trinidad, and its associated school; alas, the Methodists claimed the properties when

Figure 23.   Cornelio Molina in his home office. Vícam Switch. Photo by the author, June 2012.

Protestant branches reshuffled and consolidated spheres of influence in the 1910s.

Those in this book who remain in the region, the Yaquis, never succumbed to yori ambitions. Persistent, stalwart, resolute: the Yoemem continually lobby and even sue the Mexican government to force it to abide by its previous recognition of their territory and natural resources. Jaime León and Molina differ in their approach, yet each worked with an outside researcher—a yori stumbling along rocky paths, accustomed to library stacks and not the Sonoran sun—to help him understand the nature of Yaqui sovereignty and the ways in which the Yoemem survived in aquel entonces. Some Yaquis today, as in the distant past, distrust outsiders. One can only respect this hesitation given the dynamics of their history. Just as caujomem attacked the efficiencies of industrialized agriculture, in the forms of railroads and telegraph wires and irrigation ditches, so, too, do certain contemporary Yoemem avoid speaking with unknown historians, effectively blocking attempts to give order to the past, to shape Yaqui heritage into linear sentences and grid-like paragraphs, to make legible what must be defended.

Appendix: Incidents of "Depredations" Compiled from Volumes in Oficialía Mayor, Fondo Ejecutivo, 1911–1913, AGES

(Asterisks denote mortal encounters)

Date	Location	Actions	Vol.
14-Jan-11	Cumuripa	livestock killed	2664
31-Jan-11	Aguilita	1 hurt	2783
26-Mar-11	Rancho Aguaje	cow killed	2664
5-Apr-11	Ortiz	3 carbines, 3 horses, corn, mules, clothes, and 13 workers taken	2664
5-Apr-11	Cruz de Piedra	peones, mules, horses	2664
20-Apr-11	Labor de Camon	provisions (corn, beans, cigarettes, matches)	2664
24-May-11	Camon	4 cattle stolen	2664
31-May-11	Yaqui pueblo	items stolen	2664
15-Jun-11	Buenavista	Yaquis destroying everything	2664
16-Jun-11	Congregación de San Isidro	2 horses taken	2664
24-Jun-11	Congregación de San Isidro	4 horses and corn stolen	2664
*29-Jun-11	"La Cuesta"	robbed, abandoned property; 4 peones dead	2829

(continued)

Date	Location	Actions	Vol.
4-Jul-11	between Bácojorit and Las Labores		2664
17-Jul-11	Rancho de la Junta	stolen livestock	2664
17-Jul-11	Tienda de Raya	killed 2 cattle, taking clothes and provisions	2664
20-Jul-11	Yaqui pueblo	took livestock, destroyed things	2664
*31-Jul-11	Dist. Guaymas	stolen livestock; ranchers retaliated, one dead on each side	2664
Aug-11	Pótam	stolen livestock	2664
15-Aug-11	San Marcial	stolen livestock	2664
*25-Aug-11	Hacienda La Granja	firefight; 1 dead indian	2664
25-Aug-11	Rancho El Caballo	2 women taken, then returned	2664
26-Aug-11	Cruz de Piedra	33 mules taken	2664
29-Aug-11	Pótam	stolen livestock	2664
21-Sep-11	Guásimas	set barracks and house on fire	2664
22-Sep-11	Empalme	8 indians chased cowboys	2664
26-Sep-11	near Punta de Agua	fired at man, hurt horse, stole rifle and ammunition	2664
27-Sep-11	Tomatal	4 guns taken	2664
29-Sep-11	Campo Bojórquez near La Colorada	2 guns taken, destroyed saddles	2664
*Oct-11	Cócorit	American dead with 4 bullet wounds	2664
*3-Oct-11	Represo near La Colorada	timber merchant killed (of white origin), stolen donkey and horses	2664
7-Oct-11	Hacienda de Oros	stolen livestock	2664
7-Oct-11	5 leagues from La Colorada	pistol, watch, and clothes taken	2664

Date	Location	Actions	Vol.
10-Oct-11	Hacienda del Huamúchil	4 horses stolen	2664
14-Oct-11	Hacienda Águila	cattle taken	2664
14-Oct-11	Puerto del Represa near La Colorada	mules, provisions taken	2664
20-Oct-11	Cócorit	livestock stolen	2664
23-Oct-11	Bordo Nuevo	mules taken; firefight	2664
24-Oct-11	Hacienda La Misa	livestock and mules taken; firefight	2663
24-Oct-11	Pref. de Suaqui	horses, hats, and mounts stolen	2664
27-Oct-11	Pótam	5 horses taken	2664
30-Oct-11	San Isidro	took man's clothes	2664
Nov-11	Mr. Oroz's property	53 cattle, 4 oxen, 12 horses, 80 mules, 10 young mules, 41 mares, 22 harnesses, 6 saddles stolen	2782
17-Nov-11	near Bácum	horses, mules, money, and cattle taken	2664
17-Nov-11	near Pótam	23 cattle, other items	2664
21-Nov-11	Bácum	hat and coat stolen	2664
4-Dec-11	Bácum	mail traffic interrupted	2664
6-Dec-11	Punta de Agua	telephone line cut	2664
*11-Dec-11	Yaqui pueblo	Juan Rivera killed, shot at Pedro Pasos	2784–2785
*13-Dec-11	near Zubiate	one person named Machado killed	2784–2785
*16-Dec-11	Punta de Agua	horse, livestock, and clothes stolen; in response, 7 indians and 1 woman dead, 2 horses dead, 1 guard hurt	2783
18-Dec-11	Yaqui pueblo	horse stolen	2664
*20-Dec-11	Bardo Alto, near Cajeme	corn stolen; 1 killed	2783

(continued)

Date	Location	Actions	Vol.
22-Dec-11	Huiguichi	horse taken	2783
23-Dec-11	Huiguichi	guns stolen	2783
*23-Dec-11	Buenavista	killed 2 neighbors	2783
25-Dec-11	Río Mayo	horses stolen	2783
26-Dec-11	near Ures	shot at cowboy	2784–2785
29-Dec-11	Empalme	4 cattle stolen	2783
1-Jan-12	San Antonio de Abajo	30 cattle stolen from Maytorenas	2783
*2-Jan-12	near Estación Esperanza	Yaquis killed 2 men and 1 woman	2950
*20-Jan-12	Campo Ballesteros, near Mapoli	3 dead found	2783
22-Jan-12	El Águilar	livestock stolen	2783
23-Jan-12	Bácum	4 mules stolen	2783
24-Jan-12	between Jites and San Antonio	two killed, hurt captain	2783
*25-Jan-12	Estación Mapoli	robbed train of workers and provisions; 4 killed, 7 missing	2783
*27-Jan-12	San German	killed an old man	2783
27-Jan-12	Cócorit	livestock stolen	2783
*16-Feb-12	Cruz de Piedra	livestock stolen; 6 dead	2783
16-Feb-12	Galaz	families taken to Sierra	2783
16-Feb-12	between Lencho and Corral	Yaquis robbed workers	2783
22-Feb-12	Cumuripa	2 cattle stolen	2783
24-Feb-12	Buenavista	19 cattle taken, one killed	2783
25-Feb-12	La Misa	shootout with a cowboy	2783
26-Feb-12	Hacienda La Misa	livestock taken; in response, 1 guard hurt, 7 dead horses	2782
26-Feb-12	Tuquizon	livestock stolen	2783
29-Feb-12	Bácum	money taken, 23 cows, 4 mules, and 1 horse stolen	2783

Date	Location	Actions	Vol.
4-Mar-12	Huírivis	provisions and wardrobe stolen, took 14 men and 4 girls	2783
*6-Mar-12	Huírivis	goods from merchant stolen; manager killed	2783
6-Mar-12	Yaqui pueblo	1 cow and 1 mule killed	2784-2785
7-Mar-12	Huírivis	all families requesting help were taken by Sibalaume's men	2782
*9-Mar-12	Médano	families killed	2783
9-Mar-12	near Bácum	took valuables, one mule	2784-2785
15-Mar-12	El Carrizo, near San Marcial	100 cattle stolen, 3 cows killed	2784-2785
18-Mar-12	El Sauz	a few mule drivers hurt; one soldier hurt	2784-2785
22-Mar-12	Santa María y San Antonio	350 cattle, 50 horses taken	2782
25-Mar-12	near Oroz	35 pesos stolen	2784-2785
27-Mar-12	Pótam	hacienda set on fire	2784-2785
1-Apr-12	near Bácum	livestock and a cart stolen	2784-2785
Apr-12	Pitahaya	Yaquis burned bridge and telegraph line	2664
3-Apr-12	San Marcial	all livestock stolen or killed	2784-2785
*10-Apr-12	between Pitahaya and Mapoli	set fire to train; 1 killed, 2 women and 1 man hurt	2784-2785
*10-Apr-12	near the 50 km marker on the railroad	two bridges burned; 3 dead, 2 Yaquis dead	2784-2785
*11-Apr-12	Cumuripa	train and bridge burned; engineer y stokers dead	2782
*12-Apr-12	near San Marcial	3 soldiers dead, one missing	2784-2785
12-Apr-12	Labor Porfírio Castro	provisions stolen, damage	2784-2785

(continued)

Date	Location	Actions	Vol.
13-Apr-12	Cumuripa	horses and saddles taken, arms	2784–2785
15-Apr-12	near Hacienda Santa María	attacked, 1 cow taken	2784–2785
23-Apr-12	near the 50 km marker on the railroad	bridge burned	2784–2785
26-Apr-12	Rancho "La Pirinola"	livestock killed	2784–2785
27-Apr-12	Tórim	3 servants, 4 mules, 1 horse, and donkeys taken	2784–2785
27-Apr-12	Buenavista	municipal president hurt	2784–2785
28-Apr-12	Yaqui pueblo	garbanzo beans stolen	2664
*28-Apr-12	near San Javier	1 dead, 2 hurt	2784–2785
29-Apr-12	Buenavista	1 hurt	2784–2785
29-Apr-12	near Cócorit	made workers strip naked; horse and mule taken	2784–2785
1-May-12	Buenavista	shot at train; took 10 whites, all escaped	2663
May-12	El Oregano	took beans and livestock	2663
4-May-12	near the 40 km marker on the railroad, near Div. Tomichi	5–6 telegraph poles burned	2784–2785
*6-May-12	La Misa	1 cadaver found: Benjamin Valenzuela	2784–2785
7-May-12	near Corral	a gun, a young boy, and things from house stolen; cow killed	2784–2785
13-May-12	near Bácum	man attacked, horse killed	2784–2785
14-May-12	Santa María	beans and melons taken	2664
14-May-12	Tonichi	military firefight with Yaquis	2784–2785

Date	Location	Actions	Vol.
15-May-12	Santa María	3 cattle killed; 1 boy taken prisoner	2664
15-May-12	Los Limones	9 people fixing canal taken	2784–2785
15-May-12	Cócorit	one man shot/hurt	2784–2785
*16-May-12	San Rafael	3 runners killed	2784–2785
*17-May-12	Bácum	two horses, saddles, and a firearm taken; killed Manuel Ozuna	2784–2785
*17-May-12	San José de Gracia, El Gabilán	carts attacked; three people dead	2784–2785
*24-May-12	Cócorit	workers taken; 2 Yaquis dead	2784–2785
25-May-12	Baviácora	mail disrupted	2784–2785
25-May-12	Rancho Cobachi	9 horses and 4 guns stolen	2784–2785
25-May-12	Estación Vega	timber merchants stripped	2784–2785
26-May-12	Sapochopo	families abused and haciendas looted	2784–2785
26-May-12	Bácum	Chinese mercantile goods robbed	2784–2785
26-May-12	Asliazaran and Bojorques	Yaquis present, resisted; one person hurt	2784–2785
27-May-12	Santiago (Ures)	part of a house burned	2784–2785
27-May-12	La Misa	foreman, livestock, mules, and horses taken	2784–2785
29-May-12	Labores San Eduardo	garbanzo beans stolen, property destroyed	2784–2785
31-May-12	Suaqui	Anoris Espinosa stripped, took animals	2783
31-May-12	between Corral and Cócorit	planted fields damaged	2784–2785
31-May-12	Obiachi	corn destroyed	2784–2785
1-Jun-12	Ramal del Yaqui	bridge burned	2782

(continued)

Date	Location	Actions	Vol.
3-Jun-12	La Misa	horses stabbed	2784–2785
3-Jun-12	near Cumuripa	2 men, 2 women, and 1 boy (loyalists) taken	2784–2785
*5-Jun-12	Santa María	provisions taken; firefight, Yaqui chief dead	2784–2785
5-Jun-12	Yaqui pueblo	livestock and horses taken	2784–2785
*6-Jun-12	Santa María	2 dead indians	2782
6-Jun-12	Chupeuti (?)	all clothes, 7 carbines, 1 gun taken	2784–2785
7-Jun-12	Yaqui pueblo	attack	2782
7-Jun-12	Labor del Rafael Esquer	everything in house taken	2784–2785
9-Jun-12	near Horcasitas	travelers stripped, cow killed; cowboy and another person hurt	2784–2785
*12-Jun-12	between Limones and Potrero	train attacked, wires cut, bridges burned; 8 Yaquis dead, several hurt	2784–2785
13-Jun-12	near Ortiz	property destroyed	2784–2785
13-Jun-12	near Buenavista	cattle and horses stolen	2784–2785
15-Jun-12	Buenavista	bridges burned, telegraph and telephone lines cut	2664
15-Jun-12	near Chinal	property destroyed	2784–2785
19-Jun-12	Compañía Minera del Oro	cart driver attacked	2784–2785
20-Jun-12	Tornatal	73 piles of garbanzo beans and watermelons taken	2664
*21-Jun-12	Fábrica de Hilados (Ures)	Spanish hacendado and 2 others killed	2784–2785
21-Jun-12	Labor de Florencio Maytorena	garbanzo plants destroyed	2784–2785
21-Jun-12	Labor del Tomatal	property destroyed, watermelon taken	2784–2785
22-Jun-12	ramal de Tonichi	bridge 169A and cars burned; workers chased away	2784–2785

Date	Location	Actions	Vol.
22-Jun-12	Pótam	loyalists distributing provisions taken, clothes taken	2784–2785
22-Jun-12	Estación Cócorit	4 cows killed	2784–2785
23-Jun-12	near the 169 km marker on the railroad (Tonichi?)	repair team	2782
*24-Jun-12	between Limones and Potrero	fired, returned fire; bridges burned; telegraph and phone wires cut; 7 dead Yaqui, one horse	2784–2785
26-Jun-12	near La Sandía	steer slaughtered	2784–2785
27-Jun-12	near El Carmen and Fábrica Los Ángeles	threshing machine parts taken	2664
27-Jun-12	Casa de Jesus Sanchez	watermelons eaten and taken	2664
27-Jun-12	near San Eduardo	summer dress stripped from a woman	2784–2785
27-Jun-12	Hacienda Santa Emilia	guns stolen	2784–2785
*28-Jun-12	Yaqui pueblo	seeds stolen; 4 Chinese killed, 2 hurt	2782
28-Jun-12	near the 149 km marker on the railroad, the Tonichi segment	shots fired at train; attempted derailment at the 52 km marker	2784–2785
29-Jun-12	Rancho La Cuesta, near Tecoripa	1 woman fell	2784–2785
*1-Jul-12	Mesa Atravesada	Mr. Robinson's milkman killed	2784–2785
2-Jul-12	near the 52 km marker on the railroad	train derailment attempted	2784–2785

(continued)

Date	Location	Actions	Vol.
*3-Jul-12	San Marcial	horses stolen, cattle killed, everything destroyed; 4 men killed	2784–2785
7-Jul-12	Tórim	workers stolen; firefight in response; 8 troops, 2 horses, 20 hurt	2782
*7-Jul-12	near Oroz	animals and garbanzo stolen, fight in return; 10 Yaquis dead, 5 soldiers dead, 9 hurt, Yaquis left animals and garbanzo	2783
*11-Jul-12	near Pótam	3 Yaquis dead	2783
12-Jul-12	near the 80 km marker on the railroad	guns fired at the train	2783
*13-Jul-12	Cumuripa	Librado Casanova killed	2783
13-Jul-12	San Marcial	dead livestock, horse, mule, cows, 12 head	2783
14-Jul-12	El Mezquite Yaqui (Ures)	destroyed a group of livestock	2784–2785
*14-Jul-12	Tecoripa, Suaqui Grande	killed Manuel Verdugo, hurt neighbor	2784–2785
17-Jul-12	Tuquison	12 mules and horses killed	2664
18-Jul-12	between the 50-51 km markers on the railroad	telegraph insulators destroyed	2783
19-Jul-12	near Oroz	items stolen	2783
*20-Jul-12	Cumuripa	four good neighbors killed	2783
26-Jul-12	Punta de Agua	mule eaten	2783
27-Jul-12	Tórim	12 head of cattle, 100 sacks of seeds stolen	2782
27-Jul-12	otros lugares	thefts	2782
27-Jul-12	near Guaymas	train turned around by armed Yaquis	2783
27-Jul-12	Estación Llano	cow killed	2784–2785

Date	Location	Actions	Vol.
*28-Jul-12	Las Piedras Verdes	Antonio Ivarra and Pablo Fuentes killed	2784–2785
31-Jul-12	El Coyote	attack, horse hurt	2784–2785
*5-Aug-12	Buenavista	Ramon Gutierrez killed	2783
5-Aug-12	John Symonds	51 livestock stolen	2829
10-Aug-12	near San Marcias	livestock taken and more	2783
15-Aug-12	Santa Rosalía	1 person hurt	2784–2785
16-Aug-12	La Mina, el Bajío Opadepe	merchant goods stolen, cars attacked	2784–2785
25-Aug-12	near Corral	attempt to burn bridge	2783
27-Aug-12	Pótam	attack on Chinese; at least 5 dead	2829
Sep-12	near Bácum	4 workers forced to get nude	2783
Sep-12	Cumuripa	everything taken from Realito	2783
*Sep-12	Colonia Pesqueira	stealing and killing; 1 dead indian	2783
4-Sep-12	Tecoripa	robbery	2784–2785
8-Sep-12	Realito	goods and house taken	2783
*8-Sep-12	Barrio de la Colonia	goods stolen, people made to leave houses; 1 Yaqui dead, 5 others dead, 2 hurt, 4 soldiers dead, 5 hurt	2783
8-Sep-12	Suaqui Grande	10 cowboys attacked	2784–2785
*11-Sep-12	near La Colorada	two passersby killed	2784–2785
*11-Sep-12	Colonia Pesqueira	attacked, returned fire; 30 dead residents; 13 soldiers dead, 11 hurt	2784–2785
11-Sep-12	La Misa	15–25 cows stolen	2784–2785
*13-Sep-12	San Javier	carts belonging to Gregorio del Hago attacked, provisions and 8 mules stolen; two carreras dead	2784–2785
*15-Sep-12	near La Colorada	2 neighbors killed	2784–2785

(continued)

Date	Location	Actions	Vol.
17-Sep-12	near Pótam	matches burned, 6 blankets and clothes taken	2784–2785
18-Sep-12	La Puerta Ranch	provisions stolen from Luis Giroux	2784–2785
18-Sep-12	El Alamito	everything stolen in house and left	2784–2785
*18-Sep-12	San José de Pimas	took town by gun, thefts; 2 neighbors killed	2784–2785
20-Sep-12	Estación Roman Tonichi	bridge 121B and station burned, two cars derailed	2783
24-Sep-12	Ranchos in Cobachi y Galera Vecinos de Mátape	ranches stormed	2784–2785
24-Sep-12	La Misa	shooting at livestock	2784–2785
25-Sep-12	Punta de Agua	8 cattle slaughtered	2784–2785
*27-Sep-12	Hacienda La Cabaña y Represo Tapia	20 arms, clothes of servants, all men and women in Tapia taken; two servants killed	2784–2785
*28-Sep-12	Lomas de la Guásima	carriages and seeds taken, doors burned, 3 hostages taken; 8 dead servants from Tapia	2784–2785
*29-Sep-12	various places	thefts and murders	2782
29-Sep-12	San Marcial	town totally destroyed and burning	2784–2785
30-Sep-12	Cócorit	thefts, public havoc; 4 Indians, 3 soldiers hurt	2950
*2-Oct-12	near Buenavista	killed neighbor	2784–2785
*15-Oct-12	between Movas and Rosario	killed 4 at Despensa Ranch	2783
*19-Oct-12	San Jose de Pimas	firefight; 6 dead Yaquis, 1 soldier hurt	2784–2785
20-Oct-12	Buenavista	livestock stolen	2784–2785
22-Oct-12	Opodepe	cow killed, firefight	2784–2785

Date	Location	Actions	Vol.
*23-Oct-12	Tórin	3 national guard killed	2784–2785
23-Oct-12	La Misa	thefts	2784–2785
23-Oct-12	Cócorit	three horses killed, several more taken from federal soldiers	2784–2785
25-Oct-12	near Tonichi	bridge 118a and 106 burned	2784–2785
26-Oct-12	Tonichi	thefts	2784–2785
27-Oct-12	La Barranca	destroyed files, books, money	2781
29-Oct-12	near Buenavista	livestock stolen	2784–2785
1-Nov-12	San Eduardo	many livestock and mules stolen	2784–2785
*6-Nov-12	Buena Vista	Yaquis stole corn and livestock; Longino Muñoz killed	2784–2785
*12-Nov-12	El Gavilán	1 soldier, 1 neighbor dead; 2 hurt, 5 horses dead, 7 guns lost	2784–2785
*16-Nov-12	Mazatlán	7 neighbors dead, 4 Yaquis dead	2784–2785
20-Nov-12	San Blaseño	corn stolen	2784–2785
24-Nov-12	San José de Guaymas	4 runners threatened, their clothes taken	2784–2785
30-Nov-12	Buenavista	1 horse taken	2783
2-Dec-12	Suaqui Grande	4 soldiers hurt	2784–2785
9-Dec-12	Rancho del Capitán	one person hurt	2784–2785
11-Dec-12	San Isidro	corn and beans stolen	2784–2785
*16-Dec-12	Suaqui Grande	tried to enter property; 1 dead Indian	2950
*19-Dec-12	Hacienda Tinajera	hacienda attacked; two people killed	2784–2785
22-Dec-12	near Rancho La Guasima	fired on cowboy, livestock and horses taken	2950

(continued)

Date	Location	Actions	Vol.
*26-Dec-12	Yaqui pueblo	soldiers chased, firefight; six dead soldiers	2784–2785
13-Jan-13	La Misa	four cows, one mare taken; one soldier hurt	2950
*16-Jan-13	Tórim	Yaquis killed 3 people	2950
*17-Jan-13	Bajio	horse taken, 4 mules and a few cows dead; 1 Yaqui hurt, 5–6 dead, 10 hurt, dead includes Francisco Preciado, a leader	2950
19-Jan-13	San Antonio de la Huerta	two neighbors taken and stripped of clothes, guns taken	2950
20-Jan-13	near Estación Lencho	two bridges burned	2950
25-Jan-13	Punta de Agua	thefts	2950
*27-Jan-13	San Javier	1 dead, 1 kidnapped	2950
27-Jan-13	Punta de Agua	20–25 cows stolen	2950
27-Jan-13	near Las Sandías	thefts	2950
3-Feb-13	Nogales	firefight; 2 Yaquis hurt	2950
11-Feb-13	Palo Verde	many horses stolen	2950
11-Feb-13	Ortiz	barren of mules taken	2950
11-Feb-13	between Nacori Brande and Batue	mail carrier assaulted; 1 hurt	2950
13-Feb-13	West of Opodepe	mules and cargo taken	2783
*13-Feb-13	Bátuc	men attacked Yaquis; 2 dead, 1 hurt	2950
13-Feb-13	n/a	robbed	2950
15-Feb-13	Encino Bonito	Yaquis took 20 loads of personal effects and mules	2950
*28-Feb-13	Punta de Agua	livestock stolen; killed hacendado	2950
*10-Mar-13	San Eduardo	livestock stolen; 1 Yaqui killed	2950
14-Mar-13	near Ortiz	thefts	2950

Date	Location	Actions	Vol.
26-Mar-13	La Misa	one soldier hurt	2950
*27-Mar-13	"Rancho Labores"	Yaquis attacked; 17 workers killed, 1 woman killed	2950
27-Mar-13	Empalme	bomb and theft	2950
11-Apr-13	La Misa	livestock stolen	2950
1-Sep-13	Pótam	thefts, Chinese stores attacked, livestock killed	2950
*2-Sep-13	Tórim	12 dead, 10 injured	2950
*2-Sep-13	Lo Pomposo Vasquez	attacked pueblo; 2 dead Chinese found	2950
*2-Sep-13	n/a	body of French citizen found; 1 dead local	2950
6-Sep-13	Tórim	town attacked; dead soldiers, two neighbors, French citizen, 2 Chinese; 3 Yaquis dead, another hurt	2950
7-Sep-13	near Buenavista	cattle stolen	2950
10-Sep-13	near el Cerro de las Buerras	timber merchants chased	2950
7-Oct-13	Cócorit	75 stole saddles, clothes, seeds and livestock	2950
*10-Oct-13	Cócorit	crimes; 4 soldiers dead, 4 hurt, 8 dead indians	2950
10-Oct-13	La Colorada	53 Yaquis robbed everything	2950
*10-Oct-13	Pótam	6 dead Yaquis, 4 soldiers dead	2950
20-Oct-13	Hacienda near Agua Nueva	hacienda attacked	2950
30-Oct-13	n/a	demanded money and provisions	2950
*14-Nov-13	Cumuripa	ranch attacked; 2 soldiers killed, 5 hurt	2950

Notes

Introduction

1. Gen. B. J. Viljoen, "Tribe at War for a Century," II, 10.
2. Frederick Burnham to H. A. Sibbet, n.d. [response to letter of April 22, 1912], box 13, Frederick Russell Burnham Papers, Manuscripts and Archives, Sterling Memorial Library, Yale University (hereafter FRB-Yale).
3. See Turner, "The Significance of the Frontier in American History," and esp. Wrobel, *The End of American Exceptionalism*; and Klein, *Frontiers of Historical Imagination*.
4. See esp. Bolton, "The Epic of Greater America."
5. Borderlands (geographical and methodological) research that informed the early development of this book includes numerous works by David J. Weber, but in particular his *Bárbaros*; Spicer, *Cycles of Conquest*; Lamar, *The Far Southwest*; Adelman and Aron, "From Borderlands to Borders"; Johnson, *Revolution in Texas*; Foley, *The White Scourge*; Deutsch, *No Separate Refuge*; Truett, *Fugitive Landscapes*; DeLay, *War of a Thousand Deserts*; Jacoby, *Shadows at Dawn*; Hämäläinen, *The Comanche Empire*; Mora, *Border Dilemmas*; St. John, *Line in the Sand*; and Truett and Hämäläinen, "On Borderlands."
6. The field is now strong and immense. Key texts include Kaplan and Pease, eds., *Cultures of United States Imperialism*; Rosenberg, *Spreading the American Dream*; Streeby, *American Sensations*; Thelen, ed., "The Nation and Beyond"; Tyrrell, "American Exceptionalism in an Age of International History"; and Kramer, "Empires, Exceptions, and Anglo-Saxons," and *The Blood of Government*.
7. Emily Rosenberg follows the similar lines of thought that connected Turner's thesis with American expansion after 1890 in her influential *Spreading the American Dream*, though Mexico specifically does not garner significant attention in the analysis.
8. Nugent, *Habits of Empire*. See also Nugent's "Frontiers and Empire in the Late Nineteenth Century."
9. Smith, *American Empire*, 24.
10. Jason Ruiz also recently noted this deficiency in his *Americans in the Treasure House*. Ruiz's analysis corroborates much of my first chapter, though

I respectfully disagree on his acceptance of the term "empire" as used by González in his *Culture of Empire*, for reasons stated in chapter 1. Another work that has captured, albeit briefly, the role of Mexico to U.S. expansion is Robbins, *Colony & Empire*, esp. chapter 2, "The U.S.-Mexico Borderlands: Tradition versus Modernization."

11. Salvatore, drawing on Stephen Greenblatt's "representational machine," argues for this approach in the context of South America, but his insights apply all the more to the United States and Mexico. Salvatore, "The Enterprise of Knowledge," 70; Greenblatt, *Marvelous Possessions*.

12. Recent examples that investigate connections between the American West and other frontier zones include Melillo, *Strangers on Familiar Soil*; Brechin, *Imperial San Francisco*; Gobat, *Confronting the American Dream*; Chang, *Pacific Connections*; and Teisch, *Engineering Nature*.

13. Wrobel, *Global West, American Frontier*; Rico, *Nature's Noblemen*; MacDonald, *Sons of the Empire*; and Campbell, *In Darkest Alaska*. Charles van Onselen's recent *The Capitalist Cowboy* shows how the mining engineer John Hays Hammond used his experience in the West to enrich himself and to become a controversial figure attached to the Jameson Raid of 1896 in southern Africa as well as the Yaqui Valley of Mexico. Previous efforts by scholars to contextualize the American West within international processes include the study of settler colonialism, and it should be no surprise that these influential works came from scholars working in the former British Commonwealth. See Denoon, *Settler Capitalism*; and Belich, *Replenishing the Earth*. For an argument on connecting the West and the world, see Limerick, "Going West and Ending Up Global."

14. A large body of comparative scholarship has examined the U.S. and South African pasts. See Fredrickson, *White Supremacy*, and also his *Black Liberation*; Lamar and Thompson, eds., *The Frontier in History*; Gump, *The Dust Rose Like Smoke*; Cell, *The Highest Stage of White Supremacy*; Marx, *Making Race and Nation*; Legassick, "The Frontier Tradition in South African Historiography"; and Beinart and Coates, *Environment and History*.

15. Frederick Burnham to Harris Hammond, June 10, 1925, box 6, FRB-Yale.

16. Theodore Roosevelt to Frederick Burnham, December 27, 1926, box 8, FRB-Yale.

17. Scharff and Brucken, *Home Lands*. This interpretive framework complements Julie Greene's discussion of the role of women and the domestic sphere in the construction of the Panama Canal. Greene, *The Canal Builders*.

18. As South Africans will recognize, "homelands" (one word) has a pejorative connotation, referring to the reservations created by the Bantu Authorities

Act in 1951, which set aside lands for indigenous Africans in the days of apartheid.

19. On the long durée of Yaqui interaction with yorim and successive empires and administrations, see Folsom, *The Yaquis and the Empire*. On strategies used to maintain sovereignty, see Erickson, *Yaqui Homeland and Homeplace*; Shorter, *We Will Dance Our Truth*; and Padilla Ramos, *Progreso y libertad*.

Chapter 1. The Titian in Tzintzuntzan

1. Smith, *A White Umbrella in Mexico*, 195, 1.
2. Warner, "Mexican Notes," 443.
3. Ibid., 446, 447.
4. Ibid., 447.
5. Ibid.
6. Smith, *A White Umbrella in Mexico*, 195, 196.
7. Ibid., 158.
8. Similarly Ruiz has noted a "fixation on natural resources," which "helped to construct Mexico as a logical extension of the American frontier" in his *Americans in the Treasure House*, 14.
9. Stephen Haber's analysis of Mexican economic history suggests that railroads, mining, and agriculture provided the much-needed spark for economic development during the Porfiriato. His contention that the imported technology led to overproduction and hence to uneven development and dependency on foreign manufactured imports supports what I consider to be the gilded nature of intensified U.S. economic expansion into Mexico after 1880. Haber, *Industry and Underdevelopment*, esp. 13–31. On the dilemma between Porfirio Díaz's strong ties to foreign investors and the problems of power this created, see Haber, "The Commitment Problem and Mexican Economic History," in Bortz and Haber, eds., *The Mexican Economy, 1870–1930*, 324–36.
10. Smith, *A White Umbrella in Mexico*, 199–200.
11. Ibid., 207.
12. Ibid., 219.
13. Ibid., 219–20.
14. Ibid., 220.
15. Ibid., 222.
16. Jebb, *A Strange Career*, 203.
17. Ibid., 191.

18. Ibid., 200, 321.

19. Ibid., 321.

20. Johnstone, "Tzintzuntzan and Its 'Titian'"; "Painting Called a Titian in a Remote Mexican Hamlet," 2; and Borton, *The Call of California*, 60.

21. "Not a 'Titian' After All." Nicolás León's analysis of the painting can be found in his *Nota Acerca de Una Pintura*.

22. The character of King Twala closely follows that of Dingane, the Zulu successor to Shaka.

23. Johnstone, "Tzintzuntzan and Its 'Titian.'"

24. Poole, "Landscape and the Imperial Subject," in Joseph, LeGrand, and Salvatore, eds., *Close Encounters of Empire*, 112, 110.

25. Butler, unpublished autobiography, Howard Russell Butler Papers, 1874–1936, Archives of American Art, Smithsonian Institution, Washington, D.C., microfilm edition, reel 93.

26. The anthropologist George M. Foster, working in the 1960s, noted that "few people believe the painting was burned: it now is exhibited in a famous museum in New York City, they say." Foster, *Tzintzuntzan*, 29. A recent article concurs with Foster's reporting of the painting's destruction by fire as well as locals' skepticism of its actual burning. Martínez Aguilar, "El Tiziano de Tzintzuntzan, el lienzo que se convirtió en leyenda," 103–12.

27. Recent scholarship has unpacked the meaning of adventure novels, stories, and histories to the expansion of empire. These works principally examine the British Empire, but many of them draw parallels to expansion in the American West and the perceived closing of the frontier at the end of the nineteenth century. See Brantlinger, *Rule of Darkness*; Phillips, *Mapping Men and Empire*; Kutzer, *Empire's Children*; Bristow, *Empire Boys*; and especially Green, *Dreams of Adventure, Deeds of Empire*.

28. Literary critic Nair María Anaya Ferreira points to these lost treasure tales as drawing on and fueling the British economic exploitation of Latin America. Anaya, *La Otredad del Mestizaje*, 94–95.

29. Her only biographer notes that, on Fisher's maternal side, she inherited "a rich heritage of public service" to North Carolina, a sentiment that drove a message of Catholic uplift throughout Fisher's fiction. Becker, *Biography of Christian Reid*, 6.

30. Reid, *The Picture of Las Cruces*, 41. The entire novel also ran in *Lippincott's Monthly Magazine* (February 1894) and was also translated as a serial in *L'Illustration*, beginning in August 1894. Like *The Picture of Las Cruces*, Fisher's *The Lost Lode* reproduces the metaphor of unclaimed wealth and women. Two male protagonists compete to find a lost mine and to conquer

the heart of a Mexican beauty. One of the men worried, Fisher wrote, "that if he could not soon wrest that secret from nature's dark depths, the woman he loved might be placed forever beyond his reach." Reid, *The Lost Lode*, 11.

31. The Titian-in-Tzintzuntzan story is named explicitly. Reid, *The Picture of Las Cruces*, 7, 10.

32. Ibid., 10.

33. Ibid., 41.

34. Ibid., 12.

35. Ibid., 121.

36. The classic analysis of this is Smith's *Virgin Land*.

37. Southworth, *Sonora Ilustrado* (Nogales, Ariz.: Oasis Printing and Publishing House, 1897), n.p.; Cole, *Mexico*. Cole's lyrics continue, "Tho' years may come and go / I'll constant be / Oh Mexico / I dearly love you so! / And I would like to know / If you love me."

38. Southworth, *Sonora Ilustrado*, n.p.

39. Annette Kolodny called the repetition of the landscape-as-woman to be "probably America's oldest and most cherished fantasy: a daily reality of harmony between man and nature based on an experience of the land as essentially feminine—that is, not simply the land as mother, but the land as woman, the total female principle of gratification—enclosing the individual in an environment of receptivity, repose, and painless and integral satisfaction." Furthermore, Kolodny argues that "the success of settlement depended on the ability to master the land, transforming the virgin territories into something else—a farm, a village, a road, a canal, a railway, a mine, a factory, a city, and finally, an urban nation." Kolodny, *The Lay of the Land*, 4, 7. For an astute analysis of the gendered implications of imperial adventure novels, particularly Haggard's *King Solomon's Mines*, see McClintock, *Imperial Leather*, 21–74.

40. Ober, *The Knockabout Club in Search of Treasure*, 66. Munroe's *The White Conquerors* comprised part of another series that included tales of India, the Western Plains, Egypt, and a juvenile adaptation of Henry Morton Stanley's *In Darkest Africa*.

41. Aguirre, *Informal Empire*, 138.

42. Baxter, *Spanish-Colonial Architecture in Mexico*, 217.

43. Pollard, *Taríacuri's [sic] Legacy*.

44. Bouligny, *Brief Sketches in Mexico*, cover.

45. James Tiernan to Frances Fisher, March 12 and March 15, 1894, Fisher Family Papers, 1758–1896, folder 25, Southern Historical Collection, University of North Carolina at Chapel Hill. Available in the microfilm collection,

Slavery in Ante-Bellum Southern Industries (University Publications of America), Series B, reel 29 (hereafter Fisher Papers).

46. Rogers, *Tar Heel Women*, 41.

47. James Tiernan to Frances Fisher, February 28, 1894, Fisher Papers.

48. James Tiernan to Frances Fisher, March 12 and March 15, 1894, Fisher Papers.

49. James Tiernan to Frances Fisher, April 21, 1894, Fisher Papers.

50. James Tiernan to Frances Fisher, April 21 and April 24, 1894, Fisher Papers.

51. James Tiernan to Frances Fisher, April 29, 1894, Fisher Papers. The identity of the mill worker remains unclear. Fisher refers to him as "of the lowest order of Englishmen."

52. Pollard, *A Busy Time in Mexico*, 67, 68.

53. Harper, *A Journey in Southeastern Mexico*, 52, 65. Harper especially faulted, in the strongest possible terms, the promotional brochures that sold impossible American dreams. As he said, "Pure cream cannot be extracted from chalk and water."

54. Romero, *Geographical and Statistical Notes on Mexico*, 127–28.

55. Barron, *The Mexican Problem*, 130–31.

56. Pletcher, *Rails, Mines, and Progress*, 300, 302.

57. Coatsworth, *Growth Against Development*, 119.

58. Trollope explored the duplicitous and foolish investments that British and American capitalists were all too eager to make in his satire *The Way We Live Now*. Trollope called attention to the loose morals and vapid culture of Gilded Age societies by narrating the unquestioned fraud perpetrated by his fictional character Augustus Melmotte and his promotion of a new "South Central Pacific and Mexican Railway," which would purportedly run between Salt Lake City and Vera Cruz.

59. While I remain skeptical on equating economic indicators with American influence, this does not preclude the growth of cultural relations during and after the dawn of the twentieth century. For an excellent study that connects this period of investments with later cultural and intellectual ties, see Delpar, *The Enormous Vogue of Things Mexican*.

60. Department of Commerce and Labor, Bureau of Statistics, *Special Consular Reports*, 175.

61. On the Spanish and Mexican empires, see esp. Weber, *The Spanish Frontier in North America* and his *The Mexican Frontier*. Recent works have contributed nuanced histories of competing peoples in the borderlands. On the confluence of Native American and European imperial struggles,

see esp. DeLay, *War of a Thousand Deserts*; Hämäläinen, *The Comanche Empire*; Blackhawk, *Violence Over the Land*; and Jacoby, *Shadows at Dawn*.

62. Fuller, *The Movement for the Acquisition of All Mexico*.

63. St. John, *Line in the Sand*, 63–89.

64. Bancroft, *The Life of William H. Seward*, 2:429.

65. Wrobel, *The End of American Exceptionalism*, 21–22.

66. Bancroft, *The Works of Hubert Howe Bancroft*, 16:673.

67. Roberts, *With the Invader*, 138, 122. Emphasis added.

68. One prospector wrote that Baja California "has lain comparatively idle in the sea, but by degrees the heave of modern progress has turned it over almost into the center of the populated globe, and it must soon play fully as important a part as Upper California, which lies above it, and more so than the luxurious provinces of the decaying empire to which it never more than nominally belonged." Janes, "Lower California," 23. For another parallel between Baja California and California, see Nordhoff, *Peninsular California*, 6, 62.

69. Browne, *Adventures in the Apache Country*, 173.

70. Pletcher, *The Diplomacy of Trade and Investment*, 102; and Pletcher, *Rails, Mines, and Progress*, 313.

71. Logan, *Yaqui Land Convertible Stock*, 3–4.

72. Hammond, *The Autobiography of John Hays Hammond*, 1:32.

73. Hammond and others linked to Cecil Rhodes and Barney Barnato were blamed for facilitating the Jameson Raid, a failed attempt by British (and American) foreigners to wrest political control of the Transvaal (and its golden riches) from the Boer Republics. The abysmal failure landed Hammond in prison, where he faced capital punishment before careful diplomacy and politicking freed him and required him to return to the United States.

74. Lummis, *The Land of Poco Tiempo*, 3.

75. Mexican Central Railway Company, *Facts and Figures*, 6.

76. Hager, ed., *The Filibusters of 1890*, 55. For another first-person view of the relationship between mineral frontiers in both Californias, see Buffum and Caughey, *Six Months in the Gold Mines*.

77. Stephens, *The Gold Fields of Lower California*, 43. Despite lofty dreams, investors could not make the colony a reality.

78. Le Duc, *Report of a Trip of Observation*, 4.

79. Roberts, *With the Invader*.

80. Bishop, *Old Mexico and Her Lost Provinces*, 316.

81. Ibid., 318–19.

82. For all of Turner's glaring omissions, his theory tapped prevailing beliefs at the end of the nineteenth century. His thesis later collapsed by ignoring Native Americans and the malignant effects of conquest, but it also necessarily omits what it could not predict: that the frontier as an economic process would continue beyond the Pacific shore.

83. LaFeber, *The New Empire*, 24–31.

84. See especially Bartlett, *Personal Narrative*; and St. John, *Line in the Sand*, 23–38.

85. D. W. Meinig's notion of the copper borderlands is picked up and expanded upon by Truett, *Fugitive Landscapes*, 6.

86. Bishop, *Old Mexico and Her Lost Provinces*, 87.

87. Matthews, *The Civilizing Machine*, 12.

88. Powell, *The Railroads of Mexico*, 1.

89. *Pennsylvania Tours*, 3.

90. Clarence W. Barron, quoted in Powell, *The Railroads of Mexico*, 130.

91. See, for example, Church, *Diary of a Trip Through Mexico and California*; and Roberts, *With the Invader*.

92. Le Duc, *Report of a Trip of Observation*, 5.

93. Anderson, *The American and Mexican Pacific Railway*, 10.

94. Box, *Capt. James Box's Adventures and Explorations*, 13–14, 16. Such ideology continued well after the Civil War. These calls for a benevolent conquest all but disappeared with the outbreak of the Civil War. But soon thereafter writers again returned to push for southern expansion in charitable terms. Said one Nevada expansionist in 1867, "Our necessities . . . upon this continent, as well as insecurity to life and property in Mexico and the oppressions of the poor in other lands, all bid us make some practical, just and general . . . provisions for the accession to our protection and sway of territories not now included within our boundaries," *Radical Reconstruction on the Basis of One Sovereign Republic*, 8.

95. Bishop, *Old Mexico and Her Lost Provinces*, 71, 94–95.

96. William Henry Bishop Papers, MS 83, box 13, folder 18 (Mexico Journal #6), Manuscripts and Archives, Yale University; Bishop, *Old Mexico and Her Lost Provinces*, 276–77.

97. Richard White notes these fears and debate on both sides of the issue in *Railroaded*, 51–55.

98. Logan, ed., *A Mexican Night*, 54.

99. Romero, "The Future of Mexico and Its Relations with the United States," in Logan, ed., *A Mexican Night*, 20.

100. Le Duc, *Report of a Trip of Observation*, 4; Anderson, *The American and Mexican Pacific Railway*, 10.

101. Logan, *Irrigation on the Yaqui River*, 22.

102. *Pennsylvania Tours*, 4.

103. LaFeber's *The New Empire* makes a strong and convincing case for the connection between fears about the frontier's closing and the new foreign policy with economic empire at its core. LaFeber places Mexico alongside Alaska and Hawaii as similar imperial venues, uniting them in the chapter titled "Years of Preparation," but he does not examine in depth the expanding American interests in Mexico.

104. Logan, ed., *A Mexican Night*, 62.

105. For more on the commercial relations between England and Mexico, see Aguirre, *Informal Empire*.

106. Turner based his speech, which fixed the closing of the frontier, on the 1890 U.S. federal census.

107. Born in 1851, he graduated from St. Michael's College in Santa Fe and moved to southern New Mexico, growing up during a time of cultural realignment in the borderlands. He had worked as a clerk selling dry goods for a Prussian immigrant and merchant, and within ten years Chávez had opened his own mercantile business. At the age of thirty-four he had married Luisa González, of Chihuahua, and over the next decade the couple had raised one boy and seven girls. They oversaw a thriving mercantile business, purchased a two-story home from an Irish immigrant and merchant, and very quickly paid off the mortgage on their home. By 1893 Chávez had been appointed U.S. postmaster of Mesilla; probate judge, treasurer, and collector of Doña Ana County; and regent and treasurer of the new agricultural college. Anderson, *History of New Mexico*, 574; National Archives and Records Administration (NARA); *Schedules of the New Mexico Territory Census of 1885*, Series: M846, roll 2; United States of America, Bureau of the Census, *Twelfth Census of the United States, 1900* (Washington, D.C.: National Archives and Records Administration, 1900), T623, 1854 rolls.

108. Nathan Boyd, "La Cenci," reprint from *The New Mexican Magazine* (1914), National Gallery of Art, 5, 26.

109. Boyd purchased the paintings from Chávez for an undisclosed sum and sent them to London for restoration. Just as Boyd had recognized their potential wealth from within an "old-time adobe house" when light was finally cast on darkness, so, too, did modern science remove the haze of doubt to reveal the paintings' past. Experts determined that "the removal of the old varnish had revealed flesh-tones of wonderful purity and transparency, especially in

the portrait of Beatrice, which was found to bear the signature of [Giuseppe] Mazzolini," a nineteenth-century Italian painter. Boyd, "La Cenci," 7.

110. Boyd's two portraits were loaned to the National Gallery of Art for two years, after which they were to be returned. The historical record runs cold after 1915. Smithsonian Institution, *Report*, 142.

Chapter 2. Working Frontier Dreams

1. This anecdote comes from Burnham, *Scouting on Two Continents*, 118; and from Blanche Burnham to Phoebe Blick, May 30, 1893, in Bradford and Bradford, eds., *An American Family on the African Frontier*, 54.
2. Burnham refers to cowpunchers, or cowboys, of the short-grass prairie in the central United States.
3. Burnham, *Scouting on Two Continents*, 118.
4. Charter of the British South Africa Company, No. 1, Papers Relating to the Administration of Matabeleland and Mashonaland, South African National Archives (SANA), Pretoria, C-7383. In the formalized charter the company's mission regarding native land had less of a social Darwinist bent in Clause 28: "The Company shall retain the mineral rights in, over, or under all land so assigned to natives; and, if the Company should require any such land for the purpose of mineral development, it shall be lawful for the Company to make application to the Land Commission, and upon good and sufficient cause shown, the Commission may order the land so required, or any portion thereof, to be given up, and assign to the natives concerned just compensation in land elsewhere, situate in as convenient a position as possible, and, as far as possible, of equal suitability for their requirements in other respects." An Agreement between Her Majesty's Government and the British South Africa Company relative to Matabeleland and Mashonaland, SANA, C-7383.
5. The company provided the administrative structure that would enable other privately held ventures to exploit mineral resources, and it would then levy taxes on any gold produced as well as profit from shares of approved concessions. Phimister, *An Economic and Social History of Zimbabwe 1890–1948*, 6–7.
6. Blanche Burnham to Phoebe Blick, May 30, 1893, in Bradford and Bradford, eds., *An American Family*, 54.
7. Frederick Burnham to Mother, January 15, 1893, in Bradford and Bradford, eds., *An American Family*, 5.
8. The Burnhams lived in a cabin owned by Moses Bennett, one of the first settlers along the Le Seur River a few miles southeast of Mankato. Hughes, *History of Blue Earth County*, 97.

9. Rev. Hall to Rev. D. B. Coe, February 17, 1858, American Home Mission Society Papers (hereafter AHMS Papers), Microfilm Edition.

10. Burnham, *Taking Chances*, 280, 281. Such stories drove Burnham to read the works of Speke, Baker, Livingstone, Du Chaillu, Henry Morton Stanley, and Captain Riley.

11. A. Kingsley Macomber, who connected with Burnham in California and southern Africa, reminisced of his early years when he "used to hide behind a Chinese laundry and read dime novels on African adventures etc." Macomber to Frederick Burnham, April 4, 1940, box 7, FRB-Yale.

12. Salvatore, "The Enterprise of Knowledge," 88.

13. Frederick Burnham to Blanche Burnham, May 30, 1890, and June 17, 1890, box 1, FRB-Yale.

14. "Blade," 1.

15. Burnham, *Scouting on Two Continents*, 80, 85.

16. Frederick Jackson Turner's famous presentation at the American Historical Association conference that year announced, for many, the end of the American frontier. For some, like Burnham, who would chase his own frontiers across continents, Turner's message would not have resonated. There is no evidence that Burnham was ever aware of Turner's proclamation. See Turner, "The Significance of the Frontier to American History."

17. Darter, *The Pioneers of Mashonaland*, 113; quoted in Phimister, *An Economic and Social History of Zimbabwe*, 7.

18. Thompson, *A History of South Africa*, 115.

19. On the mineral rushes and their resulting effects of South African history, see esp. Worger, *South Africa's City of Diamonds*; van Onselen, *Studies in the Social and Economic History*; Wheatcroft, *The Randlords*; and Rotberg, *The Founder*.

20. Wrobel, *Global West, American Frontier*, 3.

21. Burnham, *Scouting on Two Continents*, 127.

22. Ibid., 179.

23. Ibid., 159, 163.

24. Brechin, *Imperial San Francisco*, 53.

25. van Onselen, *The Cowboy Capitalist*.

26. Burnham, *Scouting on Two Continents*, 78.

27. Arthur Orner to Frederick Burnham, December 19, 1940, box 5, FRB-Yale.

28. Blanche Burnham to Mother, June 1, 1900, box 2, FRB-Yale.

29. "Engineer James Visits Prescott," 1; "Movements of Mining Men," *Mineral Wealth*, March 1, 1905, 9.

30. Frederick Burnham to Harris Hammond, June 10, 1925, box 6, FRB-Yale.

31. Burnham, *Scouting on Two Continents*, 265, 271.

32. These clubs, often located in metropolitan areas, fostered interpersonal connections among people (mostly men) with experience in countless regions. Burnham, for example, would write to his wife about meeting one person "at the Rocky Mt. Club—& O. B. Sarry from Klondike & a lot of other women, men & Englishmen from S.A. & Australia." Frederick Burnham to Blanche Burnham, November 1908, box 2, FRB-Yale; Grace Blick Ingram to the Blicks, April 20, 1896, and May 28, 1896, in Bradford and Bradford, eds., *An American Family*, 279.

33. Burnham, *Scouting on Two Continents*, 101, 99, 206. The entrepreneur, Zeederburg, organized a stage line between Natal and Johannesburg, "nearly as fast as our famous Pony Express."

34. Frederick Burnham to Rebecca Burnham, June 14 1893, Bradford and Bradford, eds., *An American Family*, 65; Frederick Burnham to Rebecca Burnham, April 14, 1896, Bradford and Bradford, eds., *An American Family*, 266; Frederick Burnham to Josiah Russell, August 5, 1894, Bradford and Bradford, eds., *An American Family*, 162; Burnham, *Scouting on Two Continents*, 128.

35. Blanche Burnham to the Blicks, April 24, 1893, Bradford and Bradford, eds., *An American Family*, 38. Blanche gives these details in the context of their drive seventy-five miles north of Durban, and by "coconut feathers" she is referring to the fibrous material found covering coconut shells.

36. Victorian readers, in general, interpreted Great Zimbabwe as the creation of a lost white race. On the development of this larger myth and its particular relevance to Southern Rhodesia, see Robinson, *The Lost White Tribe*, 108–19.

37. Ranger, *Revolt in Southern Rhodesia*, 23–42. Hole, *Selous*; Gann, *A History of Southern Rhodesia*; Galbraith, *Crown and Charter*; Mason, *The Birth of a Dilemma*; Mtshali, *Rhodesia*; Hole, *The Making of Rhodesia*.

38. Frederick Burnham to Rebecca Burnham, April 11, 1895, in Bradford and Bradford, eds., *An American Family*, 221–22.

39. Frederick Burnham to Charles Holder, November 24, 1913, box 6, FRB-Yale.

40. The field of literature around race and whiteness is large, but Matthew Jacobson's *Whiteness of a Different Color* gives an excellent analysis of the shifting notions of race and immigration in the United States in the Gilded Age and Progressive Era.

41. Burnham, *Scouting on Two Continents*, 319; Frederick Burnham to Richard Harding Davis, July 30, 1906, box 5, FRB-Yale.

42. John Blick to James Blick, January 22, 1895, in Bradford and Bradford, eds., *An American Family*, 211.

43. John Blick to Phoebe Blick, June 7, 1896, in Bradford and Bradford, eds., *An American Family*, 288.

44. Blanche Burnham to Blick Family, February 6, 1894, in Bradford and Bradford, eds., *An American Family*, 121.

45. Burnham, *Scouting on Two Continents*, 83.

46. Ibid., 218.

47. Frederick Burnham to Blanche Burnham, June 1908, box 2, FRB-Yale.

48. For an extended analysis of the virtues of masculinity forged in the western and imperial tradition, see Jacobson, *Barbarian Virtues*.

49. Rebecca Russell Burnham, Diary, July 4, 1895, FRB-Yale.

50. Davis, *Real Soldiers of Fortune*, 214.

51. Haggard, *Nada the Lily*, 5.

52. Grace Blick to Blick Family, November 29, 1894, in Bradford and Bradford, eds., *An American Family*, 192.

53. Blanche Burnham to Frederick Burnham, June 13, 1900, box 2, FRB-Yale; Blanche Burnham to Frederick Burnham, September 2, 1907, box 2, FRB-Yale; Blanche Burnham to Mother, February 3, 1901, box 2, FRB-Yale; Blanche Burnham to Frederick Burnham, September 2, 1907, box 2, FRB-Yale.

54. Frederick Burnham to Rebecca Burnham, August 18, 1895, in Bradford and Bradford, eds., *An American Family*, 236. This is, to my knowledge, the only instance of violence unrelated to imperialist goals in Burnham's memoirs, but his racial views, needless to say, were ever present and consistent. On the first steamer to Natal Burnham made reference to there being "plenty of savages, . . . closely allied to the monkey. In fact it is a question whether the savage has not deteriorated from a respectable tribe of monkeys." Frederick Burnham, likely to Josiah Russell (fragment), ca. September 1893, in Bradford and Bradford, eds., *An American Family*, 89. My thanks to Ben Kline for first calling my attention to this episode of branding, discussed in his senior paper for my class at Yale University in 2014.

55. Haggard, *King Solomon's Mines*, 47.

56. Burnham, *Scouting on Two Continents*, 202.

57. This is not the only instance of his amusement of astonishing indigenous audiences with technology that seemed banal to Burnham. In *Scouting on Two Continents* Burnham relates several such stories, including his wife's revealing of a sewing machine: "Whenever she started this mechanical wonder, sometimes as many as a hundred natives would come running from all directions and stand around in an awed circle so long as the needle moved. It was witchcraft of a high order, they decided; in fact, very strong medicine!"; and when a telegraph operator in Rhodesia uses telegraph wires and a bucket of water to shock an indigenous person; 126, 115, see also

154. On his own sense of adventure as a swashbuckling hero of his literary imagination, he wrote to his uncle in 1894, "I have only one thing more to do to free up the cup of romantic adventure here and that is to find the hidden treasure of King Lobengula," and he claimed to have "the thread of its unravelling in hand," Bradford and Bradford, *An American Family*, 198. An Arizona newspaper also noted that Burnham had "reached the ruins . . . of King Solomon's mines, made famous by Rider Haggard," "Burnham in Cananea," 3.

58. The device of the recently found treasure map was inspired by Robert Louis Stevenson's *Treasure Island*. Monsman, *H. Rider Haggard*, 74; Etherington, *Rider Haggard*, 39.

59. Etherington argues that Haggard's time in Natal shaped his beliefs in the potential for coexistence between the British and Zulus, and that Haggard "repudiates without fuss the whole notion of the white man's burden." Etherington, *Rider Haggard*, 4; Sandison, *The Wheel of Empire*, quoted in Etherington, *Rider Haggard*, 122.

60. Burnham's first published narrative of Wilson's Shangani Patrol was published in a two-part series in the *Westminster Gazette* in 1895.

61. This appears to be their first meeting, as Blanche describes Haggard giving the Burnhams his photo and several novels. Blanche Burnham to Rebecca Russell Burnham, May 12, 1895, in Bradford and Bradford, eds., *An American Family*, 226. Haggard, "Wilson's Last Fight," in Lang, ed., *The Red True Story Book*, 3–18.

62. Blanche Burnham to Mother, June 1, 1900, box 2, FRB-Yale.

63. Haggard wrote, "To the Memory of the Child, Nada Burnham, who 'bound all to her' and, while her father cut his way through the hordes of the Ingobo Regiment, perished of the hardships of war at Buluwayo on May 19, 1896, I dedicate this tale of faith triumphant over savagery and death," *The Wizard*, dedication.

64. Kemper, *A Splendid Savage*, 386. And Ranger offers a harsher assessment of Burnham's truthfulness, he first proposed that Burnham's killing of the M'Limo harmed more than it helped fight the resistance, a conclusion supported by Ian Phimister. See Kemper, "Appendix," in *Splendid Savage*, 373–86; Ranger, *Revolt in Southern Rhodesia*; Phimister, "Burnham, Frederick Russell (1861–1947)."

65. Rod Atkinson, a descendant of Burnham, has researched his ancestor's history in southern Africa deeply and maintains a position in accordance with Kemper's biography. This chapter does not focus at length on the controversy of Burnham's experiences in Rhodesia, but Atkinson makes an informed

argument that the Scout's exploits have been misinterpreted by historians for some time.

66. Frederick Burnham to Josiah Russell, ca. January 1894, in Bradford and Bradford, eds., *An American Family*, 115.

67. Frederick Burnham to Blanche Burnham, June 1900, box 2, FRB-Yale. Burnham began sharing outlines of his chapters by 1901. Arthur Bent to Fred Burnham, August 31, 1901, box 5, FRB-Yale.

68. Burnham, *Taking Chances*, vii.

69. See "Was Decorated by the King: Wonderful Career of Major Fred Burnham, Son of Sterling Pioneer," *Blue Earth County Enterprise*, May 17, 1907.

70. Burnham, *Scouting*, 1–2. Burnham repeated this tale in his memoirs (quoted here) as well as in private correspondence. See Frederick Burnham to H. Rider Haggard, May 9, 1922, box 6, FRB-Yale.

71. Lass, "The Removal from Minnesota of the Sioux and Winnebago Indians," 353.

72. The lands set aside for the Ho-Chunk, or Winnebago, Reservation, were Townships 106 and 107 in Ranges 24 and 25, located two miles from Burnham's home in Tivoli. "Treaty with the Winnebago, 1859," in Kappler, ed., *Indian Affairs*, 790; Chapman, "Map of Blue Earth County, Minnesota, 1865." My thanks to Cole Sutton for his assistance in obtaining the map.

73. Hughes, *History of Blue Earth County*, 7.

74. Thanks to Ruth Hansen of Brown County Recorder's Office and to Lorna Mutzke of the Nicollet County Recorder's Office for their assistance in checking their holdings for relevant land deeds. Michelle Johnson of the Waseca County Recorder's Office, a fellow history enthusiast and generous researcher, scoured both Waseca and Blue Earth County holdings.

75. In correspondence with Haggard in 1922, before publication of his memoir, Burnham claims that his mother, "being fleet of foot, escaped into the timber lands of the Minnesota River," a location far removed from both Sterling Center and Wilton. Frederick Burnham to Rider Haggard, July 18, 1922, Frederick Russell Burnham Papers, Stanford University (hereafter FRB-Stanford). This detail also appeared in Burnham's unpublished and ghostwritten memoir by Charles F. Holder, which specifies that Rebecca Burnham "reached the Minnesota River." "Manuscript by Prof. Holder," box 4, FRB-Stanford.

76. For these reports, see the collection at the Minnesota Historical Society, "Statistics concerning the Sioux Massacre: collected by town assessors for the county auditor to be filed with the Minnesota Historical Society, in accordance with the law passed March 7, 1881," Dakota Conflict of 1862

Manuscripts Collections, Minnesota Historical Society (St. Paul, Minn.). Available at http://www2.mnhs.org (last accessed April 21, 2017).

77. Neither Russell (mother) nor Burnham (father) appears as a claimant for compensation. Bakeman, *Index to Claimants for Depredations.*

78. Hall, "Journey into Southern Minnesota," 5. Curtis Dahlin also notes that "several thousand" fled their homes in Blue Earth County, but that "no large Dakota raiding parties made it into the county" during the attacks of 1862. Dahlin, *A History of the Dakota Uprising,* 61. One attack did take place in Tivoli in 1865, when a party of four raiders killed a nine-year-old boy, Frank York, but Burnham's story is clearly set in the 1862 attacks.

79. Child, *Child's History of Waseca County,* 130. The Ho-Chunk "had taken little or no part in the Sioux War," and though anxieties were understandably high at this time there was never an alliance with the Dakota. Carley, *The Dakota War of 1862,* 76. The word "further" here refers to the original attacks around New Ulm in Blue Earth County; rumors were rife (albeit incorrect) that the initial attack would lead to other violence to the east and south in Blue Earth County.

80. Quarterly Report from Edwin Burnham, April 24, 1860, AHMS Papers, Microfilm Edition.

81. There is some room to argue—but no direct evidence—that the Burnhams could have relocated to land owned by their in-laws in Sterling Center and thus were closer (but still far removed from) to Dakota attacks. Warrant No. 89,798 of the General Land Office transferred this land from Mary McIntyre, widow of Lieutenant Daniel McIntyre, to William Russell, April 20, 1862. I am convinced, however, that the Burnhams lived in Winona, given that Edwin had the deepest roots there. A family genealogy suggests this as well. Roderick H. Burnham, *Genealogical Records of Thomas Burnham,* 251. The 1865 state census places them there as well, but by 1869 they returned to Sterling Center, where Edwin Burnham purchased William Russell's general store and served as postmaster. Hughes, *History of Blue Earth County,* 295.

82. No correspondence from other family members repeats Burnham's origin story. Some mention a fire, but none in relation to any Dakota or Ho-Chunk attack. Transcript of "Statement of Mrs. Caroline Elizabeth Kinney" (original in Yale holdings), FRB-Stanford; Annie R. Reese to Mrs. Burnham, July 23, 1948, and November 30, 1953, box 1, FRB-Stanford.

83. "Burnham the Scout: Remarkable Career of a Minnesota Boy," 19; "Burnham Remembered," 2. My thanks to Heather Harren of the Blue Earth County Historical Society for locating the latter article, and to Linda Taylor of the Waseca History Center, for their assistance.

84. "Manuscript by Prof. Holder," box 4, FRB-Stanford.

85. Hughes, *History of Blue Earth County*, 295.

86. Born "on" an Indian reservation: Burnham, *Scouting on Two Continents*, 51.

87. Ibid., 10.

88. Frederick Burnham to Will Rogers, 1933, box 7, FRB-Yale.

89. Frederick Burnham, likely to Josiah Russell (fragment), ca. September 1893, in Bradford and Bradford, eds., *An American Family*, 89.

90. Frederick Burnham to Mother, May 3, 1893, in Bradford and Bradford, eds., *An American Family*, 43.

91. Burnham also writes to his brother-in-law that he closed on thirty-three square miles of land, or twenty thousand acres, in 1895. Frederick Burnham to James Blick, April 10, 1895, in Bradford and Bradford, eds., *An American Family*, 218. Interestingly, he also floated an idea to Rhodes and his personal secretary that the BSA Company should break up the lands into small farms and cultivation. One wonders if Burnham's pride was injured when Rhodes "laughed & ridiculed the idea," preferring "cattle colonization." J. W. Dove to Fred Burnham, September 4, 1895, box 9, FRB-Yale; Ricarde-Seaver to Cecil Rhodes, March 13, 1896, box 9, FRB-Yale.

92. Burnham, *Scouting on Two Continents*, 211. For a contemporary account of the creation of his northern explorations, see Hall and Neal, *The Ancient Ruins of Rhodesia*; see also Burnham, *Scouting on Two Continents*, 211.

93. Burnham visited the Cawston Ostrich Farm in Pasadena in 1911 to learn the basics of ostrich breeding, with an eye toward importing birds himself. Frederick Burnham to Honorable Willet M. Hays, April 23, 1911, box 6, FRB-Yale.

94. Frederick Burnham to Lincoln Fowler, March 23, 1907, box 9, FRB-Yale; Frederick Burnham to Blanche Burnham, June 12, 1908, box 2, FRB-Yale.

95. See Frederick Burnham to John Hays Hammond, September 1, 1910, box 9, FRB-Yale.

96. Frederick Burnham to John Ainsworth, December 10, 1906, box 5, FRB-Yale.

97. Frederick Burnham to H. Rider Haggard, April 21, 1922, box 6, FRB-Yale.

98. John Hays Hammond to Frederick Burnham, April 2, 1905, box 6, FRB-Yale; H. Rider Haggard to Frederick Burnham, box 6, FRB-Yale.

99. Frederick Burnham to John Hays Hammond, April 4, 1905, box 6, FRB-Yale.

100. Burnham used the phrase to characterize Harry Payne Whitney, a major financier and investor in the scheme. Frederick Burnham to Blanche Burnham, November 5, 1908, box 2, FRB-Yale.

101. Frederick Burnham to Blanche Burnham, November 18, 1908, box 2, FRB-Yale; Frederick Burnham to Blanche Burnham, November 2/3, 1908, box 2, FRB-Yale.

102. Burnham, *Scouting on Two Continents*, 357.

103. H. Rider Haggard to Frederick Burnham, May 22, 1909, box 6, FRB-Yale.

104. Frederick Burnham to Robert Baden-Powell, July 10, 1900, box 5, FRB-Yale.

105. Ibid.

106. Robert Baden-Powell to Frederick Burnham, September 28, 1900, box 5, FRB-Yale. Baden-Powell wrote in Burnham's second memoir, "Now a new age is sending our free farm folk swarming into cities. Our very chest measurements are shrinking. . . . The cavalry should be the strong eyes of the British Army. We need for it the efficiency of the Canadian Mounties, the endurance of your Indian scouts, the celerity of the Texas Rangers, the craftiness of the Hill Tribes of India." Burnham, *Taking Chances*, xxiii.

107. The People, Akron, Ohio, "Boy Scout Hypocrisy," 7.

108. "Scout Body Hit by Labor," 1; "Attacks the Innocent Boy Scouts," 1.

109. "Misrepresenting Organized Labor," 4; Cumming, "Asking Mr. Weber," 4; "The Boy Scouts," 2; Sanger, "The Boy Scout Movement," 16–21. Scholars, too, have debated the origins of the scouting movement within the context of the British Empire. Macleod, "Original Intent," in Block and Proctor, *Scouting Frontiers*, 13–27. The historiography of the scouting movement is large, given its multinational history. See esp. Jordan, *Modern Manhood and the Boy Scouts of America*; and Parsons, *Race, Resistance, and the Boy Scout Movement*. On the southern African origins of the scout movement, see Parsons, *"Een-Gonyama Gonyama!"* 57–66.

110. Frederick Burnham to Robert Baden-Powell, September 18, 1909, box 5, FRB-Yale.

111. Theodore Roosevelt to Frederick Burnham, May 16, 1927, box 8, FRB-Yale.

112. Burnham, *Taking Chances*, ix.

113. Ibid., xxi. He identifies this conversation with Baden-Powell as the first discussion on scouting that would lead to the creation of the Boy Scout movement.

114. Frederick Burnham to Uncle, January 13, 1896, box 1, FRB-Yale.

115. Burnham noted that Henry Labouchere's *Truth*, a British anti-imperialist paper, "stigmatized us as land pirates, hired assassins and murderers of the deepest dye." Frederick Burnham to Josiah Russell, February 17, 1894, in Bradford and Bradford, eds., *An American Family*, 126.

116. Frederick Burnham to Rebecca Russell Burnham, September 1, 1893, in Bradford and Bradford, eds., *An American Family*, 92–93.

Chapter 3. A Borderless Faith

1. Eaton, *Life Under Two Flags*, 76, 78.
2. Eaton to Strong, March 29, 1883, American Board of Commissioners for Foreign Missions Archives (hereafter ABCFM), Microfilm Edition, reel 723. To some degree Eaton expected never to return to his previous congregations. In a parting sermon to his pastorate in New Jersey, Eaton commented on being "about to take my leave for a long parting which, probably, will not suffer us to meet again as pastor and people." Eaton, "The First Martyrdom," 8.
3. Eaton to Clark, April 26, 1882, ABCFM, reel 723.
4. Eaton to Clark, May 4, 1882, ABCFM, reel 723.
5. The specific context of Gertrude Eaton differs somewhat from Greene's analysis, since Eaton worked in lockstep with her husband and was, by all measures, the driving force of the mission, and since Eaton did not advance a secular nationalist mission but rather a global, sacred, one. Greene, *The Canal Builders*, 228.
6. Previous work has noted the importance of female missionaries to overseas Protestant missions, but less so as an explicit strategy for entrance into the lives of men, as is the case with the Eatons in Chihuahua. On women missionaries abroad and the progressive impulse of the United States, see Hunter, *The Gospel of Gentility*. On expanding Protestantism in the American past, see especially Reeves-Ellington, Sklar, and Shemo, eds., *Competing Kingdoms*; Bays and Wacker, eds., *The Foreign Missionary Enterprise at Home*; and Pruitt, *A Looking-Glass for Ladies*. For the cultural work of foreign missions, among others, see Sanneh, *Translating the Message*.
7. Strong, *The Story of the American Board*, 7, 9.
8. The London Mission Society ultimately declined the proposed partnership.
9. Strong, *The Story of the American Board*, 35.
10. Studies on the history of Protestantism in Latin America are much more numerous than those that analyze Protestant ideologies as they relate to Mexico and specifically the Revolution. The standard text continues to be Baldwin, *Protestants and the Mexican Revolution*. See also her "Broken Traditions"; and Miller, "Protestantism and Radicalism in Mexico." Several previous dissertations also contribute to the subject. See especially

Helms, "Origins and Growth of Protestantism in Mexico to 1920"; and Penton, "Mexico's Reformation."

11. Ober, *Travels in Mexico*, 301.

12. Almada, *Resumen de historia del estado de Chihuahua*, 324–25.

13. Vaughan, *The State, Education, and Social Class in Mexico*, 42–44.

14. Eaton to Clark, July 12, 1884, ABCFM, reel 724.

15. Eaton to Clark, September 18, 1882, ABCFM, reel 723.

16. Eaton to Clark, December 30, 1882, ABCFM, reel 723.

17. Because many local families refused to help the Eatons learn Spanish on account of their Protestant heresy, it was only through Pratt's connections with her liberal-minded students that James Eaton first made contacts for the study of Spanish. Gertrude C. Eaton, "A Sketch of the Mission Work in Chihuahua," 496.

18. Eaton to Clark, December 30, 1882, ABCFM, reel 723.

19. Case to Clark, March 23 and May 19, 1885, ABCFM, reel 723. Case's own recounting of the *demonios* incident, in his letters, says the message was written on his window. A published version of this story, written much later, claims the message appeared in charcoal along the entirety of his house. See Case, *Thirty Years with the Mexicans*, 35.

20. *Reports of the Stations of the Mexico Mission of the American Board, 1900– 1901*, 21.

21. The missionary publication *Life and Light for Woman* reported several instances of outright violent threats against the Protestant missionaries in Mexico. See, for example, "Persecution in Mexico."

22. Eaton to Rev. J. O. Means, April 10, 1883, ABCFM, reel 723.

23. Eaton to Rev. J. O. Means, May 22, 1883, ABCFM, reel 723.

24. Eaton to E. K. Alden, July 31, 1883, ABCFM, reel 723. Gertrude's quote is paraphrased by James.

25. Eaton to E. K. Alden, August 17, 1883, ABCFM, reel 723. Eaton elaborated that a married missionary "seems to me to be an essential in this R. Cath. Country where the celibate priests so generally live with women not wives."

26. Eaton to Alden, September 9, 1883, ABCFM, reel 723.

27. Eaton to Clark, October 13, 1883, ABCFM, reel 723. See also Gertrude C. Eaton to E. K. Alden, September 14, 18, and 25, 1883, ABCFM, reel 724.

28. Eaton to Clark, October 22, 1883, ABCFM, reel 723.

29. Carrasco began work with the Eatons as a "Bible woman" in February 1884, an "intelligent convert" from San Luis Potosí, and spent five days a week going house to house and spreading the Protestant faith. The priests, Eaton wrote, denounced her. Eaton to Clark, August 18, 1884, ABCFM, reel 724.

30. The passing observation that the Mexicans sat near the back of the church, near the door, does not imply an implicit or explicit segregation. Rather, as Eaton had noted in previous correspondence, many—at the beginning of the mission work—preferred to stay on the literal outskirts of the ceremonies so as to not jeopardize their social standing with Catholic friends and neighbors.

31. Eaton to Clark, November 28, 1883, ABCFM, reel 723.

32. Eaton to Clark, March 14 and February 6, 1884, ABCFM, reel 724. James and often Gertrude traveled throughout Chihuahua to sell publications and check on the mission's "out stations"—less established centers of mission activity often directed by native lay preachers. The travel constituted a regular portion of their work, and, when possible, James relied on Gertrude's presence while in the field as much as he did in Chihuahua City. On a tour of the field in 1885 to visit other Protestant missions as far away as Mexico City he recorded that "Mrs. E's presence was of great value. It opened various house-doors, probably enabled me to secure the private room, and of course attracted to the service, with the singing. Where there are found so many 'American' adventurers, the company of my wife greatly increased the confidence of the people." Eaton to Clark, April 28, 1885, ABCFM, reel 724.

33. Gertrude C. Eaton, "A Sketch," 498.

34. Eaton to Clark, March 14, 1884, ABCFM, reel 724; Pascoe, *Relations of Rescue*, 113.

35. Rodriguez, *Creating the Practical Man of Modernity*, 32–33. On the deeper historical tensions between U.S. Protestantism and Mexican Catholicism and the cultural assumptions this difference enabled, see esp. Pinheiro, *Missionaries of Republicanism*.

36. Eaton to Clark, March 14, 1884, ABCFM, reel 724. Eaton also feared for his wife's health: "Mrs. Eaton is undertaking too much I fear. . . . She does not know how to spare herself, where she has an object to attain." Eaton to Clark, May 20, 1884, ABCFM, reel 724.

37. "Extracts from Mrs. J. D. Eaton's Letters," June 16, 1884, ABCFM, reel 724.

38. Eaton to Clark, July 12, 1884, ABCFM, reel 724. Eaton wrote to Clark from Lancaster, Wisconsin, and quoted his wife's letters to strengthen his request for an additional female missionary in Chihuahua.

39. Case, *Thirty Years with the Mexicans*, 19.

40. Eaton to Clark, August 18, 1884, ABCFM, reel 724.

41. Eaton to Clark, February 11, 1885, ABCFM, reel 724.

42. Romney, *The Mormon Colonies in Mexico*, 54–55.

43. Ibid., 43.

44. Ibid., 26.

45. The earliest form of their education endeavors began a year before in "a little room with a few rude benches," but what became the Colegio Chihuahuense began in earnest with the arrival of its first full-time teacher, a Miss Ferris, and with the new property secured in 1885. Gertrude C. Eaton, "A Sketch," 499.

46. Eaton to Clark, February 11, 1885, ABCFM, reel 724.

47. Eaton to Clark, September 21, 1885, ABCFM, reel 724.

48. Dunning, "Boarding School at Chihuahua," 207.

49. These figures are extracted from the annual reports of the Mission to Northern Mexico, and later of the Mission to Mexico, available in the ABCFM archives on reels 723, 724, and 726, in addition to the published reports held in the Special Collections Division of Yale Divinity School, New Haven, Conn.

50. Eaton to Rev. J. O. Means, April 10, 1883, ABCFM, reel 723.

51. "Summary Report of the Northern Mexico Mission (1890)," reel 726.

52. The inroads made through gender and through the presence of missionaries' families were repeated in other regions of Mexico. Hattie J. Crawford, writing from Hermosillo in 1887, noted the utility of having children in her mission work. "I have already calling acquaintances among several ladies of upper class," she wrote. "We call our little two yr. old, Mabel, the 'little missionary.' People are attracted to her, & thus led to speak to us. Often on the street, they stop to notice her, & take her into their houses, her mother naturally following. We have thus found entrance into several homes." Hattie Crawford to Clark, May 23, 1887, ABCFM, reel 723.

53. "Report of the Colegio Chihuahuense for 1896 & 1897," ABCFM, reel 726. The report stated that those who were not clean became "the subject of not at all complimentary remark."

54. Eaton to Clark, June 1, 1885, ABCFM, reel 724. Dutton eventually died from the disease, though it did not spread to others on the mission compound.

55. Burke, *Lifebuoy Men, Lux Women*; Dangarembga, *Nervous Conditions*.

56. "Report of the Colegio Chihuahuense for 1896 & 1897," ABCFM, reel 726. *Carretas* refers to horse-drawn carriage rides or races.

57. Eaton, *Life Under Two Flags*, 167; Eaton to Clark, May 19, 1886, ABCFM, reel 724; "Mission to Mexico Annual Report, July 1, 1885, to July 1, 1886," ABCFM, reel 723.

58. Eaton to Clark, March 14, 1884, and May 20, 1884, ABCFM, reel 724.

59. Eaton to Clark, April 28, 1885, ABCFM, reel 724.

60. Eaton to Clark, October 24, 1885, ABCFM, reel 724.

61. Eaton to Clark, February 23, 1886, ABCFM, reel 724.

62. Eaton to Clark, January 1, 1886, ABCFM, reel 724. By June Eaton's concern about denominationalism had subsided somewhat, as he claimed that the Southern Methodists in Chihuahua only made the Congregationalist followers "more loyal." Eaton to Clark, June 1, 1886, ABCFM, reel 724.

63. Eaton to Clark, April 1, 1884, ABCFM, reel 724.

64. Eaton to Clark, February 11, 1885, ABCFM, reel 724; Alden Case to Clark, March 18, 1889, ABCFM, reel 723.

65. News of the arrival of Miss Ferris came when Gertrude Eaton "was feeling worn and almost disheartened," her husband wrote, "with so much crying to be done, and only one pair of hands and one nervous system to respond to the call!" Eaton to Clark, January 30, 1886, ABCFM, reel 724. These moments indicate that even though the mission grew with continued success, the strain weighed heavy on both of the Eatons.

66. Report of 1887–88, ABCFM, reel 723.

67. For a history of the church building and the mission itself, see Breach, *El Templo "La Trinidad" en Chihuahua*. In addition to a significant American presence, Chihuahua had many immigrant Germans within the city proper.

68. *Eighty-Second Annual Report*, 21.

69. Ibid., xix.

70. James Eaton to Catherine Eaton, November 16, 1892, Private Collection of Mary Edgar, Lakewood, Colorado, 3–4. Always looking for signs of future growth through gendered networks, Eaton wrote to his mother, "All seats were taken, and some two hundred men stood during the whole time. We were especially pleased to see so many ladies."

71. James Eaton to Catherine Eaton, December 3, 1892, Private Collection of Mary Edgar, Lakewood, Colorado, 1.

72. Romero, "Mexico," 353.

73. "Report for the Year Ending June 30, 1903: Chihuahua and Out-Stations," ABCFM, reel 730.

74. Eaton to Barton, April 19, 1904, ABCFM, reel 731.

75. Eaton to Barton, October 14, 1903, ABCFM, reel 731.

76. Barton to Eaton, March 11, 1904, ABCFM, reel 102.

77. Offord, "The Boon of Health," 90.

78. Eaton to Barton, October 6, 1904, ABCFM, reel 731.

79. Barton to Eaton, January 15, 1905, ABCFM, reel 104.

80. Barton to Eaton, January 15, 1905, ABCFM, reel 104. Gertrude Eaton wavered between desperation and despair during her stay at Clifton Springs.

While she recovered, James Eaton took occasional side trips to attend board meetings in Boston. Gertrude's letters to him, infrequently quoted in Eaton's reports to Boston, capture her feelings of helplessness. "Many people have gone away from here," she wrote, "nearly every one who can get away, apparently. Up on this floor, there are only the old and chronic sufferers, who cannot get away. I class myself among them; for while I have no bodily suffering, (except the failure of eyesight), I seem to be a fixture, very much to my distress. Have you forgotten that you promised to come for me? Miss Dunning has offered to be of service to me in the journey; but would you advise as to return while in my present frame of mind? . . . You have never failed me before; can you not help me now? . . . I wonder where am I to spend the remainder of my days, now 'so long and dreary.' Oh I must find some way to peace and joy and love? For my soul abhors the evil, . . . Shall I soon be going?" Eaton to Barton, December 8, 1904, ABCFM, reel 731.

81. Eaton to Barton, February 3, 1905, ABCFM, reel 731.

82. Lennox, *The Health and Turnover of Missionaries*, 151. This study, appearing decades later than the focus of this chapter, drew on data starting in the middle nineteenth century.

83. Lennox, *The Health and Turnover of Missionaries*, 151. Mental disorders, the study claimed, appeared most frequently within the first ten years of mission work.

84. "Signs of the Times," 646.

85. Scharlieb, "An Address on the Care of the Health," 918.

86. Ibid.

87. In a communiqué written after arriving in Chihuahua Eaton lamented what he called Gertrude's "crazy talk" at the transfer point in Chicago. "She begged me to abandon her there," he wrote, and she "asked whether if she were to tell a policeman that she was an escaped murderess, he would not lock her up." Eaton to Barton, January 21, 1905, ABCFM, reel 731.

88. Eaton to Barton, February 11, 1905, ABCFM, reel 731.

89. Eaton to Barton, February 17, 1905, ABCFM, reel 731.

90. Twice before Gertrude had attempted to flee James's company, and he—for lack of an alternate strategy—played along to test her resolve. Once, in Chicago, when she threatened to turn herself in to a policeman, James encouraged her to do so, only for her to shy away at the last minute. Similarly, in Chihuahua, Gertrude revealed to James that she had hoped that the three of them (including Howard) would drown themselves in a lake near Estación Laguna. When James agreed and suggested they rather seek a lake north of the border, for practical purposes, Gertrude backed away from her plans.

91. Eaton to Barton, February 28, 1905, ABCFM, reel 731.

92. Eaton to Barton, March 7, 1905, ABCFM, reel 731.

93. Reports of the Stations of the Mexico Mission of the American Board, 1908–1909 (Chihuahua: Imprenta El Norte 1909), 26.

94. Ibid., 9.

95. On the redistribution of properties and regions of influence in Mexico among Protestant denominations, see Baldwin, *Protestants and the Mexican Revolution*, 155–75; and "A Forward Step in Mexico."

96. The Iglesia La Trinidad still stands and is operated by the Methodist Church today.

97. Long, "The Passing of Colegio Chihuahuense," 52.

98. Baldwin, "Broken Traditions," 255.

99. The Chicano activist Bert Corona identified the education of his mother, Margarita Escápite Salayandía, in the Colegio Chihuahuense as an influence in the formation of his subsequent political activism. See García, *Memories of Chicano History*.

100. This contrasts sharply with the claim that "the logic of women influencing women did not bring about converts." Welter, "She Hath Done What She Could," 637.

Chapter 4. Boers Without Borders

1. Portions of this chapter about the Boer experience in Mexico first appeared as "Outlanders and Inlanders: Boer Colonization in the U.S.-Mexican Borderlands, 1902–1905," in Brian Cannon and Jessie Embry, eds., *Immigrants in the Far West: Historical Identities and Experiences* (University of Utah Press, 2015); parts of the Boer history in New Mexico were published in "Cultural Imperialism and the Romanticized Frontier: From South Africa and Great Britain to New Mexico's Mesilla Valley," *Amerikastudien/American Studies* 59, no. 4, 535–52. Reproduced with permission.

2. Brian M. du Toit has written on the history of various Boer colonies. See his *Colonia Boer*; *The Boers in East Africa*; *Boer Settlers in the Southwest*; "A Boer Settlement That Was Never Settled"; and "Boers, Afrikaners, and Diasporas."

3. De Kay, "Mexico's Latent Wealth Awaiting Development."

4. Merritt was a cousin-in-law to President Theodore Roosevelt, who met with the Boer leaders on occasion. As a partial Dutch descendant, Roosevelt sympathized with their cause but was silent publicly out of political necessity.

5. Bond, Jr., *Gold Hunter*, 82.

6. Marshall Bond to Amy Bond, Oct. 27, 1902, Marshall Bond Papers, Beinecke Library, Yale University, WA MSS S-2358. Several of Bond's letters
are reprinted in Bond, Jr., *Gold Hunter*, 89–91.

7. De Kay, "Mexico's Latent Wealth."

8. Francisco Muñoz to Gral. Luis E. Torres, February 10, 1903; [?] to Lorenzo
Torres, February 10, 1903; Tomo (vol.) 1869, Archivo General del Estado de
Sonora (hereafter AGES).

9. To date, a few scholars have acknowledged the history of the Boer colony,
although it remains largely unknown. It teeters on the edge of several
historiographies—African, imperial, Mexican, and western—and would
appear to constitute little more than a quirky episode in the history of the
U.S.-Mexican borderlands. Published works include du Toit's *Boer Settlers
in the Southwest*; Hansen, "La Colonización Boer"; and Maluy, "Boer
Colonization in the Southwest." Each of these discusses the colony's residence in the U.S. Southwest in detail but does not offer much in terms of the
Mexican colony or the reasons for its failure.

10. "Snyman's Family Here," 1.

11. Railroads facilitated this growth in exports to Mexico. Over the same time
period this figure as a percentage of gross domestic product grew from
1.2 percent to 3.0 percent. These figures are compiled from the Bureau of
Statistics, *Commercial Relations of the United States with Foreign Countries*
for the years covered.

12. The two independent states were the South African Republic, or Zuid-
Afrikaansche Republiek, and the Orange Free State, or Oranjevrijstaat. For
a balanced overview of the war, see Nasson, *The War for South Africa*.

13. Thompson, *A History of South Africa*, 141. For a new interpretation of the
Jameson Raid that places much more emphasis on the participation of John
Hays Hammond, see van Onselen, *The Cowboy Capitalist*.

14. Lowry, "'The World's No Bigger than a Kraal,'" in Omissi and Thompson,
eds., *The Impact of the South African War*.

15. Thompson, *A History of South Africa*, 142.

16. Ibid., 143.

17. Marie Snyman Kroenig, "Minga's Life," Bill Brookreson family archive.

18. Interview with JoAnn Tessandori and John Stinnet, October 22, 2010. JoAnn's
and John's grandfather, John Snyman, was the brother of Martha and Marie.

19. Viljoen, *An Exiled General*, 49–50.

20. Barker, "Farm & Orchard." In American newspapers an exoticism also characterized the Boer colony in Mexico. News of the colony's founding constituted filler material for small papers throughout the United States. In

Owingsville, Kentucky, for example, a short news item describing the arrival of Boer colonists in Mexico ran alongside other earth-shattering headlines: "Attacked by an Angry Lion," "His Heart Cut in Two," and "He Killed a Bystander," *Owingsville Outlook*, 2. When looking at the Boer colony in historical perspective, though, its establishment in the borderlands around the dawn of the twentieth century connects the historiographies of Latin America and the U.S. West. The colony's past acquires new historical import.

21. Viljoen, *My Reminiscences*.

22. "Cause of Boers Given Approval," 9. See also American Transvaal League, *An Appeal to the Citizens of the United States*. It appears that most of the support for the national American Transvaal League came from immigrants or U.S. citizens with ties to Ireland and the Catholic Church, and Boer speakers often courted southerners by drawing parallels between the war and the U.S. Civil War.

23. "Mediation for Boers." The movement stalled for fear of angering England in an age of increasing U.S.–Anglo rapprochement.

24. See Kramer, "Empires, Exceptions, and Anglo-Saxons."

25. "Mason Denounces Boer War." Mason sought to change the U.S. policy of neutrality, and his resolution was forwarded to the Committee on Foreign Relations.

26. *New York Journal*, December 24, 1899; cited in Warwick, ed., *The South African War*.

27. "Eight Thousand Cry Sympathy for Boers."

28. Pro-Boer activists in the United States mounted an intensive campaign that changed "public opinion in the US overwhelmingly in favor of the Boers." Ferguson, *American Diplomacy and the Boer War*, ix. See esp. Ferguson's chapter "A Challenge to Isolation"; and Kettenring, *Krugerism in America*, 17–25.

29. "Boys' Letter to Krueger [*sic*]."

30. Davis, *With Both Armies*, 149.

31. "Boers with Buffalo Bill."

32. "Cheers for Boers"; "Fair Skies for Paraders"; "Snyman as a Guest"; "Boer and Briton"; "Cheers for Boers"; "Will Lecture in Boston"; "Citizens to Aid County Service"; "Santa Catalina Island."

33. "General Viljoen Delivers Lecture," 1; also "Un Boero Heroico," 1.

34. "General Viljoen Delivers Lecture," 1.

35. "Por qué perdió el Transvaal su Autonomía?"

36. On U.S. colonialism and the railroads, see esp. Robbins, *Colony and Empire*, 34.

37. Van der Merwe, "Sirkusbaas Frank Fillis."
38. "South African Boer War," 4. For more on the Boer War Spectacle, see Sutton, "'Transvaal Spectacles'"; van der Merwe, *Die Boere Sirkus van St. Louis*; and Hinckley, "When the Boer War Came to St. Louis."
39. "Boer War Spectacle Pleases Secretary Taft," 8.
40. Viljoen's memoir and novel were neither historical nor literary masterpieces, though his *My Reminiscences of the Anglo-Boer War* was reviewed widely due to his wartime fame.
41. For a biography of Viljoen that is more thorough regarding his preemigration days, see Meijer, *Generaal Ben Viljoen*.
42. Viljoen, *An Exiled General*, ix–x.
43. Other works that fit within this subgenre include Roosevelt, *The Rough Riders*; Burnham, *Scouting on Two Continents*; Conan Doyle, *A Desert Drama*; and many volumes in the western dime novel tradition. Books from southern New Mexico and the borderlands in this vein are Davis, *El Gringo*; Remington, *Pony Tracks*; Ruxton, *Adventures in Mexico*; Box, *Capt. James Box's Adventures*; and Harris, *By Path and Trail*.
44. The Wild West circuit was explicitly global at times. Buffalo Bill's "Congress of Rough Riders of the World," for example, gathered cowboys with other similarly romanticized figures ("Sons of the Soudan," "Cossacks of the Caucasus," etc.), thereby linking the American West with overseas frontiers.
45. "Roosevelt Beats a Boer at Shooting," 1; "Roosevelt a Crack Shot at Target," 1.
46. For two provocative works on fin de siècle masculinity and empire, see Hoganson, *Fighting for American Manhood*; and Bederman, *Manliness and Civilization*.
47. "Mr. Kipling's Homily."
48. For Rogers's letters from South Africa, see Wertheim and Bair, eds., *The Papers of Will Rogers*. "Texas Jack" was the adopted son of Texas Jack Omohundro, a close associate of Cody and other Western entertainers.
49. Viljoen wrote a number of articles in the *Los Angeles Times* and for several other adventure periodicals. See esp. his "The Story of a Piebald Horse"; "Pathos and Humor of War-Time"; and "Red Days in South Africa."
50. Viljoen, *Vierkleur*, 225.
51. The British were infamous for instituting a system of "refugee camps" as a way to control Boer families and, more important, the resources available to soldiers who persisted with guerilla warfare and extended the South African War until the bitter end.
52. Viljoen, *Vierkleur*, 378.
53. Ibid., 384–85.

54. On the closing frontier, see especially Wrobel, *The End of American Exceptionalism*.

55. In the context of the United States, Virginia Scharff has emphasized women and mobility. See her *Twenty Thousand Roads* and *Taking the Wheel*.

56. "Boer's Love Story," A7. Viljoen and Belfort had met at least twice before this encounter, the first in 1898, when he toured London before the breakout of war, and the second time in October 1902, when, fresh from St. Helena, Viljoen gave a talk at Queen's Hall in London.

57. "Boer's Love Story," A7.

58. Ancestry.com. UK Incoming Passenger Lists, 1878–1960 [database online]. Provo, UT, USA: Ancestry.com Operations Inc., 2008. Original data: Board of Trade: Commercial and Statistical Department and successors: Inwards Passenger Lists. Kew, Surrey, England: The National Archives of the UK (TNA). Series BT26, 1,472 pieces. Class: BT26; Piece: 221; Item: 74.

59. "Actress Shows Love Letters of a Man She Once Horsewhipped," 9.

60. "Boer's Love Story," A7.

61. "Viljoen and Bride Will Reside Here," 1. Helena claimed that Benjamin had deserted her in July 1903; "Viljoen Sued by His Wife," 6; "Deserted by General," 3.

62. "Actress Shows Love Letters of a Man She Once Horsewhipped," 9.

63. "General Viljoen Is Horsewhipped," 2.

64. "Boer Hero on Divorce Suit," 2.

65. "Actress Shows Love Letters of a Man She Once Horsewhipped," 9.

66. Viljoen to Belfort, October 27, 1904, published in "Actress Shows Love Letters of a Man She Once Horsewhipped," 9. Viljoen at first attempted to deny writing the letters but later confessed to his authorship; "General Viljoen Admits Writing the Letters," 2.

67. "General Viljoen Is Horsewhipped," 2.

68. "Boer General Is Thrashed," 1.

69. The *Tribune* ran a brief story that claimed, as did Viljoen, that the whipping was a planned media stunt to garner attention to Belfort's stateside performances.

70. "General Viljoen Is Horsewhipped," 2.

71. Infuriated by Viljoen's disavowal of their romance, Belfort gave a stack of their love letters to willing journalists. Excerpts from the letters ran from Washington, D.C., to San Francisco.

72. "The Mexican Budget," 2.

73. Bartlett, *Personal Narrative of Explorations*, 445.

74. See Wasserman, *Capitalists, Caciques, and Revolution*.

75. Snyman, in fact, arrived in Chihuahua little more than fifteen years after Mormon immigrants established a series of colonies there. The placement of the Mormon colonies in Mexican historiography occupies the same general space as the Boer colony. For a brief historical sketch of the two, in conversation with the Mennonite colonies established much later, see Lawrence Douglas Taylor Hansen, "La colonización con extranjeros."

76. "Establecimiento de colonias agrícolas," 91–96. He and Viljoen were contractually obligated to locate fifty families within three years, but Snyman, convinced of the colony's success, considered an option of an additional 363,800 acres and reportedly expected a thousand families to immigrate. By 1904 he would reduce this expectation to 80. "Boer Colony in Mexico," 4; "Boers Go to Mexico," 1.

77. C. J. Viljoen, *The Huguenot.*

78. Wasserman, *Capitalists, Caciques, and Revolution*, 106–8.

79. On the railroad, for example, a front-page news article boasted in 1899 that "if the railroads are clear signs of progress, Chihuahua proves its course through its progressive byways, thanks to the energy, honor, and labor not just of the government but of all its residents." "Chihuahua y sus Ferrocarriles," 1.

80. "Gen. Snyman Back," 5.

81. "Says It's Fixed," 1.

82. "Roosevelt a Crack Shot at Target."

83. Descriptions of the property come from James Demarest Eaton to James Barton, October 14, 1903, Archives of the ABCFM, Microfilm Edition (Detroit: Gale Group), reel 731.

84. Honeij, "Boers in Mexico," 3. Honeij's details about the colony are based on a letter by Lieutenant W. Malan.

85. Eaton, "The Boer Colony in Mexico," 807.

86. Details from the family's private religious service come from a contemporary journalist who visited the colony. See "Boers Successful."

87. James Demarest Eaton to James L. Barton, February 6, 1904, ABCFM, reel 731.

88. James Demarest Eaton to James L. Barton, August 25, 1904, ABCFM, reel 731. Eaton saw in the colony the chance to expand his mission work beyond Mexicans—as it had been limited—in the state.

89. For a concise snapshot of the Creel and Terrazas interests in Chihuahua and how they worked with foreign capitalists, see Wasserman, *Pesos and Politics*, 31–57.

90. José de Jesús Carmona Delgado quoted (with lyrics) in "La inundación de 1904," in Guillermo de la Paz Soto, ed., *Meoqui.*

91. "A Boer Colony's Industry," 15; "Boers Thriving in North Mexico," 15.

92. "Boer Colony is Prospering," 10.

93. "Boers Successful."

94. Honeij, "Boers in Mexico," 3.

95. Whetten, 19, quoted in Johnson, *Heartbeats of Colonia Diaz*; Johnson, *Heartbeats of Colonia Diaz*, 12; "New Mexico Likes Boers," I18.

96. Johnson, *Heartbeats of Colonia Diaz*, 55. Emphasis added.

97. A defining moment related in several Mormon memoirs occurs when the colony's president stands up to revolutionary orders to evacuate their settlements: "No, we will not leave the country. . . . This is our country as well as yours. We've lived here many years; our sons and daughters have been born here and some of our wives and children have been buried here. This is our home and the country is dear to us. We did not come here to fight, but to live in peace, to make homes and build up the country." Joseph C. Bentley, quoted in Hatch, *Colonia Juarez*, 219.

98. Romney, *The Mormon Colonies in Mexico*, 147.

99. Sutton, "Transvaal Spectacles," 271–72.

100. International Bureau of the American Republics, "Monthly Bulletin," 531.

101. Wasserman, *Capitalists, Caciques, and Revolution*, 121.

102. "Boer Colony Prospering."

103. Interview with Benjamin Viljoen III, May 10, 2010; Interview with JoAnn Tessandori and John Stinnett, October 22, 2010.

104. "Boers Buncoed."

105. Crawford, "Boers Leave Ortiz Colony."

106. Viljoen and Snyman agreement, Joann Ganoe papers.

107. James Demarest Eaton to James L. Barton, October 28, 1905, ABCFM, reel 731.

108. "Boers Thriving in North Mexico," 15.

109. James Demarest Eaton to James L. Barton, October 28, 1905, ABCFM, reel 731. The editor of the *Chihuahua Enterprise* published a notice of the colony's demise sympathetic to Snyman and cool, if indifferent, to the future of Viljoen. Viljoen complained in a letter to the editor, saying that the article contained "allegations capable of misleading the public at large and injuring me and my people who were compelled to abandon the colony." "General Viljoen Makes Brief Statement," 13.

110. Viljoen and others settled in the corridor between Fabens and El Paso, Texas, and Las Cruces, New Mexico. Families splintered off to all areas of the Southwest after the first generation of immigrants.

111. Quoted in James Demarest Eaton to James L. Barton, October 28, 1905, ABCFM, reel 731.

112. José M. Ponce de León, report in the *Periódico Oficial*, October 8, 1905. Those signing the agreement were Francisco Armendáriz, (Vicente) Hilario Guzmán, Serapio Jiménez, Merced Núñez, Máximo González, Benigno Armendáriz, Lázaro Caballero, Antonio Mata, Esteban Núñez, Dolores Ríos, Francisco Aragón, Candelario Tinajero, Alejandro Corrales, Aniceto Aragón, José Ramírez, Amado Mendoza, Zeferino Quiniones, Hipólito Mendoza, Justiniano Márquez, Alberto Armendáriz, Juan Flores, Cleofas Ontiveros, Dolores Núñez, Hipólito Castor, and José Cano. I include these names because descendants living on these lands today recall the German presence but not the South African.

113. On the transfer of property and the impressive scientific agriculture that Hoffmann brought to the new Hacienda de Humboldt, see "Scientific Agriculture Will Yield Best Results."

114. See, for example, Viljoen, "The Boer War," 12.

115. Giliomee, *The Afrikaners*, 45.

116. E-mail correspondence with Bill Brookreson.

117. Lummis, *The Land of Poco Tiempo*, 3.

118. Boyd, *Statehood for New Mexico*, 5.

119. Nicholl, *Observations*, 27.

120. Here I draw on Scott, *Weapons of the Weak*; and especially Joseph and Nugent, *Everyday Forms of State Formation*.

121. Lamar, *The Far Southwest*, 13; Holtby, Forty-Seventh Star, Chapter 2.

122. Nicholl, *Observations*, 27. Robert Campbell has written on a similar historical practice relating to colonial cultures and the exploration of Alaska. See his *In Darkest Alaska*.

123. Bureau of Immigration of the Terr. of New Mexico, *Dona Ana County*, 2.

124. Nicholl, *Observations*, 5–6.

125. Sargeaunt and Matthew, "Bradley, George Granville (1821–1903)." See esp. Nicholl Ellison, *A Child's Recollections of Tennyson*; and Nicholl, "Reminiscences of Royalty."

126. Ancestry.com, *1900 United States Federal Census* [database online], District 44, Precinct 8, La Mesa (Provo: Ancestry.com Operations Inc., 2004). Original data: United States of America, Bureau of the Census, *Twelfth Census of the United States, 1900* (Washington, D.C.: National Archives and Records Administration, 1900), T623, 1854 rolls. The regions break down as follows: Texas (5), Missouri (3), Tennessee (3), Ohio (2), Indiana (2), Poland (2), North Carolina (2), and Alabama, Arkansas, England, Ireland, Kentucky, and Pennsylvania (1).

127. Benjamin and Myrtle Viljoen, "Ignorance Abroad," private journal held by Benjamin and Letitia Viljoen, Fallon, Nevada.

128. Nicholl, *Observations*, 21. See especially her description of the Mexican peon in ethnographic terms (30–32) and her photo titled "Typical Mexicans" (21 ff.) in chapter 2, "The Mexican in New Mexico" (20–49).

129. On petty disagreements, see Rodgers, "La Mesa Primary," 7; and the responses by H. R. Hannum, C. T. Bartlett, and H. B. Holt the letter provoked two days later.

130. The book is in possession of Joann Ganoe of Palm Desert, California.

131. "Romance of Viljoen"; "Gen. Viljoen, Boer War Hero."

132. "Gen. Viljoen, Boer War Hero."

133. Studies on the origins of the Mexican Revolution form a mountain of scholarly work that has debated, among other aspects, the causes of the Revolution's outbreak, its regional variations, its reliance on landed elites dissatisfied by Porfirian cronyism as well as the significance of foreign capital to the emergence of armed conflict. Early studies trumpeted the transformative nature of the Revolution. These studies came under attack in the late 1960s from a number of revisionist scholars who looked at key figures and regions within Mexico to reveal the fractured nature of revolution. For a discussion of the arc of this historiography, see esp. Knight, "Interpreting the Mexican Revolution"; and Joseph and Nugent, "Popular Culture and State Formation in Revolutionary Mexico," in Joseph and Nugent, eds., *Everyday Forms of State Formation*. Hart's two studies are especially relevant to the conception of the West turning south vis-à-vis the Mexican Revolution. See his *Revolutionary Mexico* and *Empire and Revolution*. Regional analyses on the ties between U.S. capitalist expansion and social agitation include, among others, Wasserman, *Capitalists, Caciques, and Revolution*; Ruiz, *The People of Sonora and Yankee Capitalists*; Joseph, *Revolution from Without*; Tinker Salas, *In the Shadow of the Eagles*; and Evans, *Bound in Twine*. The most far-reaching and nuanced study of the Revolution remains Knight's *The Mexican Revolution*.

134. The Taft–Díaz meeting remains understudied in the borderlands literature, though one work has viewed the history through the frame of clandestine politics and international security. See Harris and Sadler, *The Secret War in El Paso*.

135. Madero's brother, Gustavo, described his meeting on March 18, 1911, with the "famous General . . . known in Europe for his heroic resistance against the English." This quote, taken from a letter written by Francisco Madero Sr., to Federico González Garza, was reprinted twenty-five years later and documents that Viljoen approached the Maderos twice to assist their cause. Valades, "No Se Exigía La Caída De Don Porfirio," 9.

136. "Arrest Two Who Tried to Kill Madero," 7; "Devilliers Confiesa Su Participación," 2.

137. "Viljoen Tells Story of Plot," 1. For more on the plot to assassinate Madero and its Boer connections, see esp. "Plot on Life of Madero Alleged," 1; "Plot to Murder Madero and Seize Republic Exposed at El Paso," 2; "Arrests in Plot to Slay Madero," 1; "Pascual Orozco y Viljoen Se Dejaron Sobornar," 1; and "Alfred Henry Lewis Discusses the Anti-Madero 'Plot,'" 1.

138. Madero, *La sucesión presidencial*, 187–98.

139. Plasencia, *Obras Completas de Francisco Ignacio Madero*, 198.

140. "Viljoen Gets a Federal Offer," 2.

141. Viljoen, "Tribe at War for a Century," II, 10.

Chapter 5. Frontier in the Borderlands

1. Portions of this chapter first appeared as "When the West Turned South: Making Home Lands in Revolutionary Sonora," *Western Historical Quarterly* 45 (Autumn 2014), 299–319. Copyright by Western History Association. Reprinted by permission.

2. Viljoen, "Tribe at War for a Century," II, 10.

3. Edward Spicer's three volumes on Yaqui culture and history established a strong foundation for the development of recent Yaqui historiography. See his *Potam*; *The Yaquis*; and *People of Pascua*. For a general history of the Yoemem and the Yaqui Valley, see Hu-DeHart, *Missionaries, Miners, and Indians* and her *Yaqui Resistance and Survival*; as well as Dabdoub, *Historia de el valle del yaqui*.

4. On early Yaqui–Mexico interactions, see Folsom, *The Yaquis and the Empire*.

5. This is not to be confused with the false distinction between *pacíficos* (pacified Yaquis) and *broncos* (rebels) identified by contemporary officials. Hu-DeHart, *Yaqui Resistance and Survival*, 123. On Yaqui resistance, see also Velasco Toro, *Los Yaquis*. A case study of acculturation and resistance can be found in Moctezuma Zamarrón, *De pascolas y venados*.

6. Sonora and Sinaloa Irrigation Company, *Report of Col. E. S. Nettleton*.

7. For more on the early formation of the SSIC, see Logan, "Yaqui Land Convertible Stock"; Bogener, *Ditches Across the Desert*, 263; Stegner, *Beyond the Hundredth Meridian*, 310.

8. Logan, "Report on the Condition of the Work on the Yaqui Canal," 1.

9. Logan, "Yaqui Land Convertible Stock," 4. In a separate but similar pamphlet Logan addresses the Yaqui as peaceful and willing collaborators with the SSIC. See Hu-DeHart, *Yaqui Resistance and Survival*, 128; and Logan, *Irrigation on the Yaqui River*.

10. Logan quotes Ward, *Mexico in 1827*, 583. Contrary to Ward's description of docility, the Yaqui leader Juan de la Cruz Banderas was leading active violence against the state in 1827.

11. Hu-DeHart, *Yaqui Resistance and Survival*, 166. For the relationship between Yaqui labor and international financial and commodity markets, see Evans, *Bound in Twine*; and Joseph, *Revolution from Without*.

12. Harris, *By Path and Trail*, 1, 6, 8, 57.

13. By 1908 Buffalo Bill adventure serials featured the Yaquis in several numbers, published by Prentiss Ingraham, including *Buffalo Bill Among the Man-Eaters*; *Buffalo Bill's Totem*; and *Cave of the Skulls*. For another fantasy novel with romanticized natives, see Coolidge, *Yaqui Drums*, 9, 69, 114.

14. For more on the colonial gaze, see esp. Pratt, *Imperial Eyes*.

15. Here I especially think of Ferdinand Oyono's *Une Vie de Boy*, a novel set in colonial French and German Cameroon. See also Britwum, "Regard, mémoire, témoignage," and Bourgeacq, "The Eye Motif and Narrative Strategy." Such metaphors and tropes emerge most forcefully in the writing of the folklorist and scholar J. Frank Dobie. Among his first works Dobie produced two volumes of treasure lore: *Coronado's Children* and *Apache Gold and Yaqui Silver*. Often characterized as a regionalist, Dobie also fits within the broader American folklore movement. His portrayal of Indians of the Southwest and Mexico and their relationship to gold stands as a bellwether for larger cultural forces. Built upon oral sources as well as secondary material in newspapers and magazines from the early twentieth century, his stories capture the perceived connections between indigenous silence, secrecy, the native gaze, and threatened violence. See Dobie, *Apache Gold and Yaqui Silver*, 157, 154–55; and also Clois Stone, "J. Frank Dobie and the American Folklore Movement."

16. Smith, *Under the Cactus Flag*, 243; Roberts, *With the Invader*, 135.

17. Folsom, *The Yaquis and the Empire*, 208.

18. Misreading the sociopolitics of Yaqui participation in a borderland (capitalist) economy was not unique to Maytorena or to the Mexican state and American capitalists. In his analysis of Quaker–Miami interactions at Fort Wayne in 1804, Daniel Richter has shown how ways of understanding Indians "proved almost impervious to contradictory evidence, in part because it so conveniently justified Euro-American expropriation of Indian land and resources." Richter, *Trade, Land, and Power*, 228.

19. Alarcón Menchaca, *José María Maytorena*, 62, 49.

20. Hu-DeHart, *Resistance and Survival*, 170.

21. Day, *Morris B. Parker's Mules, Mines and Me*, 119. Between 1902 and 1908 the Díaz administration attempted to deport all Yaquis from Sonora, sending them to plantations in central Mexico's Valle Nacional and to henequen plantations in Yucatán. This instance of ethnic cleansing contributed to growing resentment during the Porfiriato and played a significant role in the rise of revolutionary sentiment nationwide and overseas. These—the harshest—years of Yaqui persecution followed previous rebellions by Cajeme and Tetabiate in the late 1800s, both of whom rebelled in part owing to increasing encroachment on Yaqui lands. American investors exacerbated these tensions in the region after 1880, when railroads stretched south of the border, and especially after 1890 in the Yaqui River Valley.

22. The company that formed, the Yaqui Delta Land and Water Company, sold bonds for the RCC. For the sake of simplicity I continue to refer to the company by its original name.

23. Box 24, FRB-Yale.

24. Frederick Burnham to Blanche Burnham, June 24/29, 1909, box 3, FRB-Yale. These photos were taken during Charles F. Holder's visit to Burnham in 1909 to identify an Aztecan stone discovered by Burnham in the countryside while overseeing construction of irrigation canals. The photos have Burnham's handwriting on them, both at the time and after, but viewing the annotations along with temporal identifiers such as "now" suggests he was aware of the ethnic cleansing during his employment on RCC lands.

25. Wright, "Report of Touring and Evangelistic Work."

26. Horace Wagner to Secretary of the American Board, May 27, 1910, ABCFM, reel 735; Horace Wagner to ABCFM, August 14, 1911, ABCFM, reel 735.

27. Wagner to Enoch Bell, December 19, 1919, ABCFM, reel 735.

28. Velázquez Estrada, *México en la mirada de John Kenneth Turner*, 211.

29. Ibid., 76.

30. Turner, *Barbarous Mexico*, 35–36. Turner's association of Yaquis with American slavery was intentionally provocative. The conditions of the Yaquis—and certainly their labor on the henequen plantations in Yucatán—were described by contemporary observers and labor activists as slavery. See esp. Padilla Ramos, *Progreso y libertad*; and her *"Los Partes Fragmentados"* (in press with the Instituto Nacional de Antropología e Historia). Padilla Ramos looks into the accusations of slavery, real or perceived, and does not find conclusive evidence of bodies for sale. She believes that current evidence in Yaqui oral histories relating to slavery comes from a feedback loop originating in Turner's writings. Regardless, Yaquis today are convinced the experiences of their ancestors constituted slavery. In some ways it is a moot point, as slavery is

less noteworthy historically as the explicit extermination campaigns and deportations that characterize the excesses of the Porfiriato. For the Yaqui role within larger historical dynamics, see esp. Joseph, *Revolution from Without*; and Evans, *Bound in Twine*.

31. Interview with Santiago Matuz, Loma de Guamúchil, June 21, 2012.

32. Herminia Estrella López, quoted in Aguilar Zeleny, ed., *Tres procesos*, 41.

33. Interview with María Jesús Valenzuela and Teodulo Rubio Jusacamea, Pótam, June 28, 2012. Jusacamea: "Desde pequeños la mama previene al niño para estar a la defensiva del yori, desde que lo está amamantando y le dice 'mira, ahí viene el yori . . .' Valenzuela: "Viene el yori y quita el pecho." Jusacamea: "Cuidado, te va hacer daño!"

34. Jaime León, ed., *Testimonios de una mujer yaqui*, prologue.

35. Hunt, "'*Le Bebe en Brousse*';" Stoler, "Making Empire Respectable"; and chapter 3 of her *Carnal Knowledge and Imperial Power*. Intimacy and breastfeeding appear to be widely applicable to the colonial encounter. For other regional studies, see Bartlett, "Black Breasts, White Milk?"; Spear, "Colonial Intimacies"; and Nestel, "(Ad)ministering Angels."

36. Turner, *Barbarous Mexico*, 219.

37. Ricarda León Flores discussed the courting between Madero and Sibalaume as well as later attempts by Maytorena to influence the intransigent Yaqui leader. Of the eight pueblos, only Huírivis accepted Madero's invitation. Jaime León, ed., *Testimonios de una mujer yaqui*, 23.

38. This binary of *caujomem/torocoyorim* emerged in varied forms, at times as *broncos/mansos* (rebels/peaceful).

39. Jaime León, ed., *Testimonios de una mujer yaqui*, 8. León Flores says the Yaquis have stronger "razones," than *yorim*, which I interpret as "beliefs," but "reasons" or "claims [to the land]" may come closer to her intended meaning.

40. Ibid., 29.

41. Ibid., 21.

42. Erickson, *Yaqui Homeland and Homeplace*, 97. On space, gender, and the home, see also Zayas, "Tres mujeres curanderas yoremes," in Olavarría, ed., *Símbolos del desierto*; and Sánchez, "Comer y cocinar," in the same volume.

43. Jaime León, ed., *Testimonios de una mujer yaqui*, 22.

44. This statement applies only to the early months of the Revolution, when tentative peace agreements were reached. With the eventual failure of Madero's peace commissions, politically motivated violence on settlers increased.

45. W. C. Laughlin et al. to Gobernador, November 6, 1912, Archivo Histórico del Gobierno del Estado de Sonora, Ramo Oficialía Mayor, Tomo (vol.) 2784, Hermosillo, Sonora.

46. Two studies have explored the various peace commissions, although from tangential approaches. See Torúa Cienfuegos, *Frontera en llamas*; and Alarcón Menchaca, *José María Maytorena*.

47. The government expected the treaty to solve its confrontations with the Yaquis. Officials from around the country wrote to congratulate Governor Luis Torres on the monumental accomplishment. Tomo 2424, Oficialía Mayor, AGES. For an oral history of the Treaty of 1909, see Padilla Ramos, "Los Partes Fragmentados," 226.

48. For letters reporting the disturbing signs (but few depredations) of Yaquis in the fields, see Tomo 2424 and 2425, Oficialía Mayor, AGES.

49. Compiled from Tomos 2664 and 2783, Oficialía Mayor, AGES.

50. Secretaría de Relaciones Exteriores to Gobernador de Sonora, January 16, 1911, Tomo 2829, Oficialía Mayor, AGES.

51. Frederick Burnham to Sweetheart, July 27, 1911, box 3, FRB-Yale.

52. Escalante to Secretary of State of Sonora, November 21, 1911, Tomo 2664, Oficialía Mayor, AGES. The suggestion that this was a "show of power" is my own.

53. Francisco Vasques et al. to Gobernador del Estado, May 31, 1911, Tomo 2664, Oficialía Mayor, AGES.

54. [Anonymous] to Gobernador del Estado, June 29, 1911, Tomo 2829, Oficialía Mayor, AGES.

55. Benjamin Viljoen to Francisco Madero, November 22, 1911, reprinted in Fabela, ed., *Documentos Históricos de la Revolución Mexicana*, 316.

56. Pedro García to Gobernador del Estado, July 6, 1911, Tomo 2664, Oficialía Mayor, AGES.

57. "El Gobernador Maytorena y Viljoen Conferenciaron con los Yaquis," 4. Other sources place the number somewhere between two hundred and nine hundred.

58. Viljoen, "Tribe at War for a Century," II, 10.

59. Alarcón Menchaca, *José María Maytorena*, 223.

60. Flores Magón, "La Bandera Roja en Sonora," 3.

61. Flores Magón, "Adelante, Hermanos Yaquis!" 3; "Says Viljoen Has No Right in Office," 6. The strength of the Flores Magón brothers' message stands in contrast to the weakening financial position of *Regeneración*. Lomnitz, *The Return of Comrade Ricardo Flores Magón*, 398.

62. "Viljoen Meets with Chiefs of Yaquis," 5.

63. Viljoen, "Tribe at War for a Century," II, 10.

64. Ibid.

65. "Seems a Cinch for Senor Madero," 2; "Gen. Viljoen Ill in Hospital at Empalme," 2.

66. Interview with Camilo Flores, June 22, 2012, Vícam Switch, Sonora.

67. Viljoen, "Tribe at War for a Century," II, 10.

68. Ibid.

69. Flores Magón, "Notas al Vuelo," 1.

70. In the case of Madero, I define "imperial" here as the overwhelming power of the científico-Díaz-capitalist alliance.

71. Viljoen, "Tribe at War for a Century," II, 10.

72. Spicer, *Cycles of Conquest*, 511.

73. Viljoen, "Tribe at War for a Century," II, 10.

74. W. C. O., "Reyes Rebellion is Assuming Threatening Front," 4.

75. "La Verdadera Situación de los Yaquis," 6.

76. "B. J. Viljoen Said to Be Mexican Citizen Now," 1. *El País* reported that Viljoen, his translator Enrique V. Anaya, and another Boer immigrant, W. Malan, became citizens on January 31, 1912. "Nuevos Ciudadanos," 3.

77. Viljoen, "Tribe at War for a Century," II, 10.

78. "Yaqui Chiefs Settle All Troubles," 1.

79. Viljoen, "Tribe at War for a Century," II, 10.

80. "Gen. Viljoen to Go After Yaquis," 3. Viljoen wrote to deny this report in a desperate and final attempt to keep the peace. "Hace Declaraciones el Sr. General Viljoen," 1; "Los Indios Yaquis Siguen en Su Criminal Tarea," 5.

81. Viljoen to Gayou, January 31, 1912, Tomo 2783, Oficialía Mayor, AGES. Espinosa declined and signaled his intent to move further into the sierras to Torocopobampo. See Viljoen to Gayou, February 6, 1912, Tomos 2782 and 2783, Oficialía Mayor, AGES.

82. "Acierto del Gobierno en la cuestión del Yaqui," written for *La Voz de Sonora* in 1912, Tomo 2782, Oficialía Mayor, AGES.

83. Viljoen to Maytorena, March 1912, Tomo 2782, Oficialía Mayor, AGES.

84. Sources containing oral histories include Kelley, *Yaqui Women*; Aguilar Zeleny, ed., *Tres procesos de lucha*; Erickson, *Yaqui Homeland and Homeplace*; Jaime León, ed., *Testimonios de una mujer yaqui*; Padilla Ramos, *Los irredentos parias* and "Los Partes Fragmentados."

85. This includes the late Yaqui wars (1880–1909) through the Mexican Revolution (1910–20) to the last uprising (1926–27).

86. On the *testimonio*, see esp. Beverley, *Testimonio*; Gugelberger, ed., *The Real Thing*; and Gugelberger and Kearney, "Voices for the Voiceless," part of a special issue on testimonial literature.

87. Some oral histories contain clues to situate them chronologically, but most leave historians with little to pinpoint the accuracy of their powerful images. This is not meant to imply, however, that chronology does not figure as part of Yaqui conceptions of the past. Edward Spicer, in his study of

Pótam, consulted a number of historical specialists in Ráhum, Vícam, and elsewhere who compiled a list of notable events and dates that is in accordance with published history from outside the pueblos. Spicer, *Potam*, 24.

88. It became clear during my interviews and discussions that, like the oral histories I sought, I, too, drifted along currents determined by my gender. In much the same way Kirstin Erickson found herself steered toward women during her fieldwork, my contacts mostly recommended Yaqui men to participate in my research. Despite this gendered experience in the present, the emphasis on women, children, and families persisted in the vast majority of interviews I conducted. What's more, I did not focus on obtaining stories of any kind other than those about the late Yaqui wars and the Revolution. The gendered and family approach became evident only after the interview phase of this fieldwork and archival work. I told the collaborators that I sought to collect stories from the Yaqui wars and Revolution for a dissertation on capitalism and culture in the U.S.–Mexican borderlands.

89. Interview with Cornelio Molina, Vícam Switch, June 26, 2012. "Es parte, ahora, de lo que conocemos como archivos abiertos, todavía, para la reflexión sobre la continuidad de la vida del yaqui. . . . Es una narrativa de vida."

90. Interview with Teodoro Buitimea, Loma de Guamúchil, June 24, 2012; Interview with Camilo Flores, Vícam Switch, June 22, 2012. Buitimea: "No había tiempo de enterrarlos, se hinchaban ahí en el sol. Imagínate con este solazo." Flores: "Dice que lo castigaban a azotes según la falta, una cubeta como esa, con naranjas agrias partida por la mitad. Una vez que lo azotaban, el que ya estaba comisionado le daban una media naranja agria."

91. Interview with Santiago Matuz, Loma de Guamúchil, June 21, 2012. "Éste era un destacamento de soldados, tenían sitiada el agua. Entonces los yaquis para tomar agua, tuvieron que pelear contra ellos. . . . Ahí llegó un tío, Pedro Mátus, comandante. . . . Eran miles de soldados a los que tenía que enfrentar."

92. Interview with Jesús Matuz, Cócorit, June 21, 2012. "Él, al ver que morían muchos en cada guerra, vendió su alma en el *yo'o juara*. . . . Él quiso vender su alma al diablo para matar soldados. Son mil soldados los que se le dieron en el *yo'o juara* y llegando a los mil soldados, fallecería. Tal como sucedió."

93. Interview with Don "Nacho" Ignacio Ochoa Álvarez, Pótam, June 20, 2012, and June 28, 2012. "Le pusieron unas esposas o algo así. Se lo llevaron. Y le dijo el papá al hijo: 'Vete, mijito, ahorita voa volver te voa a traer unos dulces,' le dijo. Nunca volvió ni lo volvió a ver jamás, dice."

94. As told to Kirstin Erickson in her *Yaqui Homeland and Homeplace*, 46.

95. Hernández, *Las Razas Indígenas de Sonora*, 172 ff., cited in Moisés, Kelley, and Holden, *The Tall Candle*, xvii. For the other principal sources for the Yaqui wars between 1899 and 1902, see Balbás, *Recuerdos del Yaqui*; and Troncoso, *Las Guerras con las Tribus Yaqui y Mayo*.

96. Interview with María de Jesús López Valenzuela and Teodulo Rubio Jusacamea, Pótam, June 28, 2012. Jusacamea: "Y andaban sin alimentos, enfermos, mujeres embarazadas. . . . No tenían ni agua para tomar. Asi como escapar nomas, sin llevar nada: ni ropa, ni nada, ni armas. Únicamente luchar para escaparse nomás."

97. Interview with Teodoro Buitimea, Loma de Guamúchil, June 24, 2012. "Ahí en Estación Lencho, cuando las mujeres eran las gentes que eran tomadas prisioneras eran enviadas para el centro del país. Pero las mujeres eran tomadas como botín de guerra; ahí en esa casona de piedra. Y las violaban, cabrón. Las violaban las veces que quisieran. Ni les preguntaban si querían o no querían, las violaban. . . . Mi abuela fue botín de guerra, y de ese botín de guerra nació mi mamá."

98. Spicer traces the various "cycles of conquest" on peoples in the U.S.-Mexican borderlands in his influential work, *Cycles of Conquest*.

99. Moisés, Kelley, and Holden, *The Tall Candle*, xlii; Kelley, *Yaqui Women*, 35–36.

100. Erickson, drawing on Spicer, discusses the unique aspects of Yaqui *compadrazgo* in contemporary society. Erickson, *Yaqui Homeland and Homeplace*, 116–19.

101. The interviews occurred over three weeks in June 2012.

102. Flores Magón to Maytorena, May 28, 1912, Tomo 2782, Oficialía Mayor, AGES.

103. Maytorena to Ramos, July 8, 1912, Tomo 2782, Oficialía Mayor, AGES.

104. Benjamin Viljoen, Letter to the Editor, II9.

105. H. A. Sibbet to Frederick Burnham, March 11, 1912, box 13, FRB-Yale.

106. Frederick Burnham to Secretary of War, April 22, 1912, box 13, FRB-Yale. Burnham later told the Sunsetter Club in Los Angeles that "at one time, when the situation seemed very desperate, I was delegated to go to the States and bring back some bloodhounds to be used in hunting down some blood-thirsty bands that had been assassinating our people over a considerable period." Frederick Burnham, "My Life Among a Lost White Tribe in the Sierras," address delivered to the Sunsetter Club of Southern California, November 1932, box 4, FRB-Stanford.

107. Frederick Burnham to H. A. Sibbet, n.d. [response to letter of April 22, 1912], box 13, FRB-Yale, Yale University.

108. L. H. Taylor to Ignacio Quiroz, June 18, 1912, Tomo 2784–85, Oficialía Mayor, AGES.
109. Led by Victoriano Huerta and assisted by Félix Díaz, a nephew of Porfirio Díaz, the coup intensified revolutionary factionalism and fighting.
110. Sara Pérez, Madero's widow, gave an interview to the journalist Robert Murray three years later regarding her petitions for asylum. For the entire transcript, see Fabela, ed., *Historia Diplomática de la Revolución Mexicana*, 175–83. The coup against Madero divided the nation and compelled the Sonoran government not to recognize the Huerta administration. Merchants and *hacendados* felt the short-term effects most acutely through economic instability. The long-term effects of renewed upheaval eventually forced Yaqui leaders to align themselves with varied factions vying for power. Of the major revolutionary fighters, the Yaquis most forcefully supported Álvaro Obregón, a peasant who grew up eighty kilometers south of the Yaqui homelands in Mayo country and made a name for himself fighting in the Sonoran North. Obregón, like his predecessors, recognized the value of Yaqui support. He courted officials, promising to recognize indigenous lands once military triumph was achieved. For more on the Yaquis and revolutionary factions, see Ramírez Zavala, *La participación de los Yaquis en la Revolución*, 33–115.
111. The Mexican government did not recognize (parts of) Yaqui lands until a 1937 agreement reached under President Lázaro Cárdenas.
112. Frederick Burnham to H. Rider Haggard, April 21, 1922, box 6, FRB-Yale.

Epilogue

1. Marjorie Van Meter to Mother, December 14, 1912, Marjorie Van Meter Letters, 1912–16, Center for Southwest Research, University of New Mexico. For more on Van Meter and the 1913 activities in Sonora, see my "When the West Turned South."
2. "John Hays Hammond, American Miner and Millionaire," 8.
3. [Gibbon] statement, n.d., box 35, Ellen Bergman Collection of Thomas E. Gibbon Papers (hereafter EBCHL), Huntington Library, San Marino, California.
4. The arms consisted of "six Gatlin guns, poles, limbers and carriages" and three hundred boxes of ammunition. Biklaski to Webster, August 18, 1915, Investigative Case Files of the Bureau of Investigation 1908–22, NARA M1085, roll 857, page 30.
5. Blaisdell, "Harry Chandler and the Mexican Border Intrigue."

6. Translation of Maytorena to Viljoen, July 4, 1914, box 21, EBCHL. When Chandler first learned of the damaging telegraph from Maytorena to Viljoen, he wrote to Gibbon simply, "My dear Tom: Please do nothing with this until you see me. H.C." Chandler to Gibbon, July 11, 1914, box 21, EBCHL. The company subsequently crafted a statement and distanced itself from Viljoen's conflicting interests by responding, "Viljoen's friendship and military service with Madero, Carranza, Villa, Maytorena, and other Mexican leaders may have caused Aviles to assume to correspond with him during his employment by the C&M Ranch Company as if he were still connected with the Mexican army; if so, it was without the knowledge of Chandler or any other officer of the Company, who otherwise would have promptly disavowed and stopped the same," [Gibbon] statement, n.d., box 35, EBCHL.
7. Viljoen denied all such claims, calling the whole case a frame-up, though his previous scandals in the press reveal a willingness to cover up personally and professionally damaging news stories. "Viljoen Says Indictment Against Him is 'Frame Up,'" 12.
8. Gibbon to Bridge, July 17, 1919, box 20, EBCHL.
9. Adelman and Aron, "From Borderlands to Borders."
10. This included J. M. Danziger of the Compañía de la Baja California, L. Lindsay of the Esperanza Timber Company, and E. L. Doheny of the Mexican Petroleum Company. "Mexico—Mr. Doheny," box 35, Thomas E. Gibbon Papers, Huntington Library, San Marino, California.
11. Gibbon to Hudson, April 1918, box 32, Thomas E. Gibbon Papers.
12. Jaime León, ed., *Testimonios de una mujer yaqui*, 44–45.
13. Ibid., 45.
14. Ibid., 46, 47.
15. Ibid., 47.
16. "New Mexico Likes Boers," I, 18.
17. It appears that Viljoen filed papers in order to counter complaints among Mexican elites that a foreign citizen was acting on behalf of Madero and the government. When Viljoen renounced his post because of health complications, he apparently withdrew his naturalization papers, retaining his U.S. citizenship.
18. "Boer General Eager for War," 2; see also "Boer War Given Start in U.S.," 3.
19. "Snyman Ranch Saved by Official Action," 2; "Alega ahora que está convencido de la honradez de Snyman a quien había secuestrado porque compró su rancho," *El País*, March 12, 1914, 2; "Villa Saves Snyman Ranch," I2.
20. Snyman to Bond, July 27, 1916, Marshall Bond Papers, Beinecke Library, Yale University, WA MSS S-2358.

21. Interview with George M. "Dogie" Jones, Watrous, New Mexico, October 20, 2011.
22. Yaquis must purchase potable water or face the consequences of exposing their families to pesticides in the groundwater from nearby industrial agriculture.
23. For a view of how perceptions of ethnicity have shaped struggles for land and water in the Yaqui valley, see McGuire, *Politics and Ethnicity on the Río Yaqui.*

Bibliography

Institutional Archives and Libraries

Albert B. Fall Papers, Huntington Library, San Marino, California.

American Board of Commissioners for Foreign Missions Papers. Microfilm edition (Research Publications).

American Board of Commissioners for Foreign Missions Archives, 1810–1961, Houghton Library, Harvard University, Cambridge, Massachusetts.

American Home Missionary Society Papers, 1816–1936. Microfilm edition (Microfilming Corporation of America).

Ancestry Library Edition, distributed by ProQuest.

Archivo General del Estado de Sonora, Hermosillo, Sonora.

Beinecke Rare Book and Manuscript Library, Yale University, New Haven, Connecticut.

Blue Earth County Historical Society, Mankato, Minnesota.

Center for Southwest Research and Special Collections, University of New Mexico, Albuquerque, New Mexico.

DeGolyer Library, Southern Methodist University, Dallas, Texas.

Ellen Bergman Collection of Thomas E. Gibbon Papers, Huntington Library, San Marino, California.

Fisher Family Papers, 1758–1896, Southern Historical Collection, University of North Carolina at Chapel Hill. Microfilm edition, Slavery in Ante-Bellum Southern Industries (University Publications of America).

Fondo Ejecutivo, Ramo de Oficialía Mayor, Archivo General del Estado de Sonora, Hermosillo, Sonora.

Frederick Russell Burnham Papers, Manuscripts and Archives, Sterling Memorial Library, Yale University, New Haven, Connecticut.

Frederick Russell Burnham Papers, Hoover Institution Library and Archives, Stanford University, Stanford, California.

Howard Russell Butler Papers, Archives of American Art, Smithsonian Institution, Washington, D.C.

Huntington Library, San Marino, California.

Instituto Chihuahuense de la Cultura, Universidad Autónoma de Chihuahua, Chihuahua City, Chihuahua.

John Hays Hammond Papers, Manuscripts and Archives, Sterling Memorial Library, Yale University, New Haven, Connecticut.
Marshall Bond, Jr., Papers, Beinecke Rare Book and Manuscript Library, Yale University, New Haven, Connecticut.
National Archives and Records Service of South Africa, Pretoria, South Africa.
New Mexico State University Archives and Special Collections, Las Cruces, New Mexico.
Thomas E. Gibbon Papers, Huntington Library, San Marino, California.
Western Americana Collection, Beinecke Rare Book and Manuscript Library, Yale University, New Haven, Connecticut.
William Henry Bishop Papers, Manuscripts and Archives, Sterling Memorial Library, Yale University, New Haven, Connecticut.

Privately Held Archives

PAPERS RELATING TO THE VILJOEN AND SNYMAN COLONY IN THE BORDERLANDS

Michele Bottaro, Santa Rosa, California.
Bill Brookreson, Seattle, Washington.
Joann and Thomas Ganoe, Desert Springs, California.
George and Joyce Ann Jones, Watrous, New Mexico.
Hendrik Christo Viljoen, Stellenbosch, South Africa.
Jeannine Viljoen, Santa Rosa, California.
Benjamin Viljoen III and Letitia Viljoen, Fallon, Nevada.

PAPERS RELATING TO JAMES AND GERTRUDE EATON

Mary Edgar, Longwood, Colorado.
Sue Martine, Gilbert, Arizona.

Oral History Interviews

YAQUI INTERVIEWEES

Anonymous informant, Pótam, June 27, 2012.
Teodoro Buitimea Flores, Loma de Guamúchil, June 24, 2012.
José Gabriel Estrella Molina, Ráhum, June 20, 2012.
Camilo Flores Jiménez, Vícam Switch, June 22, 2012.
Guadalupe Gotogopisio, interviewed by Teodoro Buitimea, Loma de Guamúchil, June 26, 2012.
José Juan Hernández, Loma de Guamúchil, June 21, 2012.

Juan Silverio Jaime León, Ciudad Obregón, June 25, 2012.

María de Jesús López Valenzuela and Teodulo Rubio Jusacamea, Pótam, June 28, 2012.

Jesús Matuz González, Loma de Guamúchil, June 21, 2012.

Santiago Matuz Anguamea, Loma de Guamúchil, June 21, 2012.

Alejandro Molina, Pótam, June 20, 2012.

Cornelio Molina Valencia, Vícam Switch, June 26, 2012.

Ignacio Ochoa Álvarez, Pótam, June 20, 2012, and June 28, 2012.

BOER DESCENDANT INTERVIEWEES

Benjamin Viljoen III, Fallon, Nevada, May 10, 2010.

George M. "Dogie" Jones, Watrous, New Mexico, October 20, 2011.

Group interview with Benjamin Viljoen III, John Stinnett, JoAnn Tessandori, and Joann Ganoe, Lake Tahoe, Nevada, October 22, 2010.

John Stinnett and JoAnn Tessandori, Lake Tahoe, Nevada, October 22, 2010.

Newspaper Databases

Access Newspaper Archive, published by Heritage Archives, Ltd.

Hispanic American Newspapers, 1808–1908, published by Readex.

Latin American Newspapers, 1805–1922, published by Readex.

Chronicling America: Historic American Newspapers, published by the Library of Congress.

Historical Newspapers Complete, published by ProQuest.

Newspaper and Magazine Articles

"A Boer Colony's Industry." *Deseret Evening News*, March 19, 1904, 15.

"A Forward Step in Mexico." *Missionary Review of the World* 27, no. 9 (September 1914): 641–43.

"Actress Shows Love Letters of a Man She Once Horsewhipped." *Oakland Tribune*, April 4, 1905.

"Alega ahora que está convencido de la honradez de Snyman a quien había secuestrado porque compró su rancho." *El País*, March 12, 1914, 2.

"Alfred Henry Lewis Discusses the Anti-Madero 'Plot.'" *El Paso Herald*, May 30, 1911, 1.

"Arrest Two Who Tried to Kill Madero." *Tacoma Times*, May 29, 1911, 7.

"Arrests in Plot to Slay Madero." *New York Times*, May 29, 1911, 1.

"Attacks the Innocent Boy Scouts." *Daily Gate City* (Keokuk, Iowa), July 21, 1911, 1.

"B. J. Viljoen Said to Be Mexican Citizen Now." *El Paso Herald*, January 23, 1912, 1.

Barker, F. C. "Farm & Orchard: The Boer at Home." *Rio Grande Republican,* December 1, 1899.

"Blade." *Copper Era*, August 13, 1903, 1.

"Boer and Briton: Snyman and McVane on Transvaal War." *Boston Daily Globe*, April 27, 1901.

"Boer Colony in Mexico." *New-York Tribune,* June 1, 1903, 4.

"Boer Colony is Prospering." *San Francisco Call*, August 22, 1905, 10.

"Boer Colony Prospering." *Los Angeles Times*, August 28, 1905.

"Boer General Eager for War." *Ogden Standard*, September 3, 1914, 2.

"Boer General Is Thrashed." *Evening Times* (Cumberland, Md.), January 20, 1905, 1.

"Boer Hero on Divorce Suit." *Valentine Democrat*, September 15, 1904, 2.

"Boer War Given Start in U.S." *El Paso Herald*, October 21, 1914, 3.

"Boer War Spectacle Pleases Secretary Taft." *St. Louis Republic*, August 13, 1904, 8.

"Boer's Love Story." *Los Angeles Times*, December 31, 1903, A7.

"Boers Buncoed." *Los Angeles Times*, October 15, 1905.

"Boers Go to Mexico." *Minneapolis Journal*, May 12, 1903, 1.

"Boers Successful." *Chihuahua Enterprise*, August 12, 1905.

"Boers Thriving in North Mexico." *Mexican Herald*, March 13, 1904, 15.

"Boers with Buffalo Bill." *New York Times*, March 29, 1901.

"Boys' Letter to Krueger [*sic*]." *New York Times*, April 10, 1900.

"Burnham in Cananea." *Bisbee Daily Review*, March 8, 1907, 3.

"Burnham Remembered." *Mankato Daily Review*, February 3, 1900, 2.

"Burnham the Scout: Remarkable Career of a Minnesota Boy Who Has Been Appointed on Gen. Roberts' Personal Staff." *Saint Paul Globe*, January 28, 1899, 19.

"Cause of Boers Given Approval." *San Francisco Call*, February 21, 1902, 9.

"Cheers for Boers." *Boston Daily Globe*, March 6, 1901.

"Chihuahua y sus Ferrocarriles." *Correo de Chihuahua*, February 23, 1899, 1.

"Citizens to Aid County Service." *Chicago Daily Tribune,* January 13, 1903.

Crawford, W. W. "Boers Leave Ortiz Colony." *Los Angeles Times*, November 7, 1905.

Cumming, George. "Asking Mr. Weber." *Evening Times-Republican,* July 27, 1911, 4.

de Kay, Charles. "Mexico's Latent Wealth Awaiting Development." *New York Times*, December 7, 1902.

"Deserted by General." *Minneapolis Journal*, September 8, 1904, 3.

"Devilliers Confiesa Su Participación." *El Diario*, May 30, 1911, 2.

Dunning, Mary. "Boarding School at Chihuahua." *Life and Light for Woman* 24, no. 5 (May 1894).

Eaton, Gertrude C. "A Sketch of the Mission Work in Chihuahua." *Life and Light for Woman* 22, no. 11 (November 1892).

Eaton, James D. "The Boer Colony in Mexico: An Interesting Christian Settlement and Its Bearing on the Future." *Congregationalist and Christian World* 90, no. 48 (December 2, 1905).

"Eight Thousand Cry Sympathy for Boers." *New York Times*, January 30, 1900.

"El Gobernador Maytorena y Viljoen Conferenciaron con los Yaquis." *El Imparcial*, November 5, 1911, 4.

"Engineer James Visits Prescott." *Bisbee Daily Review*, July 17, 1910, 1.

"Establecimiento de colonias agrícolas en el Estado de Chihuahua." In *Anales de la Legislación Federal*, 91–96. Mexico City: Impr. de E. Dublán, 1904.

"Fair Skies for Paraders." *New York Tribune*, March 19, 1901.

Flores Magón, Ricardo. "Adelante, Hermanos Yaquis!" *Regeneración*, October 7, 1911, 3.

———. "La Bandera Roja en Sonora." *Regeneración*, October 28, 1911, 3.

———. "Notas al Vuelo." *Regeneración*, May 27, 1911, 1.

"Gen. Snyman Back." *Mexican Herald*, December 10, 1902, 5.

"Gen. Viljoen Ill in Hospital at Empalme." *El Paso Herald*, November 15, 1911, 2.

"Gen. Viljoen to Go After Yaquis." *Mexican Herald*, January 30, 1912, 3.

"Gen. Viljoen, Boer War Hero." *Washington Times*, February 24, 1907.

"General Viljoen Admits Writing the Letters." *Washington Times*, March 30, 1905, 2.

"General Viljoen Delivers Lecture." *Mexican Herald*, February 3, 1903, 1.

"General Viljoen Is Horsewhipped." *Richmond Planet*, February 25, 1905, 2.

"General Viljoen Makes Brief Statement." *Chihuahua Enterprise*, October 21, 1905, 13.

"Hace Declaraciones el Sr. General Viljoen." *Nueva Era*, February 2, 1912, 1.

Hall, Richard. "Journey into Southern Minnesota." *Home Missionary*, 36, no. 1 (May 1863): 5.

"He Killed a Bystander." *Owingsville (Ky.) Outlook*, September 24, 1903, 2.

Honeij, James A. "Boers in Mexico." *Tufts College Graduate* 2, no. 1 (April 1904).

"John Hays Hammond, American Miner and Millionaire, Has Plan to Pacify Warlike Yaquis, Whom Mexico Can't Subdue." *Arizona Republican*, January 13, 1913, 8.

Johnstone, R. Bruce. "Tzintzuntzan and Its 'Titian': My Adventures When Trying to Photograph It." *World Wide Magazine* 6 (1900): 25–31.

"La Verdadera Situación de los Yaquis: Declaraciones del Señor Gobernador del Estado de Sonora." *Nueva Era*, December 10, 1911, 6.

Long, Mary F. "The Passing of Colegio Chihuahuense." *Life and Light for Woman*
  49, no. 2 (February 1919).
"Los Indios Yaquis Siguen en Su Criminal Tarea." *El País*, February 3, 1912, 5.
"Mason Denounces Boer War." *New York Times*, December 12, 1899.
"Mediation for Boers." *Washington Post*, May 6, 1902.
"Misrepresenting Organized Labor." *Evening Times-Republican*, July 24, 1911, 4.
"Movements of Mining Men." *Mineral Wealth*, March 1, 1905, 9.
"Mr. Kipling on Shooting." *New York Times*, August 3, 1902.
"Mr. Kipling's Homily." *New York Tribune*, August 16, 1902.
"New Mexico Likes Boers." *Los Angeles Times*, March 29, 1909, I, 18.
"Not a 'Titian' After All." *New York Times*, June 28, 1891.
"Nuevos Ciudadanos." *El País*, February 7, 1912, 3.
Offord, John A. "The Boon of Health: Where Rest and Recuperation May be
  Secured—Skillful Practitioners and Congenial Company." *New York Ob-
  server*, January 18, 1912.
"Painting Called a Titian in a Remote Mexican Hamlet." *New York Sun*, May 13,
  1906, 2.
"Pascual Orozco y Viljoen Se Dejaron Sobornar Con Objeto de Conocer Todos
  Los Planes." *El Diario*, May 29, 1911, 1.
"Persecution in Mexico." *Life and Light for Woman* 20, no. 8 (August 1890): 155–57.
"Plot on Life of Madero Alleged." *El Paso Herald*, May 29, 1911, 1.
"Plot to Murder Madero and 'Seize Republic'" Exposed at El Paso." *Des Moines
  News*, May 29, 1911, 2.
"Por qué perdió el Transvaal su Autonomía?" *Correo de Mexico*, September 8,
  1902.
Rodgers, E. A. "La Mesa Primary." *El Paso Herald* August 23, 1910, 7.
"Romance of Viljoen." *Suburbanite Economist*, February 22, 1907.
"Roosevelt a Crack Shot at Target." *San Francisco Chronicle*, August 3, 1902, 1.
"Roosevelt Beats a Boer at Shooting." *St. Louis Republic*, August 3, 1902, III, 1.
Sanger, Margaret. "The Boy Scout Movement." *Il Proletario*, April 6, 1912, 16–21.
"Santa Catalina Island." *Los Angeles Times*, October 2, 1901.
"Says It's Fixed," *Mexican Herald*, April 20, 1903, 1.
"Says Viljoen Has No Right in Office." *Mexican Herald*, February 9, 1912, 6.
"Scientific Agriculture will Yield Best Results." *Mexican Herald*, December 2,
  1906.
"Scout Body Hit by Labor." *Rock Island (Ill.) Argus*, July 20, 1911, 1.
"Seems a Cinch for Senor [sic] Madero." *Bisbee Daily Review*, September 9, 1911, 2.
"Sherlock Holmes of All Outdoors." *San Francisco Sunday Call*, April 9, 1911, 11.
"Signs of the Times." *Missionary Review of the World* 21, no. 9 (September 1908).

"Snyman as a Guest." *Boston Daily Globe*, March 28, 1901.

"Snyman Ranch Saved by Official Action." *Mexican Herald,* March 24, 1914, 2.

"Snyman's Family Here: General Tells Why Boers Did Not Choose America." *New-York Tribune,* June 3, 1903.

"South African Boer War." *Perrysburg (Oh.) Journal*, September 30, 1904, 4.

"Statistics concerning the Sioux Massacre: collected by town assessors for the county auditor to be filed with the Minnesota Historical Society, in accordance with the law passed March 7, 1881." Dakota Conflict of 1862 Manuscripts Collections, Minnesota Historical Society, St. Paul, Minn. Available at http://www2.mnhs.org (last accessed April 21, 2017).

"The Boy Scouts." *Goodwin's Weekly*, October 14, 1911, 2.

"The Lure of Peril: Major Burnham, American, Fights for British in South Africa." *Marion (Oh.) Daily Mirror*, December 17, 1910, 7.

"The Mexican Budget." *Galveston Daily News*, October 19, 1902, 2.

The People, Akron, Ohio. "Boy Scout Hypocrisy." *Evening Standard*, May 11, 1911, 7.

"Un Boero Heroico." *El País*, February 3, 1903, 1.

Valades, José C. "No Se Exigía La Caída de Don Porfirio." *La Prensa* June 14, 1936, 9.

"Viljoen and Bride Will Reside Here." *St. Louis Republic*, July 16, 1905, 1.

Viljoen, B. J. "The Boer War." *El Paso Herald*, November 11, 1914, 12.

———. Letter to the Editor. *Los Angeles Times*, August 18, 1915, II, 9.

———. "Pathos and Humor of War-Time: An Article." *Adventure* (December 1916): 158–61.

———. "Red Days in South Africa." *Adventure* (January 1918): 142–49.

———. "The Story of a Piebald Horse." *Adventure* (May 1916).

———. "Tribe at War for a Century." *Los Angeles Times*, February 13, 1916, II, 10.

"Viljoen Gets a Federal Offer." *El Paso Herald*, May 18, 1911, 2.

"Viljoen Meets with Chiefs of Yaquis." *Bisbee Daily Review*, November 8, 1911, 5.

"Viljoen Says Indictment Against Him is 'Frame Up.'" *El Paso Herald*, March 18, 1915, 12.

"Viljoen Sued by His Wife." *New York Times*, September 2, 1904, 6.

"Viljoen Tells Story of Plot." *El Paso Morning Times*, May 30, 1911, 1.

"Villa Saves Snyman Ranch." *Los Angeles Times*, March 11, 1914, I, 2.

Warner, Charles Dudley. "Mexican Notes: Tczintczuntczan—Uruapan." *Harper's New Monthly Magazine* 75, no. 447 (August 1887): 443–53.

"Was Decorated by the King: Wonderful Career of Major Fred Burnham, Son of Sterling Pioneer." *Blue Earth County (Minn.) Enterprise*, May 17, 1907.

W. C. O. "Reyes Rebellion is Assuming Threatening Front." *Regeneración*, December 16, 1911, 4.
"Will Lecture in Boston." *Boston Daily Globe*, February 17, 1901.
"Yaqui Chiefs Settle All Troubles." *El Paso Herald*, December 30, 1911, 1.

Books and Journal Articles

Adelman, Jeremy, and Stephen Aron. "From Borderlands to Borders: Empires, Nation-States, and the Peoples in Between in North American History." *American Historical Review* 104, no. 3 (June 1999): 814–41.
Aguilar Zeleny, Alejandro, ed. *Tres procesos de lucha por la sobrevivencia de la tribu yaqui: Testimonios*. s.l.: PACMYC, 1994.
Aguirre, Robert D. *Informal Empire: Mexico and Central America in Victorian Culture*. Minneapolis: University of Minnesota Press, 2005.
Alarcón Menchaca, Laura. *José María Maytorena: Una biografía política*. Jalisco: El Colegio de Jalisco, 2008.
Almada Breach, Carmen Elba. *El Templo "La Trinidad" en Chihuahua: 100 Años de Historia (1892–1992)*. Chihuahua: Litho Offset Atlas, 1994.
Almada, Francisco R. *Resumen de historia del estado de Chihuahua*. Mexico City: s.n., 1955.
American Transvaal League. *An Appeal to the Citizens of the United States*. Chicago: American Transvaal League, 1901.
Anaya Ferreira, Nair María. *La Otredad del Mestizaje: América Latina en la Literatura Inglesa*. Mexico City: Universidad Nacional Autónoma de México, 2001.
Anderson, Alex D. *The American and Mexican Pacific Railway, or, Transcontinental Short Line*. Washington, D.C.: Gibson Brothers, 1883.
Anderson, George B. *History of New Mexico: Its Resources and People*. Vol. 2. Los Angeles: Pacific States, 1907.
Bakeman, Mary H. *Index to Claimants for Depredations Following the Dakota War of 1862*. Roseville, Minn.: Park Genealogical Books, 2001.
Balbás, Manuel. *Recuerdos del Yaqui: Principales episodios durante la campaña de 1899 a 1901*. Mexico City: Sociedad de Edición y Librería Franco Americana, 1927.
Baldwin, Deborah J. "Broken Traditions: Mexican Revolutionaries and Protestant Allegiances." *The Americas* 40, no. 2 (October 1983): 229–58.
———. *Protestants and the Mexican Revolution: Missionaries, Ministers, and Social Change*. Urbana: University of Illinois Press, 1990.
Bancroft, Frederic. *The Life of William H. Seward*. Vol. 2. New York: Harper and Brothers, 1900.

Bancroft, Hubert Howe. *The Works of Hubert Howe Bancroft*. Vol. 16: *History of the North Mexican States and Texas*. San Francisco: History Company, 1889.

Barron, Clarence W. *The Mexican Problem*. Boston: Houghton Mifflin, 1917.

Bartlett, Alison. "Black Breasts, White Milk? Ways of Constructing Breastfeeding and Race in Australia." *Australian Feminist Studies* 19, no. 45 (November 2004): 341–55.

Bartlett, John Russell. *Personal Narrative of Explorations and Incidents in Texas, New Mexico, California, Sonora, and Chihuahua*. New York: D. Appleton, 1854.

Baxter, Sylvester. *Spanish-Colonial Architecture in Mexico*. Boston: J. B. Millet, 1901.

Bays, Daniel H., and Grant Wacker, eds. *The Foreign Missionary Enterprise at Home: Explorations in North American Cultural History*. Tuscaloosa: University of Alabama Press, 2003.

Becker, Kate Harbes. *Biography of Christian Reid*. Belmont, N.C.: S. H. Junior College, 1941.

Bederman, Gail. *Manliness and Civilization: A Cultural History of Gender and Race in the United States, 1880–1917*. Chicago: University of Chicago Press, 1996.

Beinart, William, and Peter A. Coates. *Environment and History: The Taming of Nature in the USA and South Africa*. Abingdon: Routledge, 1995.

Belich, James. *Replenishing the Earth: The Settler Revolution and the Rise of the Anglo-World, 1783–1939*. Oxford: Oxford University Press, 2009.

Beverley, John. *Testimonio: On the Politics of Truth*. Minneapolis: University of Minnesota Press, 2004.

Bishop, William Henry. *Old Mexico and Her Lost Provinces: A Journey in Mexico, Southern California, and Arizona by Way of Cuba*. New York: Harper and Brothers, 1883.

Blackhawk, Ned. *Violence Over the Land: Indians and Empires in the Early American West*. Cambridge: Harvard University Press, 2006.

Blaisdell, Lowell L. "Harry Chandler and the Mexican Border Intrigue, 1914–1917." *Pacific Historical Review* 35, no. 4 (November 1966): 385–93.

Bogener, Steve. *Ditches Across the Desert: Irrigation in the Lower Pecos Valley*. Lubbock: Texas Tech University Press, 2003.

Bolton, Herbert E. "The Epic of Greater America." *American Historical Review* 38, no. 3 (April 1933).

Bond, Marshall, Jr. *Gold Hunter: The Adventures of Marshall Bond*. Albuquerque: University of New Mexico Press, 1969.

Borton, Francis. *The Call of California and Other Poems of the West*. Riverside: s.n., 1923.

Bouligny, Edgard. *Brief Sketches in Mexico: Its Large Cities and Points of Interest*. Mexico: Mexican Central Railway Co., 1853.

Bourgeacq, Jacques. "The Eye Motif and Narrative Strategy in Ferdinand Oyono's *Une Vie de boy*: An Ethno-Cultural Perspective." *French Review* 66, no. 5 (April 1993).

Box, James. *Capt. James Box's Adventures and Explorations in New and Old Mexico*. New York: Derby and Jackson, 1861.

Boyd, Nathan. "La Cenci: Wonderful Story of Two Rare Old Portraits Found in Mesilla by Dr. Nathan Boyd." Reprint from *New Mexican Magazine*. s.l.: National Gallery of Art, 1914.

———. *Statehood for New Mexico: Arguments on Behalf of New Mexico's Admission into the Union and in Defense of the Territory's Inherent Right to the Waters of Her Streams*. Washington, D.C.: Judd and Detweiler, 1902.

Bradford, Mary, and Richard Bradford, eds. *An American Family on the African Frontier: The Burnham Family Letters, 1893–1896*. Niwot, Col.: Roberts Rinehart, 1993.

Brantlinger, Patrick. *Rule of Darkness: British Literature and Imperialism, 1830–1914*. Ithaca: Cornell University Press, 1988.

Brechin, Gray. *Imperial San Francisco: Urban Power, Earthly Ruin*. Berkeley: University of California Press, 1999.

Bristow, Joseph. *Empire Boys: Adventures in a Man's World*. New York: Harper-Collins Academic, 1991.

Britwum, Kwabena. "Regard, mémoire, témoignage: ou l'oeil du sorcier dans *Une Vie de boy* de F. Oyono." *Présence Francophone* 14 (1977).

Browne, J. Ross. *Adventures in the Apache Country: A Tour through Arizona and Sonora, with Notes on the Silver Regions of Nevada*. New York: Harper and Brothers, 1869.

Buffalo Bill Among the Man-Eaters; Or, The Mystery of Tiburon Island. London: James Henderson and Sons, 1908.

Buffalo Bill's Totem, or the Mystic Symbol of the Yaouis [sic]. London: James Henderson and Sons, 1908.

Buffum, E. Gould, and John W. Caughey. *Six Months in the Gold Mines from a Journal of Three Years' Residence in Upper and Lower California 1847-8-9*. s.l.: Ward Ritchie Press, 1959.

Bureau of Immigration of the Terr. of New Mexico. *Dona Ana County, New Mexico: The Mesilla Valley—the Garden of New Mexico. Mineral Wealth in*

Picturesque Mountain Ranges. Cattle, Sheep and Goats by the Thousands. An Ideal Winter Climate. Santa Fe: New Mexican Printing, 1901.

Bureau of Statistics. *Commercial Relations of the United States with Foreign Countries.* Volumes for 1853–1910. Washington, D.C.: Government Printing Office, 1853–1910.

Burke, Timothy. *Lifebuoy Men, Lux Women: Commodification, Consumption, and Cleanliness in Modern Zimbabwe.* Durham: Duke University Press, 1996.

Burnham, Frederick Russell. *Scouting on Two Continents.* New York: Doubleday, 1926.

———. *Taking Chances.* Los Angeles: Haynes Corporation, 1944.

Burnham, Roderick H. *Genealogical Records of Thomas Burnham, the Emigrant, Who Was Among the Early Settlers at Hartford, Connecticut, U.S. America, and His Descendants.* 1884.

Campbell, Robert. *In Darkest Alaska: Travel and Empire Along the Inside Passage.* Philadelphia: University of Pennsylvania Press, 2007.

Carley, Kenneth. *The Dakota War of 1862: Minnesota's Other Civil War,* 2nd ed. St. Paul: Minnesota Historical Society Press, 1976.

Case, Alden Buell. *Thirty Years with the Mexicans: In Peace and Revolution.* New York: Fleming H. Revell, 1917.

Cave of the Skulls, or, the Secret Hoard of the Yaquis. London: James Henderson and Sons, 1908.

Cell, John W. *The Highest Stage of White Supremacy: The Origins of Segregation in South Africa and the American South.* Cambridge: Cambridge University Press, 1982.

Chang, Kornel. *Pacific Connections: The Making of the U.S.–Canadian Borderlands.* Berkeley: University of California Press, 2012.

Child, James E. *Child's History of Waseca County, Minnesota.* s.l.: Whiting and Luers, 1905.

Church, John H. C. *Diary of a Trip Through Mexico and California.* Pittsfield, Mass.: Marcus H. Rogers, 1887.

Clois Stone, Paul. "J. Frank Dobie and the American Folklore Movement: A Reappraisal." PhD diss., Yale University, 1995.

Coatsworth, John H. *Growth Against Development: The Economic Impact of Railroads in Porfirian Mexico.* DeKalb: Northern Illinois University Press, 1981.

Cochrane, Leon John. "A Social Survey of Doña Ana County." M.A. thesis, New Mexico College of Agriculture and Mechanic Arts, 1915.

Cole, Bob. *Mexico.* New York: J. W. Stern, 1904.

Coolidge, Dane. *Yaqui Drums: An Authentic Western Novel*. New York: E. P. Dutton, 1940.

Dabdoub, Claudio. *Historia de el valle del yaqui*. Mexico City: Manuel Porrua, 1964.

Dahlin, Curtis. *A History of the Dakota Uprising*. Roseville, Minn., 2012.

Dangarembga, Tsitsi. *Nervous Conditions*, 2d ed. Emeryville, Calif.: Avalon, 2004.

Darter, Adrian. *The Pioneers of Mashonaland*. London: Simpkin, Marshall, Hamilton, Kenty, 1914.

Davis, Richard Harding. *Real Soldiers of Fortune*. New York: Charles Scribner's Sons, 1906.

———. *With Both Armies*. New York: Charles Scriber's Sons, 1900.

Davis, W. W. H. *El Gringo: New Mexico and Her People*. New York: Harper, 1857.

Day, James M., ed. *Morris B. Parker's Mules, Mines and Me in Mexico, 1895–1932*. Tucson: University of Arizona Press, 1979.

de la Paz Soto, Guillermo, ed. *Meoqui: historias, anécdotas y leyendas*. Vol. 2. Mexico City: Doble Hélice, 2006.

DeLay, Brian. *War of a Thousand Deserts: Indian Raids and the U.S.–Mexican War*. New Haven: Yale University Press, 2006.

Delpar, Helen. *The Enormous Vogue of Things Mexican: Cultural Relations Between the United States and Mexico*. Tuscaloosa: University of Alabama Press, 1992.

Denoon, Donald. *Settler Capitalism: The Dynamics of Dependent Development in the Southern Hemisphere*. Oxford: Oxford University Press, 1983.

Department of Commerce and Labor, Bureau of Statistics. *Special Consular Reports: Emigration to the United States* 30. Washington, D.C.: Government Printing Office, 1904.

Deutsch, Sarah. *No Separate Refuge: Culture, Class, and Gender on an Anglo-Hispanic Frontier in the American Southwest, 1880–1940*. New York: Oxford University Press, 1987.

Dobie, J. Frank. *Apache Gold and Yaqui Silver*. Boston: Little, Brown, 1939.

Doyle, Arthur Conan. *A Desert Drama, Being the Tragedy of the* Korosko. Philadelphia: J. B. Lippincott, 1898.

du Toit, Brian M. "A Boer Settlement That Was Never Settled: Tamaulipas, Mexico." *Historia* 49, no. 1 (May 2004): 48–70.

———. "Boers, Afrikaners, and Diasporas." *Historia* 48, no. 1 (May 2003): 15–54.

———. *Boer Settlers in the Southwest*. El Paso: University of Texas at El Paso, 1995.

———. *Colonia Boer: An Afrikaner Settlement in Chubut, Argentina*. Lewiston, N.Y.: Edwin Mellen Press, 1995.

————. *The Boers in East Africa: Ethnicity and Identity.* Bergin and Garvey, 1998.

Dwyer, John. *The Agrarian Dispute: The Expropriation of American-Owned Rural Land in Postrevolutionary Mexico.* Durham: Duke University Press, 2008.

Eaton, James D. *Life Under Two Flags.* New York: A. S. Barnes, 1922.

————. " 'The First Martyrdom': A Farewell Sermon Preached by Rev. James D. Eaton in the Congregational Church, Bound Brook, N.J., on Sunday Evening, July 31, 1881." Somerville, N.J.: Somerset Gazette Steam Printing House, 1881.

Eighty-Second Annual Report of the American Board of Commissioners for Foreign Missions. Boston: ABCFM, 1892.

Erickson, Kirstin C. *Yaqui Homeland and Homeplace: The Everyday Production of Ethnic Identity.* Tucson: University of Arizona Press, 2008.

Etherington, Norman. *Rider Haggard.* Woodbridge, Conn.: Twayne Publishers, 1984.

Evans, Sterling. *Bound in Twine: The History and Ecology of the Henequen-Wheat Complex for Mexico and the American and Canadian Plains, 1880–1950.* College Station: Texas A&M University Press, 2007.

Fabela, Isidro, ed. *Historia Diplomática de la Revolución Mexicana.* Vol. 1. Mexico City: Fondo de Cultura Económica, 1958.

Ferguson, John. *American Diplomacy and the Boer War.* Philadelphia: University of Pennsylvania Press, 1939.

Foley, Neil. *The White Scourge: Mexicans, Blacks, and Poor Whites in Texas Cotton Culture.* Berkeley: University of California Press, 1999.

Folsom, Raphael. *The Yaquis and the Empire: Violence, Spanish Imperial Power, and Native Resilience in Colonial Mexico.* New Haven: Yale University Press, 2014.

Foster, George M. *Tzintzuntzan: Mexican Peasants in a Changing World.* New York: Little, Brown, 1967.

Fredrickson, George. *Black Liberation: A Comparative History of Black Ideologies in the United States and South Africa.* Oxford: Oxford University Press, 1996.

————. *White Supremacy: A Comparative Study in American and South African History.* Oxford: Oxford University Press, 1981.

Fuller, John D. P. *The Movement for the Acquisition of All Mexico, 1846–1848.* Baltimore: Johns Hopkins University Press, 1936.

Galbraith, John S. *Crown and Charter: The Early Years of the British South Africa Company.* Berkeley: University of California Press, 1974.

Gann, L. H. *A History of Southern Rhodesia, Early Days to 1934.* New York: Humanities Press, 1969.

García, Mario T. *Memories of Chicano History: The Life and Narrative of Bert Corona.* Berkeley: University of California Press, 1994.

Giliomee, Hermann. *The Afrikaners: Biography of a People.* Charlottesville: University of Virginia Press, 2009.

Gobat, Michel. *Confronting the American Dream: Nicaragua Under U.S. Imperial Rule.* Durham: Duke University Press, 2005.

González, Gilbert G. *Culture of Empire: American Writers, Mexico, and Mexican Immigrants, 1880–1930.* Austin: University of Texas Press, 2004.

Green, Martin. *Dreams of Adventure, Deeds of Empire.* New York: Basic Books, 1979.

Greenblatt, Stephen. *Marvelous Possessions: The Wonder of the New World.* Oxford: Clarendon Press, 1991.

Greene, Julie. *The Canal Builders: Making America's Empire at the Panama Canal.* New York: Penguin Press, 2009.

Gugelberger, Georg M., ed. *The Real Thing: Testimonial Discourse and Latin America.* Durham: Duke University Press, 1996.

——, and Michael Kearney. "Voices for the Voiceless: Testimonial Literature in Latin America." *Latin American Perspectives* 18, no. 3 (Summer 1991): 3–14.

Gump, James. *The Dust Rose Like Smoke: The Subjugation of the Zulu and the Sioux.* Lincoln: University of Nebraska Press, 1994.

Haber, Stephen. "The Commitment Problem and Mexican Economic History." In Jeffrey L. Bortz and Stephen Haber, eds., *The Mexican Economy, 1870–1930: Essays on the Economic History of Institutions, Revolution, and Growth.* Stanford: Stanford University Press, 2002.

——. *Industry and Underdevelopment: The Industrialization of Mexico, 1890–1940.* Stanford: Stanford University Press, 1989.

Hager, Anna Marie, ed. *The Filibusters of 1890: The Captain John F. Janes and Lower California Newspaper Reports and the Walter G. Smith Manuscript.* Los Angeles: Dawson's Book Shop, 1968.

Haggard, H. Rider. "Wilson's Last Fight." In Andrew Lang, ed., *The Red True Story Book.* London: Longmans, Green, 1895.

——. *King Solomon's Mines.* Longmans, Green, 1885.

——. *Nada the Lily.* London: Longmans, Green, 1892.

——. *The Wizard.* Bristol: J. W. Arrowsmith, 1896.

Hall, R. N., and W. G. Neal. *The Ancient Ruins of Rhodesia (Monomotapae Imperium).* London: Methuen, 1902.

Hämäläinen, Pekka. *The Comanche Empire.* New Haven: Yale University Press, 2008.

Hammond, John Hays. *The Autobiography of John Hays Hammond*. Vol. 1. New York: Farrar and Rinehart, 1935.

Harper, Henry H. *A Journey in Southeastern Mexico: Narrative of Experiences, and Observations on Agricultural and Industrial Conditions*. Boston: De Vinne Press, 1910.

Harris, Charles H., and Louis R. Sadler. *The Secret War in El Paso: Mexican Revolutionary Intrigue, 1906–1920*. Albuquerque: University of New Mexico Press, 2009.

Harris, Dean. *By Path and Trail*. Chicago: Chicago Newspaper Union, 1908.

Hart, John Mason. *Empire and Revolution: The Americans in Mexico Since the Civil War*. Berkeley: University of California Press, 2002.

———. *Revolutionary Mexico: The Coming and Process of the Mexican Revolution*. Berkeley: University of California Press, 1987.

Hatch, Nelle Spilsbury. *Colonia Juarez: An Intimate Account of a Mormon Village*. Salt Lake City: Deseret, 1954.

Helms, James Ervin. "Origins and Growth of Protestantism in Mexico to 1920." PhD diss., University of Texas, 1955.

Hernández, Fortunato. *Las Razas Indígenas de Sonora y la Guerra del Yaqui*. Mexico City: Talleres de la Casa Editorial "J. de Elizalde," 1902.

Hinckley, Ted C. "When the Boer War Came to St. Louis." *Missouri Historical Review* 61 (1967): 285–302.

Hoganson, Kristin. *Fighting for American Manhood: How Gender Politics Provoked the Spanish–American and Philippine–American Wars*. New Haven: Yale University Press, 2000.

Hole, Hugh Marshall. *The Making of Rhodesia*. London: Frank Cass. 1967.

Holtby, David V. *Forty-Seventh Star: New Mexico's Struggle for Statehood*. Norman: University of Oklahoma Press, 2012.

Hu-DeHart, Evelyn. *Missionaries, Miners, and Indians: History of Spanish Contact with the Yaqui Indians of Northwestern New Spain, 1533–1830*. Tucson: University of Arizona Press, 1981.

———. *Yaqui Resistance and Survival: Struggle for Land and Autonomy, 1821–1910*. Madison: University of Wisconsin Press, 1984.

Hughes, Thomas. *History of Blue Earth County and Biographies of Its Leading Citizens*. Chicago: Middle West, 1901.

Hunt, Nancy Rose. "'Le Bebe en Brousse': European Women, African Birth Spacing and Colonial Intervention in Breast Feeding in the Belgian Congo." *International Journal of African Historical Studies* 21, no. 3 (1988): 401–32.

Hunter, Jane. *The Gospel of Gentility: American Women Missionaries in Turn-of-the-Century China*. New Haven: Yale University Press, 1984.

International Bureau of the American Republics. *Monthly Bulletin of the International Bureau of the American Republics* 18 (October–December 1904).

Jacobson, Matthew Frye. *Barbarian Virtues: The United States Encounters Foreign Peoples at Home and Abroad, 1876–1917*. New York: Hill and Wang, 2001.

——. *Whiteness of a Different Color: European Immigrants and the Alchemy of Race*. Cambridge: Harvard University Press, 1998.

Jacoby, Karl. *Shadows at Dawn: A Borderlands Massacre and the Violence of History*. New York: Penguin, 2008.

Jaime León, Juan Silverio, ed. *Testimonios de una mujer yaqui*. s.l.: Conaculta and PACMYC, 2000.

Jebb, Mrs. John Beveridge Gladwyn [Clara Lydia Jebb]. *A Strange Career: Life and Adventures of John Gladwyn Jebb by His Widow with an Introduction by H. Rider Haggard*. London: William Blackwood and Sons, 1894.

Johnson, Annie Richardson. *Heartbeats of Colonia Diaz*. Salt Lake City: Publishers Press, 1972.

Johnson, Benjamin Heber. *Revolution in Texas: How a Forgotten Rebellion and Its Bloody Suppression Turned Mexicans into Americans*. New Haven: Yale University Press, 2003.

Jordan, Benjamin René. *Modern Manhood and the Boy Scouts of America: Citizenship, Race, and the Environment, 1910–1930*. Chapel Hill: University of North Carolina Press, 2016.

Joseph, Gilbert M. *Revolution from Without: Yucatán, Mexico, and the United States, 1880–1924*. Durham: Duke University Press, 1988.

Joseph, Gilbert M., and Daniel Nugent, eds. *Everyday Forms of State Formation: Revolution and the Negotiation of Rule in Modern Mexico*. Durham: Duke University Press, 1994.

Kaplan, Amy, and Donald E. Pease. *Cultures of United States Imperialism*. Durham: Duke University Press, 1994.

Kappler, Charles J., ed. "Treaty with the Winnebago, 1859." In *Indian Affairs: Laws and Treaties*, Vol. 2: *Treaties*. Washington: Government Printing Office, 1904.

Kelley, Jane Holden. *Yaqui Women: Contemporary Life Histories*. Lincoln: University of Nebraska Press, 1978.

Kemper, Steven. *A Splendid Savage: The Restless Life of Frederick Russell Burnham*. New York: W. W. Norton, 2016.

Kettenring, Ernest. "Krugerism in America: The United States and the Anglo-Boer War." PhD diss., University of New Hampshire, 1984.

Klein, Kerwin Lee. *Frontiers of Historical Imagination: Narrating the European Conquest of Native America, 1890–1990*. Berkeley: University of California Press, 1997.

Knight, Alan. "Interpreting the Mexican Revolution." *Texas Papers on Mexico: Pre-publication working papers of the Mexican Center Institute of Latin American Studies, University of Texas at Austin.* Paper No. 88-02 (1988).

———. *The Mexican Revolution.* 2 vols. Cambridge: Cambridge University Press, 1986.

Kolodny, Annette. *The Lay of the Land: Metaphor as Experience and History in American Life and Letters.* Chapel Hill: University of North Carolina Press, 1975.

Kramer, Paul A. *The Blood of Government: Race, Empire, the United States, and the Philippines.* Chapel Hill: University of North Carolina Press, 2006.

———. "Empires, Exceptions, and Anglo-Saxons: Race and Rule Between the British and United States Empires, 1880–1910." *Journal of American History* 88, no. 4 (March 2002): 1315–53.

Kutzer, M. Daphne. *Empire's Children: Empire and Imperialism in Classic British Children's Books.* New York: Garland, 2000.

LaFeber, Walter. *The New Empire: An Interpretation of American Expansion, 1860–1898.* Ithaca: Cornell University Press, 1963.

Lamar, Howard R. *The Far Southwest, 1846–1912: A Territorial History.* Revised Edition. Albuquerque: University of New Mexico Press, 2000.

———, and Leonard Thompson. *The Frontier in History: North America and Southern Africa Compared.* New Haven, Yale University Press, 1981.

Lass, William E. "The Removal from Minnesota of the Sioux and Winnebago Indians." *Minnesota History* (December 1963).

Le Duc, William G. *Report of a Trip of Observation over the Proposed Line of the American & Mexican Pacific Railway, through the States of Sinaloa and Sonora, Mexico.* Washington, D.C.: Gibson Brothers, 1883.

Legassick, Martin. "The Frontier Tradition in South African Historiography." In Shula Marks and Anthony Atmore, eds., *Economy and Society in Pre-Industrial South Africa.* London: Longman Group, 1980.

Lennox, William G. *The Health and Turnover of Missionaries.* New York: The Methodist Book Concern, 1933.

León, Nicolás. *Nota Acerca de Una Pintura Existente en el Antiquísimo Convento de Franciscanos en Tzintzuntzan, Atribuida al Tiziano.* Morelia: Gobierno en la Escuela de Artes, 1891.

Limerick, Patricia Nelson. "Going West and Ending Up Global." *Western Historical Quarterly* 32, no. 1 (Spring 2001): 5–23.

Logan, Walter S. *A Mexican Night: The Toasts and Responses at a Complimentary Dinner Given by Walter S. Logan, at the Democratic Club, New York City,*

December 16th, 1891, to Senor Don Matias Romero, Mexican Minister to the United States. New York: Albert B. King, 1891.

———. *Irrigation on the Yaqui River.* s.l.: s.n. [1892].

———. "Report on the Condition of the Work on the Yaqui Canal." New York: Sonora and Sinaloa Irrigation Company, 1905.

———. *Yaqui Land Convertible Stock.* s.l.: s.n. [1894].

———. *Yaqui: The Land of Sunshine and Health; What I Saw in Mexico.* New York: Albert B. King, 1894.

Lomnitz, Claudio. *The Return of Comrade Ricardo Flores Magón.* New York: Zone Books, 2014.

Lowry, Donal. "'The World's No Bigger Than a Kraal': The South African War and International Opinion in the First Age of 'Globalization.'" In D. Omissi and A. S. Thompson, eds., *The Impact of the South African War.* New York: Palgrave, 2002.

Lummis, Charles F. *The Land of Poco Tiempo.* New York: Charles Scribner's Sons, 1893.

MacDonald, Robert H. *Sons of the Empire: The Frontier and the Boy Scout Movement, 1890–1918.* Toronto: University of Toronto Press, 1993.

Macleod, David I. "Original Intent: Establishing the Creed and Control of Boy Scouting in the United States." In Nelson R. Block and Tammy M. Proctor, *Scouting Frontiers: Youth and the Scout Movement's First Century.* Newcastle upon Tyne: Cambridge Scholars, 2009.

Madero, Francisco I. *La sucesión presidencial en 1910: el partido nacional democrático.* San Pedro, Coahuila: s.n., 1908.

Maluy, Dale C. "Boer Colonization in the Southwest." *New Mexico Historical Review* 52, no. 2 (April 1977): 93–110.

Martínez Aguilar, José Manuel. "El Tiziano de Tzintzuntzan, el lienzo que se convirtió en leyenda." *Signos Históricos* 18, no. 36 (July-December 2016): 80–117.

Marx, Anthony W. *Making Race and Nation: A Comparison of South Africa, the United States, and Brazil.* Cambridge: Cambridge University Press, 1998.

Mason, Philip. *The Birth of a Dilemma: The Conquest and Settlement of Rhodesia.* Oxford: Oxford University Press, 1958.

Matthews, Michael. *The Civilizing Machine: A Cultural History of Mexican Railroads, 1876–1910.* Lincoln: University of Nebraska Press, 2013.

McClintock, Anne. *Imperial Leather: Race, Gender, and Sexuality in the Colonial Contest.* New York: Routledge, 1995.

McGuire, Thomas R. *Politics and Ethnicity on the Río Yaqui: Potam Revisited.* Tucson: University of Arizona Press, 1986.

Meijer, J. W. *Generaal Ben Viljoen, 1868–1917.* Menlopark, South Africa: Protea Boekhuis, 2000.

Melillo, Edward Dallam. *Strangers on Familiar Soil: Rediscovering the Chile–California Connection.* New Haven: Yale University Press, 2015.

Mexican Central Railway Company. *Facts and Figures About Mexico and Her Great Railroad, The Mexican Central.* Mexico City: Mexican Central Bureau of Information, 1897.

Miller, Daniel R. "Protestantism and Radicalism in Mexico from the 1860s to the 1930s." *Fides et Historia* 40, no. 1 (Winter/Spring 2008): 43–66.

Moctezuma Zamarrón, José Luis. *De pascolas y venados: Adaptación, cambio y persistencia de las lenguas yaqui y mayo frente al español.* Mexico City: Siglo XXI Editores, 2001.

Moisés, Rosalio, Jane Holden Kelley, and William Curry Holden. *The Tall Candle: The Personal Chronicle of a Yaqui Indian.* Lincoln: University of Nebraska Press, 1971.

Monsman, Gerald. *H. Rider Haggard on the Imperial Frontier: The Political and Literary Contexts of His African Romances.* Greensboro, NC: ELT Press, 2006.

Mora, Anthony P. *Border Dilemmas: Racial and National Uncertainties in New Mexico, 1848–1912.* Durham: Duke University Press, 2011.

Mowry, Sylvester. *Arizona and Sonora: The Geography, History, and Resources of the Silver Region of North America.* New York: Harper and Brothers, 1864.

Mtshali, B. Vulindlela. *Rhodesia: Background to Conflict.* New York: Hawthorn Books.

Munroe, Kirk. *The White Conquerors: A Tale of Toltec and Aztec.* London: Blackie and Son, 1893.

Nasson, Bill. *The War for South Africa: The Anglo–Boer War, 1899–1902.* Cape Town: Tafelberg, 2010.

National Archives and Records Administration. *Schedules of the New Mexico Territory Census of 1885.* Series: M846, Roll: 2. Washington, D.C.

Nestel, Sheryl. "(Ad)ministering Angels: Colonial Nursing and the Extension of Empire in Africa." *Journal of Medical Humanities* 19, no. 4 (1998): 257–77.

Nicholl Ellison, Edith. *The Desert and the Rose.* Boston: Cornhill, 1921.

———. "A Far-Away Corner." *Cornhill Magazine* 9, no. 50 (August 1900): 251–57.

———. "Reminiscences of Royalty." *The Era Magazine: An Illustrated Monthly* 11, no. 3 (March 1903).

———. *A Child's Recollections of Tennyson.* New York: E. P. Dutton, 1906.

———. *Observations of a Ranchwoman in New Mexico.* London: Macmillan, 1898.

Nordhoff, Charles. *Peninsular California: Some Account of the Climate, Soil, Pro-ductions, and Present Conditions Chiefly of the Northern Half of Lower California*. New York: Harper and Brothers, 1888.

Nugent, Daniel, ed. *Rural Revolt in Mexico: U.S. Intervention and the Domain of Subaltern Politics*. Expanded Edition. Durham: Duke University Press, 1998.

Nugent, Walter. "Frontiers and Empire in the Late Nineteenth Century," *Western Historical Quarterly* 20, no. 4 (November 1989): 393–408.

———. *Habits of Empire: A History of American Expansion*. New York: Alfred A. Knopf, 2008.

Ober, Fred. *The Knockabout Club in Search of Treasure*. Boston: Dana Estes, 1892.

———. *Travels in Mexico*. Denver: Perry Publishing, 1883.

Offenburger, Andrew. "When the West Turned South: Making Home Lands in Revolutionary Sonora." *Western Historical Quarterly* 45 (Autumn 2014): 299–319.

Olavarría, María Eugenia, ed. *Símbolos del desierto*. Mexico City: Universidad Autónoma Metropolitana, 1992.

Oyono, Ferdinand. *Une vie de boy*. Paris: Julliard, 1956.

Padilla Ramos, Raquel. "Los Partes Fragmentados: Narrativas de la Guerra y la Deportación Yaquis." PhD diss., Universitat Hamburg, 2009.

———. *Los irredentos parias: Los Yaquis, Madero y Pino Suárez en las elecciones de Yucatán, 1911*. Mexico City: Instituto Nacional de Antropología e His-toria, 2011.

———. *Progreso y libertad: Los yaquis en la víspera de la repatriación*. Her-mosillo: Programa Editorial de Sonora, 2006.

Parsons, Timothy H. *Race, Resistance, and the Boy Scout Movement in British Co-lonial Africa*. Athens: Ohio University Press, 2004.

———. *"Een-Gonyama Gonyama!*: Zulu Origins of the Boy Scout Movement and the Africanisation of Imperial Britain." *Parliamentary History* 27, no. 1 (February 2008): 57–66.

Pascoe, Peggy. *Relations of Rescue: The Search for Female Moral Authority in the American West, 1874–1939*. Oxford: Oxford University Press, 1990.

Patterson, Orlando. *Slavery and Social Death: A Comparative Study*. Cambridge: Harvard University Press, 1982.

Pennsylvania Tours to the Golden Gate and Mexico. Philadelphia: Allen, Lane and Scott, 1891.

Penton, Marvin James. "Mexico's Reformation: A History of Mexican Protes-tantism from Its Inception to the Present." PhD diss., University of Iowa, 1965.

Phillips, Richard. *Mapping Men and Empire: A Geography of Adventure.* New York: Routledge, 1997.

Phimister, Ian. "Burnham, Frederick Russell (1861–1947)." *Oxford Dictionary of National Biography.* Oxford: Oxford University Press, 2004.

———. *An Economic and Social History of Zimbabwe 1890–1948: Capital Accumulation and Class Struggle.* London: Longman, 1988.

Pinheiro, John C. *Missionaries of Republicanism: A Religious History of the Mexican–American War.* Oxford: Oxford University Press, 2014.

Plasencia, Adela Pinet. *Obras Completas de Francisco Ignacio Madero, Discursos 1. 1909–1911.* Mexico City: Clío, 2000.

Pletcher, David M. *Rails, Mines, and Progress: Seven American Promoters in Mexico, 1867–1911.* Ithaca: Cornell University Press, 1958.

———. *The Diplomacy of Trade and Investment: American Economic Expansion in the Hemisphere, 1865–1900.* Columbia: University of Missouri Press, 1998.

Pollard, Helen Pearlstein. *Taríacuri's [sic] Legacy: The Prehispanic Tarascan State.* Norman: University of Oklahoma Press, 1993.

Pollard, Hugh B. C. *A Busy Time in Mexico: An Unconventional Record of Mexican Incident.* London: Constable, 1913.

Poole, Deborah. "Landscape and the Imperial Subject: U.S. Images of the Andes, 1859–1930." In Gilbert M. Joseph, Catherine C. LeGrand, and Ricardo D. Salvatore, eds., *Close Encounters of Empire: Writing the Cultural History of U.S.–Latin American Relations.* Durham: Duke University Press, 1998.

Powell, Fred Wilbur. *The Railroads of Mexico.* Boston: Stratford, 1921.

Pratt, Mary Louise. *Imperial Eyes: Travel Writing and Transculturation.* New York: Routledge, 1992.

Pruitt, Lisa Joy. *A Looking-Glass for Ladies: American Protestant Women and the Orient in the Nineteenth Century.* Macon, Ga.: Mercer University Press, 2005.

Radical Reconstruction on the Basis of One Sovereign Republic, . . . An Appeal to All Americans for New Nationality with the South and Russian America, looking also to Union with Mexico and Canada. Sacramento: Russell and Winterburn, 1867.

Ramírez Zavala, Ana Luz. *La participación de los Yaquis en la Revolución 1913–1920.* Hermosillo: Instituto Sonorense de Cultura, 2012.

Ranger, Terence. *Revolt in Southern Rhodesia, 1896–7.* London: Heinemann, 1967.

Reeves-Ellington, Barbara, Kathryn Kish Sklar, and Connie A. Shemo, eds. *Competing Kingdoms: Women, Mission, Nation, and the American Protestant Empire, 1812–1960.* Durham: Duke University Press, 2010.

Reid, Christian. *The Lost Lode*. Philadelphia: H. L. Kilner, 1892.

———. *The Picture of Las Cruces: A Romance of Mexico*. New York: J. B. Lippincott, 1894.

Remington, Frederic. *Pony Tracks*. New York: Harper and Brothers, 1900.

Report of José M. Ponce de León. *Periódico Oficial*, October 8, 1905.

Reports of the Stations of the Mexico Mission of the American Board, 1900–1901. Guadalajara: ABCFM, 1901.

Reports of the Stations of the Mexico Mission of the American Board, 1907–1908. Chihuahua: Imprenta "El Norte," 1908.

Reports of the Stations of the Mexico Mission of the American Board, 1908–1909. Chihuahua: Imprenta "El Norte," 1909.

Richter, Daniel K. *Trade, Land, and Power: The Struggle for Eastern North America*. Philadelphia: University of Pennsylvania Press, 2013.

Robbins, William. *Colony and Empire: The Capitalist Transformation of the American West*. Lawrence: University of Kansas Press, 1994.

Roberts, Edwards. *With the Invader: Glimpses of the Southwest*. San Francisco: Samuel Carson, 1895.

Robinson, Michael F. *The Lost White Tribe: Explorers, Scientists, and the Theory That Changed a Continent*. Oxford: Oxford University Press, 2016.

Rodriguez, Victor J. *Creating the Practical Man of Modernity: The Reception of John Dewey's Pedagogy in Mexico*. New York: Routledge, 2017.

Rogers, Lou. *Tar Heel Women*. Raleigh: Warren Publishing, 1949.

Romero, Matías. *Geographical and Statistical Notes on Mexico*. New York: G. P. Putnam's Sons, 1898.

———. "Mexico." *Journal of the American Geographical Society of New York* 28, no. 4 (1896).

Romney, Thomas Cottam. *The Mormon Colonies in Mexico*. Salt Lake City: Deseret, 1938.

Roosevelt, Theodore. *The Rough Riders*. New York: G. P. Putnam's Sons, 1899.

Rosenberg, Emily S. *Spreading the American Dream: American Economic and Cultural Expansion, 1890–1945*. New York: HarperCollins, 1982.

Rotberg, Robert I. *The Founder: Cecil Rhodes and the Pursuit of Power*. Oxford: Oxford University Press, 1988.

Ruiz, Jason. *Americans in the Treasure House: Travel to Porfirian Mexico and the Cultural Politics of Empire*. Austin: University of Texas Press, 2014.

Ruiz, Ramón Eduardo. *The People of Sonora and Yankee Capitalists*. Tucson: University of Arizona Press, 1988.

Ruxton, George Frederick. *Adventures in Mexico: From Vera Cruz to Chihuahua in the Days of the Mexican War*. Oyster Bay: Nelson Doubleday, 1915.

Salvatore, Ricardo D. "The Enterprise of Knowledge: Representational Machines of Informal Empire." In Gilbert M. Joseph, Catherine C. LeGrand, and Ricardo D. Salvatore, eds., *Close Encounters of Empire: Writing the Cultural History of U.S.–Latin American Relations*. Durham: Duke University Press, 1998.

Sánchez, Óscar. "Comer y cocinar: naturaleza y cultura." In María Eugenia Olavarría, ed., *Símbolos del desierto*. México, D.F.: Universidad Autónoma Metropolitana, 1992.

Sanneh, Lamin O. *Translating the Message: The Missionary Impact on Culture*. Maryknoll, N.Y.: Orbis Books, 1989.

Sargeaunt, John. "Bradley, George Granville (1821–1903)." *Oxford Dictionary of National Biography*. Oxford: Oxford University Press, 2004.

Scharff, Virginia. *Taking the Wheel: Women and the Coming of the Motor Age*. Albuquerque: University of New Mexico Press, 1992.

———. *Twenty Thousand Roads: Women, Movement, and the West*. Berkeley: University of California Press, 2002.

———, and Carolyn Brucken. *Home Lands: How Women Made the West*. Berkeley: University of California Press, 2010.

Scharlieb, Mary. "An Address on the Care of the Health of Married Women Missionaries." *British Medical Journal* 1, no. 2839 (May 29, 1915).

Scott, James C. *Weapons of the Weak: Everyday Forms of Peasant Resistance*. New Haven: Yale University Press, 1985.

Shorter, David Delgado. *We Will Dance Our Truth: Yaqui History in Yoeme Performances*. Lincoln: University of Nebraska Press, 2014.

Smith, F. Hopkinson. *A White Umbrella in Mexico*. Boston: Houghton Mifflin, 1889.

Smith, Henry Nash. *Virgin Land: The American West as Symbol and Myth*. Cambridge: Harvard University Press, 1978.

Smith, Neil. *American Empire: Roosevelt's Geographer and the Prelude to Globalization*. Berkeley: University of California Press, 2003.

Smith, Nora Archibald. *Under the Cactus Flag: A Story of Life in Mexico*. Boston: Houghton, Mifflin, 1899.

Smithsonian Institution. *Report on the Progress and Condition of the United States National Museum for the Year Ending June 30, 1914*. Washington, D.C.: Government Printing Office, 1915.

Sonora and Sinaloa Irrigation Company. *Report of Col. E. S. Nettleton on the Yaqui Irrigation Enterprise*. s.l.: The Company, 1893.

Southworth, J. R. *Sonora Ilustrado*. Nogales, Ariz.: Oasis Printing, 1897.

Spear, Jennifer M. "Colonial Intimacies: Legislating Sex in French Louisiana." *William and Mary Quarterly* 60, no. 1 (January 2003): 75–98.

Spicer, Edward H. *Cycles of Conquest: The Impact of Spain, Mexico, and the United States on Indians of the Southwest, 1533–1960.* Tucson: University of Arizona Press, 1967.

———. *People of Pascua.* Tucson: University of Arizona Press, 1988.

———. *Potam: A Yaqui Village in Sonora.* s.l.: American Anthropological Association, 1954.

———. *The Yaquis: A Cultural History.* Tucson: University of Arizona Press, 1980.

St. John, Rachel. *Line in the Sand: A History of the Western U.S.–Mexico Border.* Princeton: Princeton University Press, 2011.

Stegner, Wallace. *Beyond the Hundredth Meridian: John Wesley Powell and the Second Opening of the West.* New York: Penguin Books, 1992 [1954].

Stephens, Bascom A. *The Gold Fields of Lower California for Miners and Settlers, Being a Complete Guide Book with Official Maps, Revenue and Mining Laws, Etc., Etc.* Los Angeles: Southern California Publishing, 1889.

Stoler, Laura Ann. "Making Empire Respectable: The Politics of Race and Sexual Morality in 20th-Century Colonial Cultures." *American Ethnologist* 16, no. 4 (November 1989): 634–60.

———. *Carnal Knowledge and Imperial Power: Race and the Intimate in Colonial Rule.* Berkeley: University of California Press, 2002.

Streeby, Shelley. *American Sensations: Class, Empire, and the Production of Popular Culture.* Berkeley: University of California Press, 2002.

Strong, William E. *The Story of the American Board: An Account of the First Hundred Years of the American Board of Commissioners for Foreign Missions.* Boston: Pilgrim Press, 1910.

Sutton, Jennie. "'Transvaal Spectacles': South African Visions at the 1904 St. Louis World's Fair." *Safundi: The Journal of South African and American Studies* 8, no. 3 (2007): 271–87.

Taylor Hansen, Lawrence Douglas. "La Colonización Boer en Chihuahua y el Suroeste de Estados Unidos, 1903–1917." *Historia Mexicana* 52, no. 2 (2002): 449–89.

———. "La colonización con extranjeros en el norte de México: El caso de los mormones, los boers y los menonitas." *Vetas: Revista de El Colegio de San Luis* 6, no. 16 (January–April 2004): 107–37.

Teisch, Jessica B. *Engineering Nature: Water, Development, and the Global Spread of American Environmental Expertise.* Chapel Hill: University of North Carolina Press, 2011.

Thelen, David, ed. "The Nation and Beyond: Transnational Perspectives on United States History." *Journal of American History* 86, no. 3 (December 1999).

Thompson, Leonard. *A History of South Africa*. Third Edition. New Haven: Yale University Press, 2000 [1995].

Tinker Salas, Miguel. *In the Shadow of the Eagles: Sonora and the Transformation of the Border During the Porfiriato*. Berkeley: University of California Press, 1997.

Torúa Cienfuegos, Alfonso. *Frontera en llamas: Los yaquis y la revolución mexicana*. Hermosillo: Universidad de Sonora-CESUES, 2006.

Travern, B. *Treasure of the Sierra Madre*. New York: Alfred A. Knopf, 2010 [1935].

Trollope, Anthony. *The Way We Live Now*. London: Chapman and Hall, 1875.

Troncoso, Francisco P. *Las Guerras con las Tribus Yaqui y Mayo del Estado de Sonora*. Mexico City: Tip. del Departamento de Estado Mayor, 1905.

Truett, Samuel. *Fugitive Landscapes: The Forgotten History of the U.S.–Mexico Borderlands*. New Haven: Yale University Press, 2006.

———, and Pekka Hämäläinen, "On Borderlands." *Journal of American History* 98, no. 2 (2011): 338–61.

Turner, Frederick Jackson. "The Significance of the Frontier in American History." In John Mack Faragher, ed., *Rereading Frederick Jackson Turner: "The Significance of the Frontier in American History" and Other Essays*. New York: Henry Holt, 1994.

Turner, John Kenneth. *Barbarous Mexico*. Chicago: Charles H. Kerr, 1911.

Tyrrell, Ian. "American Exceptionalism in an Age of International History." *American Historical Review* 96, no. 4 (1991): 1031–55.

van der Merwe, Floris J. G. "Sirkusbaas Frank Fillis (1857–1921): die Barnum van Suid-Afrika." *South African Journal of Cultural History* 16, no. 2 (2002): 110–31.

———. *Die Boere Sirkus van St. Louis (1904) with English supplement, "Meet Me in St. Louis": South Africa at the World's Fair and the Olympic Games of 1904*. Stellenbosch: FJG Publikasies, 1998.

van Onselen, Charles. *Studies in the Social and Economic History of the Witwatersrand, 1886–1914*. London: Longman, 1982.

———. *The Cowboy Capitalist: John Hays Hammond, the American West and the Jameson Raid*. Johannesburg: Jonathan Ball, 2017.

Vaughan, Mary Kay. *The State, Education, and Social Class in Mexico, 1880–1928*. DeKalb: Northern Illinois University Press, 1982.

Velasco Toro, José. *Los Yaquis: historia de una activa resistencia*. Xalapa, Mexico: Universidad Veracruzana, 1988.

Velázquez Estrada, Rosalía. *México en la mirada de John Kenneth Turner*. Mexico City: UAM/INAH Azcapotzalco, 2004.

Viljoen, B. J. *My Reminiscences of the Anglo–Boer War.* London: Hood, Douglas and Howard, 1902.

———. *Under the Vierkleur: A Romance of a Lost Cause.* Boston: Small, Maynard, 1904.

———. *The Huguenot* (June 1948).

———. *An Exiled General.* St. Louis: A. Noble Printing, 1906.

Ward, H. G. *Mexico in 1827.* Vol. 1. London: Henry Colburn, 1828.

Warwick, Peter, ed. *The South African War; The Anglo–Boer War, 1899–1902.* Harlow, UK: Longman, 1980.

Wasserman, Mark. *Capitalists, Caciques, and Revolution: The Native Elite and Foreign Enterprise in Chihuahua, Mexico, 1854–1911.* Chapel Hill: University of North Carolina Press, 1984.

———. *Pesos and Politics: Business, Elites, Foreigners, and Government in Mexico, 1854–1940.* Stanford: Stanford University Press, 2015.

Weber, David J. *Bárbaros: Spaniards and Their Savages in the Age of Enlightenment.* New Haven: Yale University Press, 2005.

———. *The Mexican Frontier, 1821–1846: The American Southwest Under Mexico.* Albuquerque: University of New Mexico Press, 1982.

———. *The Spanish Frontier in North America.* New Haven: Yale University Press, 1994.

Welter, Barbara. "She Hath Done What She Could: Protestant Women's Missionary Careers in Nineteenth-Century America." *American Quarterly* 30, no. 5 (Winter 1978).

Wertheim, Arthur Frank, and Barbara Bair, eds. *The Papers of Will Rogers,* Vol. 1: *November 1879–April 1904.* Norman: University of Oklahoma Press, 1996.

Wheatcroft, Geoffrey. *The Randlords: The Exploits and Exploitations of South Africa's Mining Magnates.* New York: Atheneum, 1986.

White, Richard. *Railroaded: The Transcontinentals and the Making of Modern America.* New York: W. W. Norton, 2011.

Worger, William H. *South Africa's City of Diamonds: Mine Workers and Monopoly Capitalism in Kimberley, 1867–1895.* New Haven: Yale University Press, 1987.

Wright, A. C. "Report of Touring and Evangelistic Work." *Reports of the Stations of the Mexico Mission of the American Board, 1905–1906.* Chihuahua: Imp. El Norte, 1906.

Wrobel, David M. *The End of American Exceptionalism: Frontier Anxiety from the Old West to the New Deal.* Lawrence: University Press of Kansas, 1993.

———. *Global West, American Frontier: Travel, Empire, and Exceptionalism from Manifest Destiny to the Great Depression*. Albuquerque: University of New Mexico Press, 2013.

Zayas, Maritere. "Tres mujeres curanderas yoremes." In María Eugenia Olavarría, ed., *Símbolos del desierto*. México, D.F.: Universidad Autónoma Metropolitana, 1992.

Index

Page numbers in *italic* type indicate illustrations.

Bácum, 165
Baden-Powell, Robert, 53, 63, 72–74, 76
Baja California, 33, 165, 170, 189, 219n68
Balderas, Isabel, 105
Baldwin, Deborah, 107
Bancroft, Hubert, 32
Banderas, Juan de la Cruz, 247n10
Bantu Authorities Act, 214n17
baptism, 87–89
barbarian virtues, 57
Barbarian Virtues (Jacobson), 225n48
Barbarous Mexico (Turner), 159
Barnato, Barney, 219n73
Barron, Clarence, 29
Bartlett, John Russell, 126
Batopilas, 105
Baumea, Manuela, 179
beauty: indigenous, 59; recognition of, 23
Belém, 160
Belfort, May, 122–24, 241n56
Beloit College, 89–90
belonging, binary system of, 152
benevolent conquest, 39, 220n94
Benitez, Guadalupe, 85
Bennett, Moses, 222n8
Berlin Conference, 82
bias, historical, 11
Bible: sale of, 84, 87–88; study of, 92
Bierstadt, Albert, 18, 19
binary system of belonging, 152
Bishop, William Henry, 35–36, 38
Blackburn, Douglas, 115
Blick, John, 49, 56, 57
bloodhounds, 184, 253n106
blood of Christ, 20
Blue Earth County, Minnesota, 66–68, 228n78, 228n79
boarding schools, 92
Boer Relief Fund, 117
Boers: Chihuahua colony of, 2–4, 101–2, 109–46, 238n9, 238n20; collapse of colony, 133; defeat by British Empire,

109; exile of, 113–19; home religious services, 129; lectures by veterans, 117–18; performances of resistance, 117; recruitment of colonists, 110; social status of, 167; support leagues, 115–16; U.S. sympathy for, 115–16
Boer War Spectacle, 8, 119–25, 132–34
Bolton, Herbert Eugene, 5–6
Bond, Marshall, 109
booster literature, 4, 28–33, 111–12, 136, 218n53
border, U.S.-Mexico, 36–37
borderlands, use of term, 5
borderlands scholarship, 1–3, 213n5, 218n61
borders, permeability of, 6
Boyd, Nathan, 43, 221n109
Boy Scouts, 54, 72–74, 230n109, 230n113
breastfeeding, 158
Brechin, Gray, 53
bribery, of indigenous peoples, 15–16
Brief Sketches in Mexico (Bouligny), 27
British imperial culture, 14
British South Africa Company (BSA Company), 34, 46, 50–58, 69–75, 115, 149, 222n4, 229n91
broncos (rebels), 246n5
Broussard, Robert, 70
Brown County, Minnesota, 66
Brucken, Carolyn, 10
Bryan, William Jennings, 157
BSA Company. *See* British South Africa Company (BSA Company)
Buenamea, Juan, 173
Buffalo Bill. *See* Cody, William "Buffalo Bill"
Buitimea Flores, Teodoro, 179, *180*
Buitimea Matuz, Francisco, 191
Bulawayo, 54–59, 63
Bule, Luis, 163
Burke, Timothy, 94
Burnham, Blanche, 45, 49, 56–63, 76, 108, 156, 191–92